Palgrave Studies in Classical Liberalism

This series offers a forum to writers concerned that the central presuppositions of the liberal tradition have been severely corroded, neglected, or misappropriated by overly rationalistic and constructivist approaches.

The hardest-won achievement of the liberal tradition has been the wrestling of epistemic independence from overwhelming concentrations of power, monopolies and capricious zealotries. The very precondition of knowledge is the exploitation of the epistemic virtues accorded by society's *situated and distributed* manifold of spontaneous orders, the DNA of the modern civil condition.

With the confluence of interest in situated and distributed liberalism emanating from the Scottish tradition, Austrian and behavioral economics, non-Cartesian philosophy and moral psychology, the editors are soliciting proposals that speak to this multidisciplinary constituency. Sole or joint authorship submissions are welcome as are edited collections (conference proceedings excluded), broadly theoretical or topical in nature.

More information about this series at
http://www.palgrave.com/gp/series/15722

Mikayla Novak

Inequality

An Entangled Political Economy Perspective

palgrave
macmillan

Mikayla Novak
RMIT University
Melbourne, VIC, Australia

Palgrave Studies in Classical Liberalism
ISBN 978-3-030-07765-5 ISBN 978-3-319-89417-1 (eBook)
https://doi.org/10.1007/978-3-319-89417-1

Cover illustration: K.Ausmaa / Alamy Stock Photo

Printed on acid-free paper

This Palgrave Macmillan imprint is published by the registered company Springer International Publishing AG part of Springer Nature.
The registered company address is: Gewerbestrasse 11, 6330 Cham, Switzerland

Preface and Acknowledgements

This book is about inequality. There are, needless to say, as many definitions of inequality, as there are assessments, as to the worthiness of this issue as a legitimate matter for public concern. As I indicate in this book, I largely limit attention to inequality of income and wealth. I say "largely" in this context because some sense should be given as to how economic inequalities (i.e. skewed income and wealth distributions) shape other kinds of inequality—such as political inequality and social inequality—and *vice versa*. These considerations highlight the inherent complexities of a topic which are often overlooked by participants in contemporary public debates, wherein the pressure for analytical expediency and explanatory simplicity seems to be the norm.

Given the breadth of interest about the nature and consequences of inequality, this book is not only aimed at academics, policymakers, and representatives of interest groups and "think tanks." My hope is that this book successfully reaches out to an even broader audience, encompassing interested laypeople whose lives are unquestionably affected by how economic, social, and political actors respond to the inequality issue. In some ways this book is merely an addition to an already voluminous literature. However, in writing this book I have sought to add value, by interpreting economic inequality through the lens of "entangled political economy" theory developed by eminent George Mason University economist Richard Wagner.

A detailed discussion will clearly be reserved for the main text, but what could be said at this juncture is that inequality in entangled political economy frame is reflected less in the swings and roundabouts of aggregate statistics such as the Gini coefficient. My focus is trained more upon the "bottom up" interactions within the economic, social, and political spheres which give rise to unequal income and wealth distributions. As might already be imagined by the reader, this book reflects an interdisciplinary approach to theory and analysis, inspired by the social-scientific disciplines of economics and political economy, political science, sociology, law, and history. Drawing upon insights from multiple disciplines may not lend itself to a clean, stylised vision of human affairs, yet this unavoidably appears the best way to reflect upon life as we find it—and not as we would like it to be.

This book is organised in three parts. The first part of the book, encompassing Chaps. 1, 2, and 3, outlines the conceptual basis for economic inequality in an entangled political economy perspective. It introduces the reader to the key dimensions of the contemporary inequality debate raging across developed countries. We also provide an account of Wagner's entangled political economy framework, and explain how distributional matters may be considered using that approach. Part two of the book, which covers Chaps. 4, 5, and 6, presents case studies illuminating how entanglements between economic, social, and political actors bring out redistributive effects inconsistent with the widely held desire to reduce income and wealth inequalities. Finally, the third part of the book (Chaps. 7, 8, and 9) outlines the principles for institutional reforms to help redress inequality in appropriate and meaningful ways, and to provide concluding remarks.

There have been many influences upon my thinking, as refined over the best part of 20 years. I would like to briefly acknowledge them here, in a reflection of the idea that no person is entirely unaffected by what has been encountered during times past. The late Tomas J. F. Riha, my mentor and Honours thesis supervisor during my undergraduate years at The University of Queensland (Australia), introduced me to the works of James M. Buchanan and the twentieth-century German ordo-liberal school of law and economics. I can never thank him enough for those intellectual introductions, which well and truly propelled me onto a path of discovery and learning in the classical liberal tradition.

John Foster, Emeritus Professor at The University of Queensland, introduced me to evolutionary economics through his Honours-level macroeconomics class. His thought-provoking presentations of economic theory in a heterodox light certainly made its long-lasting impression. The work of evolutionary economist Jason Potts (RMIT University, Australia) has also proven itself as an inspiration, with the originality and profundity of his work representing a compelling intellectual combination.

I want to specifically acknowledge the efforts of others who have similarly influenced my thinking, but may barely be aware of this fact. Peter Boettke (George Mason University, United States) and Wolfgang Kasper (Emeritus Professor, University of New South Wales, Australia) have served as sources of sound economic education like no other. Richard Wagner (George Mason University, United States), whose work predominantly influences the ideas encapsulated in this book, is another exemplary figure of scholarly input to, and engagement with, the classical liberal tradition I can only hope to emulate. There are obviously other people on a personal and professional basis, too numerous to mention, who have deeply influenced my thought patterns over the years. I take this opportunity to thank them for doing so.

I wish to thank Palgrave Macmillan for the opportunity to publish this, my first book, and for the superlative assistance they provided as the manuscript took shape. I thank the editors of the Palgrave Studies in Classical Liberalism series (David Hardwick and Leslie Marsh) for their support and assistance to make this book a reality.

Two anonymous referees organised by Messrs Hardwick and Marsh lent their support for the publication of this work, and I thank them for their contributions. I would also like to thank, in alphabetical order, Vincent Geloso (Texas Tech University, United States), Stefan Kolev (University of Applied Sciences Zwickau, Germany), and Andrew Norton (Grattan Institute, Australia) for their comments on a draft version of this work. The insightful and constructive feedback by all parties is deeply appreciated and, of course, they bear no responsibility for any errors of omission or commission which appear in this publication.

Finally, I wish to thank my partner and spouse, Deanna Trainham, for her advice, love and support, and, last but certainly not least, infinite patience in allowing me to pursue my aspirations and dreams. This book is dedicated to you.

Melbourne, VIC, Australia Mikayla Novak

Contents

List of Figures

1

Introduction

Inequality as Focal Point

The concept of the "focal point" underlines much of the human discourse. A focal point refers to that issue, or sets of related issues, upon which discussion and debate are drawn together. The focal point may encompass matters of great disputation among individuals and groups; nevertheless, it tends to elicit sharing of opinions and perspectives amidst a crowded space of public concerns. In recent years, income and wealth inequality (frequently referred to here as "economic inequality") within developed countries has been raised as a critical matter in economic, social, and political debates.

A proxy measure of interest in economic inequality is the frequency of appearance of that term within the approximately 5.2 million books digitised by Google. The phrase "economic inequality," as a percentage of all two-word phrases cited in Google's digitised English-language book portfolio, increased considerably over the past two decades.[1] In 1980, there were approximately 2.5×10^{-5} references to economic inequality, increasing to over 3.5×10^{-5} by 2008. The validity of NGrams has been questioned by some (Pechenick et al. 2015; Koplenig 2017), so one should be

M. Novak, *Inequality*, Palgrave Studies in Classical Liberalism,
https://doi.org/10.1007/978-3-319-89417-1_1

cautious about drawing broad inferences using this tool and similar word-counters. Nonetheless, it can hardly be denied that interest in economic inequality, and other variants of inequality (e.g. gender, health, racial, social, spatial), appear to have escalated in recent years.

Another indication that economic inequality has become a focal point is illustrated by the fact that economists and other social scientists have published best-selling books, exploring the dimensions of the issue and advising how to deal with it. One of the leading works in the contemporary inequality literature is an English translation of *Capital in the Twenty-First Century*, written by French economist Thomas Piketty. The book quickly achieved the status as the top-selling book on Amazon and the *New York Times* listing, something of a rarity for a book whose subject is firmly situated within the intellectual confines of political economy.

Thomas Piketty's essential idea is that inequality is determined by two key economic variables growing at different rates. The first is the annual growth rate of total income generated in the economy (denoted by the letter *g*). The second is the average annual rate of capital returns (denoted by the letter *r*), which incorporates profits, dividends, interest earnings, rents, and selective other income flows from capital.[2] Piketty contends that situations whereby *r* exceeds *g* are consistent with worsening inequality: "[w]hen the rate of return on capital significantly exceeds the growth rate of the economy … then it logically follows that inherited wealth grows faster than output and income" (Piketty 2014, p. 26).

Piketty claimed a build-up in the relative importance of private sector capital to national income in several developed economies, subsequent to the Great Depression and World War II. Piketty suggests that recent trends merely affirm his fears about a "new patrimonial capitalism" (Ibid., p. 173). Drivers of this trend, as Piketty saw it, were population ageing slowing economic growth on the one hand, and privatisations and accelerating financial asset prices, which bolster returns on capital, on the other.

The future, according to Piketty, portends a worsening of the inequality trend. Assuming the rate of income growth will gradually decline to 1.5 per cent per annum, and with savings rates stabilising in the long run, Piketty forecasts returns on (pre-tax) capital to consistently exceed the growth rate in income over the course of this century. Piketty warned of powerful economic and financial forces threatening more heavily skewed income and wealth distributions:

> The overall conclusion … is that a market economy based on private property, if left to itself, contains powerful forces of convergence, associated in particular with the diffusion of knowledge and skills; but it also contains powerful forces of divergence, which are potentially threatening to democratic societies and to the values of social justice on which they are based. … The consequences for the long-term dynamics of the wealth distribution are potentially terrifying. (Ibid., p. 571)

Putting aside the riskiness of some capital ventures necessitating higher-than-average returns, Piketty nonetheless proclaims a tendency whereby *r* exceeds *g* as a reflection of "[t]he central contradiction of capitalism" (Ibid.). Without countervailing forces at play, "the entrepreneur inevitably tends to become a rentier, more and more dominant over those who own nothing but their labour. Once constituted, capital reproduces itself faster than output increases. The past devours the future" (Ibid., p. 571).

The Nobel laureate in Economics Joseph Stiglitz has emerged as another anti-inequality figure. In his best-selling book *The Price of Inequality*, Stiglitz suggests: "[o]ne of the darkest sides of the market economy that came to light was the large and growing inequality that has left the American social fabric, and the country's economic sustainability, fraying at the edges: the rich were getting richer, while the rest were facing hardships that seemed inconsonant with the American dream" (Stiglitz 2012, p. 2). Stiglitz feared that unequal distributions of income and wealth would also lead to political polarisation, in turn diminishing the possibility that citizens and policymakers would reach agreement about the most appropriate responses to the inequality problem.

Another contribution to inequality as a focal point came from the late Sir Anthony (Tony) Atkinson. In his book *Inequality: What Can Be Done?*, Atkinson surmised that "the present level of inequality is excessive" (Atkinson 2015, p. 9). Referencing trends in the United States (U.S.), Atkinson explains there has been an "Inequality Turn" from the late 1970s, with a more skewed income distribution benefiting the wealthy: "[a]t the top of the distribution, the share in total gross income of the top 1 per cent increased by one-half between 1979 and 1992, and by 2012 it was more than double its 1979 share" (Ibid., p. 18).

Atkinson suspects that an excessively skewed distribution of income and wealth not only worsens economic performance, but is morally dubious. Using the analogy of a foot race equally positioning everybody at the starting point, Atkinson claims "most people would find it unacceptable to ignore completely what happens after the starting gun is fired" (Ibid., p. 10). The inequality experienced by the present generation could detrimentally affect opportunity enjoyed by future generations because, among other things, "the beneficiaries of inequality of outcome today can transmit an unfair advantage to their children tomorrow" (Ibid., p. 11). Furthermore, a severe sense of distance between the rich and the poor creates perceptions of unwarranted injustices prevailing within society.

Concern about inequality is not restricted to members of the economics profession. Social protest movements mobilised, to some extent, as a consequence of inequality becoming a focal point of discourse (Pickerill and Krinsky 2012; Snow and Owens 2014; Corcoran et al. 2015; Della Porta 2015; Gaby and Caren 2016; for an alternative view, see Solt 2015). Arguably the most notable of those movements was the "Occupy" movement, gaining precedence in the years immediately following the 2007–08 "global financial crisis" (GFC). The issues raised by Occupy protestors varied, yet a common rallying theme was their enmity towards the economic interests of those people situated within the top one per cent of the income distribution. Referring to their being a part of the remaining 99 per cent of the income distribution,[3] Occupy protestors forcefully contributed towards the crystallisation of economic inequality as a major concern.

Since the peak of the Occupy movement other protests have organised in response to economic, political, and social problems. These include the "Black Lives Matter" movement, with a chief focus on institutionalised violence and systemic racism against members of the African-American community, and British protestors against official responses to the 2017 Grenfell Tower fire in London. Inasmuch as these social protest movements are disparate in their specific aims and objectives, many of them sought to make some connection between their unique causes and inequality issues more generally.

Disquiet about economic inequality is, to be sure, not limited to the participants of social protest movements. Opinion surveys of community attitudes suggest inequality is, indeed, a more widespread concern. An international survey undertaken by the Pew Research Center found that over half of the people surveyed living in developed countries said that inequality is a "very big problem," with similar sentiments shared by respondents in emerging and developing countries (Pew Research Center 2014).

Where the intellectuals and public sentiments go, the political class invariably follows. Political figures of diverse ideological affinities have elevated inequality as a policy problem, advancing proposals to significantly realign income and wealth distributions as they are found in their respective countries.

A candidate for presidency in the 2016 U.S. election, Bernie Sanders, galvanised numerous progressive-leaning voters to his cause by suggesting that extreme inequalities demonstrated the American economy was "rigged" against the lower and middle classes. His main rival, Hillary Clinton, ultimately selected as Democratic Party candidate for the presidency, also campaigned on the subject of fixing inequality. Clinton lost her bid to become U.S. president to the Republican candidate, businessman and television celebrity Donald Trump, despite winning a majority of the votes cast. Although inequality did not principally inform Trump's campaign strategy, most American political observers agreed he controversially tapped into a sense of disgruntlement and unease amongst voters in regions with limited prospects for upward mobility. Trump attracted a sufficient groundswell of electoral support by blaming groups—such as immigrants, and traders from emerging economies such as China and Mexico—for the relatively difficult circumstances faced by Americans in the lower echelons of the income and wealth scale (Reeves 2016).

In 2016, another Nobel laureate in economics, Peter Diamond, referred to unique ways in which economic inequality is more of a pressing issue in the U.S. than elsewhere (Diamond 2016). Even so, political concern about the distribution of income and wealth has spread far beyond America's borders. The ruling British Conservative Party lost a swathe of seats, and was obliged to form a minority coalition government with a political bloc from Northern Ireland, in 2017, partly due to the electoral persuasiveness of Labour Opposition Leader Jeremy Corbyn's campaign against inequality. Opposition labourist parties in Australia and New Zealand also found it politically advantageous to raise inequality matters as part of their respective campaigns for economic and social policy change.

Debating Recent Inequality Trends

Inequality has always been with us, more or less, for that is implied by the very concept of a *distribution* of income and wealth. Indeed, there is abundant evidence pointing to the persistence of inequality in a historical context, stretching from even ancient times (Paynter 1989; Scheidel 2017). Given this seemingly immovable part of reality we ask the following question: Why has inequality become, or at least has returned as, a leading topic in public debate now?

In no small part the growth of interest in, and concern about, inequality is the result of statistical trends pointing to more heavily skewed distributional outcomes. Since the development of modern economics from the eighteenth century, distributional questions have been at the forefront of economic investigation. The most frequently used measure indicating the extent of income inequality is the "Gini coefficient," with its numerical values ranging from zero to one. Gini coefficient values closer to zero signify a more equal distribution (i.e. everybody possessed the same level of income), whereas values closer to one signal a less equal distribution (i.e. only one person entirely possessed the available income). Although Gini coefficient values vary, they have tended to increase for a number of developed countries, implying that economic inequality in those locations has worsened (OECD 2015).

Wealth inequality has also presented as a significant concern for many years, given that the ownership of tangible and intangible assets also underpins economic well-being. There is a general lack of quality time-series Gini coefficients for wealth inequality, and so researchers have resorted to relying upon other forms of statistical evidence. Tony Atkinson and colleagues presented statistics indicating the share of net wealth—defined as (financial and non-financial) assets minus liabilities (debts)—possessed by households within the top one per cent of the wealth distribution of several advanced countries. They have shown that wealth became more concentrated in Australia, Finland, France, the Netherlands, Switzerland, and the United States since the 1980s, although the GFC temporarily reduced the values of certain financial and other assets (Atkinson et al. 2017).

The use of certain statistical measures for economic inequality has been the subject of controversy. The Gini coefficient has been criticised for several reasons—it can be difficult to accurately estimate income and wealth using historical records, a given Gini coefficient value may coincide with multiple distributions, and so on. Thomas Piketty himself criticised the use of the Gini coefficient, "which mix very different things, such as inequality with respect to labor and capital, so that it is impossible to distinguish clearly among the multiple dimensions of inequality and the various mechanisms at work" (Piketty 2014, p. 243).

Drawing upon historical income tax return data, other studies reinforce the idea that income inequality has been on the rise in recent decades (Piketty and Saez 2003; Leigh 2005). The extent to which this methodology gives a true reflection of income distribution is debatable. Critics have pointed out that tax records under-report income to the extent that taxes are avoided or evaded. Under-reporting may also occur when certain income earners (e.g. low-income earners) are not obliged to file a tax return. In other cases, records are susceptible to filing errors. Finally, inequality statistics based upon tax records are sensitive to policy changes, and to individuals' responses to those changes. A study by Auten and Splinter (2017) indicates that a consistent accounting of U.S. policy changes, such as tax cuts, suggests the increase in income share attributed to the top one per cent of earners is less than that reported in previous studies.

Other researchers doubt that income and wealth are adequate measures of *living standards*, contending that income and wealth distributions should not necessarily be emphasised as a central focus for economic discourse and policy concern. According to the proponents of these alternative perspectives, measures pertaining to such variables as consumption, housing size, or education attainment, health status, and other aspects of living standards deserve further investigation (Hassett and Mathur 2012; Eberstadt 2017; Sumner 2017).

Another issue raised recently is that inequality has not only a national dimension but a global scale. Certain inequality experts point out that a domestic, "behind-the-border" perspective gives insufficient attention to international dimensions, with some evidence pointing to a relatively stable, or in some respects declining, global distribution of income over the last few decades. Work undertaken by former World Bank economist Branko Milanović illustrates that a population-weighted Gini coefficient for incomes earned within countries shows a steady improvement (i.e. lessening inequality) from the 1990s (Milanović 2008).

The Consequences of Inequality

The complexities surrounding inequality concepts and measurements have played their part in generating sincerely held disagreements about whether income and wealth distributions are widening or compressing. Regardless of the positions in relation to these concerns, there is another question to be posed: why does a high degree of inequality, or worsening degree thereof, matter?

The economist Arthur Okun countenanced an inverse relationship between the degree of inequality and rate of economic growth (Okun 1975). Greater inequality is associated with faster growth as skilled individuals reap the rewards from greater material abundance, whereas lesser inequality is associated with slower growth as more people share what is available. From the perspective of what is now referred to as "Okun's Law," the trade-off between inequality and growth suggests that policy-makers adjust their policies to find a balance the community is willing to accept.

In *The Captured Economy*, Brink Lindsey and Steven Teles hypothesise that inequality has emerged as a focal point by virtue of an apparent economic anomaly. The residents of most developed countries find themselves living with a high, if not extreme, degree of inequality *and* persistently slow rates of economic growth. As they note, "[t]he simultaneous occurrence of sluggish growth and spiralling inequality presents us with a paradox. … What we are not supposed to see is the situation we're currently living through" (Lindsey and Teles 2017, p. 4). The breakdown of Okun's inequality-growth nexus is important because subdued economic activity effectively exposes a lack of opportunity for many to improve their economic circumstances, amplifying the degree of public disquiet over the existing distribution of economic rewards.

There is the alternative suggestion that, under certain circumstances, rising inequality is associated with a slower rate of economic growth. In other words, the apparent departure from Okun's Law perhaps should not be construed as anomalous after all. This proposition has been subjected to empirical testing, with several studies pointing to a negative correlation between economic performance and economic inequalities in developed countries (Ostry et al. 2014; OECD 2015; also Cingano 2014). Contrasting studies indicate that the relationship between growth and inequality is non-existent or, in some cases, even positive (Halter et al. 2014; Neves et al. 2016; Thewissen 2014). Although there is a lack of consensus over whether or not income and wealth inequalities are problematic from the standpoint of growth, we acknowledge the recent academic literature seems to have sparked a renewed debate over the entire matter.

There have been studies pointing to non-economic reasons to scrutinise any consistent trend of worsening inequality. One of the more influential tracts in the modern inequality literature is *The Spirit Level: Why More Equal Societies Almost Always Do Better*, by epidemiologists Richard Wilkinson and Kate Pickett (2009). The researchers contend that a range of maladies—crime, declining trust, educational underachievement, illicit drug usage, mental illness, obesity, premature mortality, and reduced social status—has been observed in developed countries with relatively great dispersions of income and wealth.

Although the key findings of the Wilkinson-Pickett study are contentious (Snowdon 2010), other investigations highlight additional problems for societies bearing a high degree of economic inequality. Some studies show the beneficiaries of concentrated income and wealth feeling, or demonstrating, less compassion, empathy, or interest towards others in vulnerable social situations (Piff et al. 2012; Stellar et al. 2012; Côté et al. 2015; Bianchi and Vohs 2016). The veracity of the conclusions is to be debated, but it could not be said that such concerns are recent. The eighteenth-century Scottish moral philosopher Adam Smith purportedly decried inequality extremes because they may encourage the well-off to ignore the desire to behave in a manner earning the approbation of lower-ranked others (Rasmussen 2016).

A hallmark of democracy is that it aims to promulgate discussion about wide-ranging issues of public interest, wherein each and every citizen-voter is politically treated as a status-equal in relation to each other (diZerega 1989; Madison 1997; Nell 2017). However, a concern has been aired that the wealthy are able to more effectively influence political decision-making than those with few resources and limited social links. People with abundant income and wealth may contribute disproportionately to campaigns and other political activities, signalling with their spending a desire to have certain interests or values promoted in policymaking. Alternatively, they may procure policy advantages by virtue of their generally more intimate knowledge about how to communicate with, and persuade, others in a policy sense (Rojas 2017). Other researchers express a concern that rich people attain disproportionate advantages because of a comparable educational background, or shared personal and professional connections, with politicians and senior bureaucrats (Canayaz et al. 2016; Brown and Huang 2017; Murray and Frijters 2017).

The Key Drivers of Inequality

It is widely held that the distribution of income and wealth is becoming more extreme in developed countries, and that there are potential economic, social, and political risks associated with worsening economic inequality. Although such interpretations have been contested by some, it remains important to enquire into the causes of inequality. What are the drivers of inequality? What broad factors influence a trend towards income and wealth being increasingly accumulated by those within the upper echelons of our economies and societies?

Researchers specialising in inequality indicate there are many non-policy and policy determinants affecting income and wealth inequality outcomes, although the prescience of governmental policy action in modern times does suggest that the boundaries between non-policy and policy factors are fuzzy. In no necessary order of importance, some of the major (and somewhat interrelated) proximate causes of inequality patterns include:

- *Greater returns to education*: People who successfully undertake further education and training tend to earn greater incomes over their lifetimes than those who have merely obtained an elementary school education. Studies have shown that the so-called wage premium associated with additional education is significant—in 1980, an American with a graduate degree earned about 50 per cent more than an American without one, rising to over 100 per cent in the 2000s (Becker and Murphy 2007). In new, niche industries it is possible for highly skilled individuals to enjoy the "superstar effect" of a substantial salary well in excess of those working in more traditional industries.
- *Declining private sector unionism*: Throughout much of the twentieth century, powerful private sector unions were able to procure significant wage gains and fringe benefits (e.g. healthcare entitlements, superannuation payments) from employers for the benefit of their members. However, subsequent declines in union membership have not only weakened employees' bargaining power but also contributed to rising inequality more generally (Atkinson 2015).
- *Changing executive remuneration techniques*: Substantial earnings increases for senior executives in major corporations—entailing a combination of generous base salary rises, attractive bonus payments, and provision of company stocks—have been cited as a key influence behind a widening income disparity. These payments are often rationalised as appropriate rewards to attract and maintain scarce entrepreneurial and managerial talent in an increasingly globalised world, though critics question the validity of such claims. The contribution of tax reductions in bolstering the remuneration of corporate executives has also been noted in the relevant literature.
- *Increasing globalisation*: In addition to highly skilled labour attracting wage premiums by relocating countries, the openness of capital, financial, and commodity markets is believed to be contributing to a worsening of intra-country inequality. For example, an influx of manufactured imports provides significant benefits for consumers but may induce

structural unemployment in some regions, thus worsening income inequality. Offsetting this somewhat, absolute poverty rates in the developing world appears to have declined as a result of globalisation (Zanden et al. 2014; Cruz et al. 2015).

- *Financial sector development and innovation*: Growth in the scale and scope of financial sector activities—known as "financialisation," and which typically follows episodes of deregulation, privatisation, and globalisation—is cited as a crucial factor informing the skewness in income and wealth. It is suggested that growth in incomes, via capital gains, dividends, and interest income, strengthened the relative position of already wealthy bank managers and executives when they bargain for even better rewards (Lin and Tomaskovic-Devey 2014).
- *Technological changes*: The displacement of labour with fewer skills and lesser workplace experiences, all else being equal, would tend to worsen economic inequality. Altered cross-border trading patterns and the advent of labour-saving information technology and robotics have been nominated as additional contributors to inequality. Most recently, there has been some unease expressed about the potential for future automation to further exacerbate income and wealth dispersions (Tarnoff 2017).
- *Growing rent-seeking pressure*: There are concerns that economic inequality has also been shaped by "rent-seeking"—the utilisation of finances, and other, resources in attempts to politically secure specific and particularised advantages at the expense of other parties. The issue is that wealthy people may influence policymakers to accord them special fiscal, regulatory, or other policies, strengthening their relative economic and financial positions even further.

Any of the aforementioned factors, and even more not mentioned here, may be influential at any given point in time. The extent to which any given driver of inequality prevails is also likely to wax and wane as the economy, society, and the polity evolve. What is important to heed in this context is that there is no single overriding determinant of inequality. Therefore, investigation and judgement are necessary to delineate—as far as existing methods and techniques allow for it—the relative importance of those factors weighing on the worsening inequality.

Sketching Inequality in a Classically Liberal Political Economy Frame

The inequality focal point encompasses intersecting debates, discussions, ideas, and suggestions propounded by numerous societal participants, each subscribing to their own ideological dispositions, pecuniary and non-pecuniary interests, or philosophical perspectives. The underlying beliefs, concerns, and values that people hold have a crucial bearing upon the extent to which inequality is conceived as a problem for economies, polities, and societies. To the extent that inequality is viewed as problematic, this leads people to give varying weight to which of the determining factors are more important to tackle.

Classical liberalism (or as it is often referred to, particularly in the U.S., libertarianism) serves as a major philosophical pivot in the contemporary inequality debate, and is the perspective embraced in this book. Although classical liberals need not agree upon the finer details of every issue, it is not unreasonable to summarise their "worldview propensities," for want of a better phrase, under three headings: freer markets, more open societies, and smaller governments. Other things being equal, a classical liberal would normatively vouch for economic, social, and political arrangements in which people freely undertake action, either individually or in collaboration with others, for as long as nobody else is coerced into undertaking certain lines of action they would otherwise not perform. In the liberal view, the freer people are, the better off they would become.

Whether it is grounded in a natural rights (deontological) perspective or utilitarian (consequentialist) perspective, classical liberalism submits that the freedom to produce, exchange, and consume goods and services is of paramount importance in the pursuit of material betterment for the masses. Directed by the emergent phenomena of relative prices, several property and profit-and-loss, economic entrepreneurs set out to discover opportunities to more effectually serve others in the marketplace. In so doing, entrepreneurship contributes to the available stock of knowledge concerning what, how, when, where, and why to make and sell. We refer to all the operational acts of production, exchange, and consumption as being performed by individuals, and groups of individuals, situated within the "economic order," and shaped by certain institutional rules which impress upon economic functioning.

Economic action does not exhaust the possibilities for human action. We also consider explicitly cooperative acts of mutual assistance—altruism, help, solidarity, and support rendered to others within a broad range of social contexts and organisations. What we have in mind here are the elements of what we describe as the "communal order"—incorporating the likes of families, neighbourhoods, charities, clubs and societies, education and health facilities, interest groups, non-government organisations, and other civic associations.

Most of the social bodies and forms within the communal order do not directly rely upon the feedback mechanisms of the market, for this would surely compromise the ability of such entities to commit to altruistic and solidaristic acts of support favouring the needy, children, and other specified community members. As some economists have noted, nonetheless, the ability of any given group within the communal order to receive esteem and support largely depends upon furnishing a good reputation in caring for others (Chamlee-Wright and Myers 2008; Boettke and Coyne 2009). Classical liberals have long endorsed the development and maintenance of the communal order, not only as a generalised arena in which to perform non-state activities but as a forum to learn tolerance and respect, even love and admiration, towards diverse others.

Classical liberals are often portrayed as having a vexed relationship with the notion of government, which is but one element of a "political order" populated by individuals and their agencies deliberating over matters of public interest and implementing policies in accordance with such interest. Government exacts coercive force to retrieve revenues, and to enforce regulations, in the pursuit of its varied policy objectives. For some liberals (especially those of the "anarcho-capitalist," natural-rights strain), the exercise of such coercion within the political order is deemed to be morally unconscionable, and so they prefer that governments partake in no conduct at all.

Most others of a classical liberal persuasion, however, agree (some more reluctantly than others) that governmental activity is necessary, and sometimes desirable, in cases whereby non-government actors are incapable of financing or delivering important goods and services for broad-scale community benefit. If the force of government has to be applied within the political realm, it is desirable that politicians and bureaucrats behave in accordance with the rule of law applicable to each and all, provide benefits to all members of the public (and not restricted to special, concentrated interests), and ensure public sector action be decentralised as much as practicably possible in accordance with subsidiarity principles.

Inequalities, perhaps even extreme inequalities, would certainly arise under circumstances whereby classical liberal principles held most sway. Each and every individual is unique—with their own abilities, beliefs, capabilities, dispositions, experiences, fears, hopes, inclinations, interests, passions, talents, and values—and they exist in an astonishingly diverse array of physical spaces, social settings, and times. In addition, features such as the uneven distribution of inherited genetics and luck also factor greatly into our considerations (Buchanan 1971, 1983). We are different for varied reasons, so inequalities will almost automatically emerge whenever humans interact.

It would be a mistake to conclude that because people are different in a practical sense, economic inequality somehow does not matter. On an anecdotal basis it may be observed that a not-inconsiderable number of classical liberals today perhaps lean towards such a viewpoint. Speculatively, the perception that certain liberals *do not* see inequality as of concern might also reflect an ideologically or politically reflexive desire to dismiss progressivist and social-democratic sentiments that largely *do* accept that inequality is real, is worsening, and is a problem.

In general terms, however, liberals have sought to constructively engage with those individuals and organisations that have elevated inequality as a focal point of socio-politico-economic discourse. These efforts have gone some distance beyond merely challenging the methodological integrity and data accuracy of prominent inequality studies, or raising doubts over the economic efficacy of redistributive policies to ameliorate inequalities of income and wealth. We argue classical liberals can concede that inequality is problematic without losing their sense of principle, with the qualification that normative assessments regarding the severity of inequality ultimately depends on the various underlying factors which shape it.

It has been previously mentioned that an important dimension of investigations regarding the significance of factors impinging upon inequality relates to their consequences. We receive guidance in this regard thanks to the contributions of economists Vincent Geloso and Steven Horwitz, who recently distinguished inequality in two basic guises—"good" (liberty-consistent) and "bad" (liberty-inconsistent). According to Geloso and Horwitz, the good inequalities are socially beneficial by nature and "result from the satisfaction of individual economic preferences or demographic changes and have no perverse impact on economic growth" (Geloso and Horwitz 2017, p. 121). On the other hand, bad inequalities are harmful from a societal perspective "because they result from limiting individual choice in ways that expand inequality by limiting overall growth and harming the least well-off" (Ibid., p. 122). For these authors, the conduct and effect of numerous forms of governmental policy are such that they often fall into the socially harmful drivers of inequality. This is a position similarly adopted by the likes of Lindsey and Teles (2017) and Watson (2015), who recount a number of key policies as key drivers of upward redistribution from the less well-off in favour of the rich and powerful.

It has been suggested recently that what the public actually objects to is the perceived lack of economic fairness, rather than unequal distributions of income or wealth *per se* (Bavetta and Navarra 2012; Starmans et al. 2017). This kind of intuition has led some to suggest that "[w]e should eliminate crony capitalism, prevent taxpayer bank bailouts, and ensure competitive markets that the public want for efficiency and fairness reasons, irrespective of their effect on inequality measures such as the Gini coefficient" (Bourne 2018). We do not contest these recently expressed positions, but merely state that inequality, despite definitional and measurement controversies, should not be ruled out as a legitimate topic of liberal concern. Indeed, the position adopted in this book is that the decomposition of inequalities by source—interpreting which are socially harmful, especially with regard to the exercise of liberties—is a far more rigorous strategy for classical liberals to embrace when engaging with the inequality issue.

The most novel feature of this book is that we do more than focus merely upon the drivers of inequality, because of our view that inequality is best considered a dynamic, interactionist phenomenon. This book situates the harmless versus harmful decomposition within a relatively new theoretical system of political economy—namely, the "entangled political economy" framework developed and refined by George Mason University economist, and public finance theorist, Richard Wagner (2007, 2010, 2014, 2016). The entangled political economy framework has already been successfully applied to issues such as taxation policy, government budgeting, public sector debt, federalism, financial sector regulation, health policy, and public administration and governance, and an important aim of this book is to construe inequality as another field in which entangled political economy may bear fruitful insights.

Entangled political economy conceptualises economic and political actors in society as engaging in a continuous process of interaction with each other. We could refer to this as a "structured living-togetherness," exemplified by competition and collaboration to discover and attain mutually advantageous benefits. The political is not divorced from the economic, and vice versa, and nor is the communal order of sociality separated from other domains of human action. Although there are distinctive ordering principles conditioning the kinds of actions undertaken within each order of society, the engagement of non-political actors with politicians and bureaucrats leads to what is best described as entangled, or knotted, political economy across orders.

The simultaneous aspects of economic, social, and political participation weighing upon human action culminate in the observance of structured relations of an endogenous character. What is particularly noteworthy is that the endogenously structured relations in an entangled political economy are necessarily incomplete, because they reflect partial and contingent attachments that are laid down by interactionist (but cognitively constrained and knowledgably bounded) economic, social, and political actors. Economic inequality arises when non-uniform patterns of income and wealth connections are forged between various players within society, as a result of both "good" and "bad" sources as previously discussed.

The entangled political economy framework illustrates, perhaps in a way like no other existing framework does, that dynamic network effects are of paramount importance towards understanding how inequality emerges and changes. This raises the prospect that inequality is rife within society, rather than being an anomaly. It follows that the challenge is not merely to assess which inequalities should be the subject of policy remediation and which should not. It is important to ensure that fiscal and regulatory actions by political players are consistent with the fundamental dynamic working principles of an open market-based economy, a vibrant civil society, and liberal-democratic political order.

To ensure that entanglement between the non-political and the political does not degenerate into a takeover by public ordering principles, Richard Wagner relies upon the principles of "order theory" (*ordnungstheorie*). These propositions were developed by German economists and legal academics, known as "ordo-liberals," primarily during the first half of the twentieth century. A key principle of ordo-liberalism is that governments can impose policies, but they must help maintain the integrity of the economic order grounded in non-interference with relative price movements, the protection of several property, maintenance of contract laws, monetary stability, and consistency in policy. This book will illustrate that appropriate economic rules should help ensure that entanglements remain consistent with liberty principles, as well as minimise the potential for unwarranted inequality extremes to emerge.

Another distinctive feature of this book is that it will explain that economic inequality does not only arise from an economic motive to receive concentrated benefits in the market sphere, or to secure specific advantages from political actors. Whereas our primary focus is upon economic inequality, it is readily acknowledged that numerous developments within society and polity can generate other forms of inequality which, in turn, feed back upon income and wealth inequalities in varied ways. Harmful, liberty-inconsistent inequality may emerge through deliberate acts of social exclusion of particular groups, for example, from opportunities to orchestrate their own value-adding networked connections with others on a voluntary basis (Novak 2016; Boettke and Candela 2017). The effects of social exclusion upon economic inequality—including through the legacies of systemic racism, sexism, and other group-based discriminations—can be accommodated within the entangled political economy framework, and will also be discussed in this book.

Structure of the Book

This book is structured in three parts. Part I outlines the theoretical foundations for the critical investigation of economic inequality animating the themes addressed in the book. Chapter 2 details the framework of entangled political economy which, as previously mentioned, is based on the interactions between economic, social, and political actors in the shared plane of human existence. We emphasise the networking features and evolutionary properties inherent in entangled political economy thinking, and how these insights influence economic, social, and political outcomes. The chapter contrasts entangled political economy with conventional approaches to political economy, which largely treat economics and politics as separate phenomena.

Chapter 3 applies entangled political economy theory to the issue of inequality. Inequality is the result of an incomplete structure of networks forged among and between actors operating within the economic, communal, and political orders. We explicitly frame inequality conceptions using a tripartite "micro-meso-macro" analytical framework (Dopfer et al. 2004; Potts and Morrison 2007; Dopfer and Potts 2008), illustrating how inequitable relationships propagate throughout the ramparts of civil society. This chapter contends that economic inequality arises not only as a result of partial attachments in the form of variable income flows and wealth stocks. Discriminatory and exclusionary social treatment of certain members of the population also contributes towards inequality-inducing network structures.

The exposition of the theoretical basis for inequality in the system of entangled political economy provides the platform for case studies, outlined throughout Part II of this book. Chapter 4 examines the potential for certain expenditure and taxation policies to exacerbate economic inequality, particularly in circumstances whereby such initiatives either provide differential advantages or constrain upward economic mobility.

Certain government regulations may intensify economic inequality, as will be discussed in Chap. 5 of this book. Regulatory settings protect the income and wealth positions of asset holders, and suppliers in product and factor markets, from competitive challenge by entrepreneurs proposing to incorporate novelties into the entangled political economy. This creates economic rents which can be captured by interest groups which enjoy better political connections with legislators and bureaucrats.

Reflecting the idea that economic inequality can intersect with other manifestations of inequality in complex ways, Chap. 6 discusses the role of discrimination and social exclusion in amplifying economic inequality. This chapter describes the processes through which discriminatory treatment towards certain groups magnifies inequality. In particular, animosity towards so-called out-groups potentially manifests itself in their exclusion from voluntary network interactions of economic worth.

Part III of this book sketches principles for pro-equality reform within an entangled political economy. Chapter 7 outlines the need for a more effective, rules-based economic policy regime to assist in the management, indeed suppression, of the worst aspects of harmful inequalities that endanger the exercise of liberty. Some degree of inequality is inevitable, and in some cases harmless, nonetheless a legal framework of institutional rules may prevent economic inequality arising from abuses of political power at the expense of open and competitive market processes. Inspired by the insights of German liberal order theory, this chapter reveals that "acceptable," socially harmless inequality is correlative with the maintenance of so-called liberty-consistent network structures.

In Chap. 8 of this book we turn to the principles underpinning a society of dignified equals, outlining how these principles will also assist in reducing the extremes of income and wealth inequalities. Whilst the removal of legal barriers against the practice of racism and sexism is unlikely to extinguish inequality in its entirety, the inequality that persists is considered more likely to be the emergent property of liberty-consistent networks forming throughout the economy, polity, and society. In other words, inequality reflects performance differentials in economic process, instead of background characteristics or group status.

Chapter 9 concludes the book by summarising the major themes outlined, and providing additional reflections about the prospect for reforms that reduce income and wealth inequality whilst preserving, and indeed in some cases promoting, our liberties.

Although entanglement may be an unavoidable, often necessary, feature of living, a highly inequitable entanglement of economic, social, and political relationships need not be, of course depending upon its underlying source. An appreciation of the dynamics of economic inequality from the perspective of entangled political economy is a compelling way to conceptually broaden out classical liberal perspectives about the key issues at stake. This book provides the intellectual platform to better understand the basis of inequality, the circumstances in which inequality is harmful to the economy, polity, and society, and the most appropriate institutional and policy reform measures to redress inequality extremes.

Notes

1. Data refer to an "NGram" of the two-word phrase "economic inequality" in the Google Ngram Viewer. An Ngram is a case-sensitive sequence of letters of any length, including words or phrases. The selections of case-insensitive English and a smoothing factor of three are applied to the Ngram word search, the results of which are presented here.
2. Piketty excludes certain forms of capital from his analysis, especially human capital, which could influence inequality trends.
3. Media coverage frequently illustrated the "We are the 99%" placards held by Occupy movement protestors. However, the distinction between those within the top one per cent of the income distribution and the bottom 99 per cent was not a new one—the one-time political speechwriter and libertarian activist Karl Hess referred to the extent of accumulation of income, wealth, and resources by the top one per cent of income earners during the 1970s. I am indebted to Roderick Long (Auburn University, United States) for pointing this out to me.

References

Atkinson, Anthony B. 2015. *Inequality: What Can Be Done?* Cambridge, MA: Harvard University Press.

Atkinson, Tony, Joe Hasell, Salvatore Morelli, and Max Roser. 2017. *The Chartbook of Economic Inequality*. Institute for New Economic Thinking. Accessed September 4, 2017. https://chartbookofeconomicinequality.com/wp-content/uploads/Chartbook_Of_Economic_Inequality_complete.pdf

Auten, Gerald, and David Splinter. 2017. Income Inequality in the United States: Using Tax Data to Measure Long-Term Trends. *Working Paper*, November 12. Accessed January 27, 2018. http://davidsplinter.com/AutenSplinter-Tax_Data_and_Inequality.pdf

Bavetta, Sebastiano, and Pietro Navarra. 2012. *The Economics of Freedom: Theory, Measurement, and Policy Implications*. New York, NY: Cambridge University Press.

Becker, Gary, and Kevin M. Murphy. 2007. The Upside of Income Inequality. American Enterprise Institute, *The American blog*, May 7. Accessed October 10, 2015. https://www.aei.org/publication/the-upside-of-income-inequality/

Bianchi, Emily C., and Kathleen D. Vohs. 2016. Social Class and Social Worlds: Income Predicts the Frequency and Nature of Social Contact. *Social Psychological and Personality Science* 7 (5): 479–486.

Boettke, Peter J., and Rosolino A. Candela. 2017. The Liberty of Progress: Increasing Returns, Institutions, and Entrepreneurship. *Social Philosophy and Policy* 34 (2): 136–163.

Boettke, Peter J., and Christopher J. Coyne. 2009. Context Matters: Institutions and Entrepreneurship. *Foundations and Trends in Entrepreneurship* 5 (3): 135–209.

Bourne, Ryan. 2018. The Leftists Have Got It Wrong—We Shouldn't Care About Inequality at All. *The Telegraph (UK)*, January 4.

Brown, Jeffrey R., and Jiekun Huang. 2017. All the President's Friends: Political Access and Firm Value. National Bureau of Economic Research, *Working Paper No. 23356*, April. Accessed September 4, 2017. http://www.nber.org/papers/w23356

Buchanan, James M. 1971. Equality as Fact and Norm. *Ethics* 81 (3): 228–240.

———. 1983. Fairness, Hope, and Justice. In *New Directions in Economic Justice*, ed. Roger Skurski, 53–89. Notre Dame, IN: University of Notre Dame Press.

Canayaz, Mehmet İhsan, Jose Vincente Martinez, and Han N. Ozsoylev. 2016. Is the Revolving Door of Washington a Back Door to Government Contracts and Excess Stock Market Returns? December 20. Accessed August 31, 2017. https://papers.ssrn.com/sol3/papers.cfm?abstract_id=2596520

Chamlee-Wright, Emily, and Justus A. Myers. 2008. Discovery and Social Learning in Non-Priced Environments: An Austrian View of Social Network Theory. *Review of Austrian Economics* 21: 151–166.

Cingano, Federico. 2014. Trends in Income Inequality and Its Impact on Economic Growth. OECD, *Social, Employment and Migration, Working*

Papers No. 163, December. Accessed September 4, 2017. http://www.oecd.org/els/soc/trends-in-income-inequality-and-its-impact-on-economic-growth-SEM-WP163.pdf

Corcoran, Katie, David Pettinicchio, and Jacob Young. 2015. Perceptions of Structural Injustice and Efficacy: Participation in Low/Moderate/High-Cost Forms of Collective Action. *Sociological Inquiry* 85 (3): 429–461.

Côté, Stéphane, Julian House, and Robb Willer. 2015. High Economic Inequality Leads Higher-Income Individuals to Be Less Generous. *Proceedings of the National Academy of Sciences of the United States of America* 112 (52): 15838–15843.

Cruz, Marcio, James Foster, Bryce Quillin, and Philip Schellekens. 2015. Ending Extreme Poverty and Sharing Prosperity: Progress and Policies. World Bank Group, *Policy Research Note 15/03*, October. Accessed September 4, 2017. http://pubdocs.worldbank.org/en/109701443800596288/PRN03Oct2015TwinGoals.pdf

Della Porta, Donatella. 2015. *Social Movements in Times of Austerity*. Cambridge, MA: Polity Press.

Diamond, Peter A. 2016. Addressing the Forces Driving Inequality in the United States. *Contemporary Economic Policy* 34 (3): 403–411.

diZerega, Gus. 1989. Democracy as a Spontaneous Order. *Critical Review: A Journal of Politics and Society* 3: 206–240.

Dopfer, Kurt, and Jason Potts. 2008. *The General Theory of Economic Evolution*. London, UK: Routledge.

Dopfer, Kurt, John Foster, and Jason Potts. 2004. Micro-Meso-Macro. *Journal of Evolutionary Economics* 14 (3): 263–279.

Eberstadt, Nicholas. 2017. Longevity, Education, and the Huge New Worldwide Increases in Equality. In *Anti-Piketty: Capital for the 21st Century*, ed. Jean-Philippe Delsol, Nicolas Lecaussin, and Emmanuel Martin, 19–28. Washington, DC: Cato Institute.

Gaby, Sarah, and Neal Caren. 2016. The Rise of Inequality: How Social Movements Shape Discursive Fields. *Mobilization: An International Quarterly* 21 (4): 413–429.

Geloso, Vincent, and Steven Horwitz. 2017. Inequality: First, Do No Harm. *The Independent Review* 22 (1): 121–134.

Halter, Daniel, Manuel Oechslin, and Josef Zweimüller. 2014. Inequality and Growth: The Neglected Time Dimension. *Journal of Economic Growth* 19 (1): 81–104.

Hassett, Kevin A., and Aparna Mathur. 2012. A New Measure of Consumption Inequality. American Enterprise Institute, *AEI Economic Studies*. Accessed

September 3, 2017. http://www.aei.org/wp-content/uploads/2012/06/-a-new-measure-of-consumption-inequality_142931647663.pdf
Koplenig, Alexander. 2017. The Impact of Lacking Metadata for the Measurement of Cultural and Linguistic Change using the Google NGram Data Sets—Reconstructing the Composition of the German Corpus in Times of WWII. *Digital Scholarship in the Humanities* 32 (1): 169–188.
Leigh, Andrew. 2005. Deriving Long-Run Inequality Series from Tax Data. *Economic Record* 81 (s1): S58–S70.
Lin, Ken-Hou, and Donald Tomaskovic-Devey. 2014. How Financialization Leads to Income Inequality. *Institute for New Economic Thinking*, October 16. Accessed September 1, 2017. https://www.ineteconomics.org/perspectives/blog/how-financialization-leads-to-income-inequality
Lindsey, Brink, and Steven M. Teles. 2017. *The Captured Economy: How the Powerful Enrich Themselves, Slow Down Growth, and Increase Inequality*. Oxford, UK: Oxford University Press.
Madison, Gary Brent. 1997. *The Political Economy of Civil Society and Human Rights*. London, UK: Routledge.
Milanović, Branko. 2008. *Worlds Apart: Measuring International and Global Inequality*. Princeton, NJ: Princeton University Press.
Murray, Cameron K., and Paul Frijters. 2017. *Game of Mates: How Favours Bleed the Nation*. Brisbane: Publicious Pty. Ltd.
Nell, Guinevere Liberty. 2017. *The Driving Force of the Collective: Post-Austrian Theory in Response to Israel Kirzner*. London, UK: Palgrave Macmillan.
Neves, Pedro Cunha, Oscar Afonso, and Sandra Tavares Silva. 2016. A Meta-Analytic Reassessment of the Effects of Inequality on Growth. *World Development* 78: 386–400.
Novak, Mikayla. 2016. Deirdre McCloskey, Kirznerian Growth and the Role of Social Netwotks: Comment. *Economic Affairs* 36 (2): 217–220.
Okun, Arthur M. 1975. *Equality and Efficiency: The Big Tradeoff*. Washington, DC: Brookings Institution.
Organisation of Economic Co-Operation and Development (OECD). 2015. *In It Together: Why Less Inequality Benefits All*. Paris, France: OECD Publishing.
Ostry, Jonathan D., Andrew Berg, and Charalambos G. Tsangarides. 2014. Redistribution, Inequality, and Growth. International Monetary Fund (IMF), *Staff Discussion Note SDN/14/02*, February. Accessed September 4, 2017. https://www.imf.org/external/pubs/ft/sdn/2014/sdn1402.pdf
Paynter, Robert. 1989. The Archaeology of Equality and Inequality. *Annual Review of Anthropology* 18: 369–399.

Pechenick, Eitan Adam, Christopher M. Danforth, and Peter Sheridan Dodds. (2015). Characterizing the Google Books Corpus: Strong Limits to Inferences of Socio-Cultural and Linguistic Evolution. *Plos One* 10 (10): e0137041. Accessed August 31, 2017. https://doi.org/10.1371/journal.pone.0137041

Pew Research Center. 2014. Emerging and Developing Economies Much More Optimistic Than Rich Countries About the Future, October 9. Accessed September 4, 2017. http://www.pewglobal.org/files/2014/10/Pew-Research-Center-Inequality-Report-FINAL-October-17-2014.pdf

Pickerill, Jenny, and John Krinsky. 2012. Why Does Occupy Matter? *Social Movement Studies* 11 (3): 279–287.

Piff, Paul K., Daniel M. Stancato, Stéphane Côté, Rodolfo Mendoza-Denton, and Dacher Keltner. 2012. Higher Social Class Predicts Increased Unethical Behaviour. *Proceedings of the National Academy of Sciences of the United States of America* 109 (11): 4086–4091.

Piketty, Thomas. 2014. *Capital in the Twenty-First Century: The Dynamics of Inequality, Wealth, and Growth.* Translated by Arthur Goldhammer. Cambridge, MA: The Belknap Press of Harvard University Press.

Piketty, Thomas, and Emmanuel Saez. 2003. Income Inequality in the United States, 1913–1938. *The Quarterly Journal of Economics* 118 (1): 1–39.

Potts, Jason, and Kate Morrison. 2007. Meso Comes to Markets: Comment on 'Markets Come to Bits'. *Journal of Economic Behavior & Organization* 63 (2): 307–312.

Rasmussen, Dennis C. 2016. Adam Smith on What is Wrong with Economic Inequality. *American Political Science Review* 110 (2): 342–352.

Reeves, Richard V. 2016. Inequality Built the Trump Coalition, Even If He Won't Solve It. *Brookings Institution blog*, September 26. Accessed August 31, 2017. https://www.brookings.edu/blog/fixgov/2016/09/26/inequality-built-the-trump-coalition-even-if-he-wont-solve-it/

Rojas, Fabio. 2017. *Theory for the Working Sociologist*. New York, NY: Columbia University Press.

Scheidel, Walter. 2017. *The Great Leveler: Violence and the History of Inequality from the Stone Age to the Twenty-First Century*. Princeton, NJ: Princeton University Press.

Snow, David A., and Peter B. Owens. 2014. Social Movements and Social Inequality: Toward a More Balanced Assessment of the Relationship. In *Handbook of the Social Psychology of Inequality*, ed. Jane D. McLeod, Edward J. Lawler, and Michael Schwalbe, 657–681. Dordrecht, Germany: Springer.

Snowdon, Christopher. 2010. *The Spirit Level Delusion: Fact-Checking the Left's New Theory of Everything*. Ripon, UK: Democracy Institute/Little Dice.

Solt, Frederick. 2015. Economic Inequality and Nonviolent Protest. *Social Science Quarterly* 96 (5): 1314–1327.

Starmans, Christina, Mark Sheskin, and Paul Bloom. 2017. Why People Prefer Unequal Societies. *Nature Human Behavior* 1 (82): 1–7.

Stellar, Jennifer E., Vida M. Manzo, Michael W. Kraus, and Dacher Keltner. 2012. Class and Compassion: Socioeconomic Factors Predict Responses to Suffering. *Emotion* 12 (3): 449–459.

Stiglitz, Joseph E. 2012. *The Price of Inequality*. New York, NY: W. W. Norton & Co.

Sumner, Scott. 2017. More Ginis Please. Liberty Fund, *EconLog blog*, May 29. Accessed September 3, 2017. http://econlog.econlib.org/archives/2017/05/the_gini_coeffi.html

Tarnoff, Ben. 2017. Robots Won't Just Take Our Jobs—They'll Make the Rich Even Richer. *The Guardian*, March 2. Accessed September 1, 2017. https://www.theguardian.com/technology/2017/mar/02/robot-tax-job-elimination-livable-wage

Thewissen, Stefan. 2014. Is It the Income Distribution or Redistribution That Affects Growth? *Socio-Economic Review* 12 (3): 545–571.

Wagner, Richard E. 2007. *Fiscal Sociology and the Theory of Public Finance*. Cheltenham, UK: Edward Elgar.

———. 2010. *Mind, Society, and Human Action: Time and Knowledge in a Theory of Social Economy*. London, UK: Routledge.

———. 2014. Entangled Political Economy: A Keynote Address. *Advances in Austrian Economics* 18: 15–36.

———. 2016. *Politics as a Peculiar Business: Insights from a Theory of Entangled Political Economy*. Cheltenham, UK: Edward Elgar.

Watson, William. 2015. *The Inequality Trap: Fighting Capitalism Instead of Poverty*. Toronto, Canada: University of Toronto Press.

Wilkinson, Richard G., and Kate Pickett. 2009. *The Spirit Level: Why More Equal Societies Almost Always Do Better*. London, UK: Allen Lane.

van Zanden, Jan Luiten, Joerg Baten, Marco Mira d'Ercole, Auke Rijpma, Comal Smith, and Marcel Timmer. 2014. *How Was Life? Global Well-Being Since 1820*. Paris, France: OECD Publishing.

Part I

Theoretical Foundations

2

Entangled Political Economy: A General Introduction

Introduction

An interpretation of what gives modern humans the self-ascribed Latin name, *Homo sapiens* ("wise man"), is their ability to render some sense of the world about us through acts of theorising. Among the astonishing array of theories that people have devised are social theories or, in other words, frameworks or paradigms used to describe and assess features of shared human existence. The merit of social theory is that it provides the theorist—who incidentally happens to be a participant within the society about which they theorise—an array of organised thought-patterns for comprehending complex human behaviour and practices.

The mainstream economic position developed during the twentieth century emphasises the choices exercised by fully knowledgeable, perfectly informed individuals who rationally engage in optimising behaviour subject to constraints. The seamless operation of the economy in the mainstream frame is, in effect, dependent upon heavily simplified bundles of theoretical assumptions about preferences, optimisation, markets, knowledge, and coordination (Potts 2000). Should actions undertaken by economic actors within markets not conform with

M. Novak, *Inequality*, Palgrave Studies in Classical Liberalism,
https://doi.org/10.1007/978-3-319-89417-1_2

underlying mainstream assumptions—that is, if individuals behave less-than-rationally, are not perfectly knowledgeable or informative, and have incoherent preferences—it is said the market "fails" because there are still unexploited opportunities for economic gains to be made.

In mainstream economic theory there is a prominent role for policymakers (implicitly advised by economists) to ensure that choices made by individuals yield better, more efficient resource-allocation outcomes. According to one reflection of the development of twentieth-century economic thought, "economists needed no persuading that the market had little capacity for self-correction and adjustment to disequilibrium; thus, they treated the state as a *deus ex machina* that could close the gap between theory and reality" (Boettke 1997, p. 43). Essentially, the policymaker is unrealistically treated as a distant, alien agent estranged from society that, nonetheless, exogenously "acts on economy to shift its equilibrium" (Wagner 2014, p. 21).

Mainstream economics is often lauded for its analytical tractability and conceptual clarity, but it also comes in for methodological criticism. Over the past decade or so a novel theoretical framework of human action, labelled as "entangled political economy,"[1] has assumed its place within the economics literature. Posed as an alternative to the mainstream perspective, entangled political economy illuminates the networked features and evolutionary properties inherent in a more realistic conception of political economy, and how these features influence economic, political, and social outcomes.

This chapter outlines the key principles underpinning the entangled political economy framework. In the next section, we contrast the mainstream approach to political economy against entangled political economy. This is followed by a discussion about the nature of economic, social, and political activities within entangled political economy. Although the "structured living-togetherness" of entanglement is endemic throughout human existence, the interdependencies that emerge have significant implications for the vitality of effective, workable orders of human action. The implications of such matters are also canvassed in this chapter. This chapter concludes by reinforcing the key foundations and insights of entangled political economy theory.

Entangled Political Economy as Alternative, and Antidote, to Mainstream Political Economy

An emblematic feature of mainstream, conventional economics is its theoretical treatment of the concepts of economy and polity as both holistic and separate entities. Both economy and polity are reduced to entities occupying the field of political-economic consideration—the economy being reduced to a representative economic agent, and the polity reduced to a single entity (oftentimes, the representative, median voter of public choice theory). What distinguishes the economic from the political is that the unitary political agent exogenously acts in a unidirectional fashion to alter previously generated economic outcomes. Convention paints a comparative static portrait of an omniscient, benevolent planner, aloofly injecting fiscal and regulatory interventions into markets which supposedly fail to achieve optimal resource allocations or desirable distributional outcomes (Novak 2017).

Think of an economy as a block of Swiss cheese. The economy-as-Swiss-cheese is entirely adequate on its own account, yet it is filled with holes (or the bubbles of carbon dioxide produced by bacteria in the cheese, otherwise known as "eyes"). For our purpose, let us suppose the eyes in the cheese are perceived as a manifestation of "failure," somehow conceived. The "political-actor-as-cheese-perfector" elects to redress the failure by making the block of cheese "blind," doing so by filling the holes with additional cheese. There are other metaphorical ways of describing the way in which a separate, disinterested polity tries to perfect the allocational (or distributional) situation of the economy, and these have crept into the economic literature. The position of policymakers in mainstream thinking has been depicted as, variously, "engineers," "surgeons," "plumbers," "craftsmen," and so on (Duflo 2017).

The illustrative examples presented here are consistent with a vision of political economy wherein economic and political entities are separable. This is referred to as "additive political economy," and it gives rise to a notion that equilibrium is conceptualised prior to politics but that political activity seeks to modify that equilibrium later (Wagner 2014).

This mode of thinking is pervasive in conventional economic theory and analysis, insofar as it portrays a role for governmental action altering economic conditions, *ex post*, with their taxes, spending initiatives, or regulatory edicts.

Additive political economy, presumptively consisting of fallen economic agents on the one hand and enlightened political agents on the other, has been challenged at least since the last quarter of the twentieth century. Austrian economic thought emphasises interaction and process within markets, as opposed to the static, equilibrium theorising of orthodoxy, reflecting the inherent inquisitiveness of human beings to discover and realise new sources of economic value. An Austrian-style process approach is just as conceivable for describing political activity, as some economists have suggested (DiLorenzo 1988; Wohlgemuth 1995, 2002). Public choice theory has also arisen as an important strand of thought, stressing the existence of a motivational equivalence in economics and politics whereby people acting in both arenas may respond to self-interest and public-interest impulses (Buchanan [1979] 1999).

Developments in complexity science, evolutionary theory, and networking analysis have also laid bare the conceptual simplicity of additive political economy. These insights reveal diverse interactional ecologies consisting of heterogeneous individuals, fallible yet capable of seeking relationships and grafting advantages, and whose actions unfold in both time and space. The works of Richard Wagner have reflected a desire to absorb insights from these, and similar, theoretical advances to present a credible alternative to additive political economy. As previously mentioned, Wagner challenges the mainstream orthodoxy by emphasising an evolutionary political economy wherein commingled economic, political, and other agents relate to one another on the same social plane. This theoretical framework is called "entangled political economy."

Given there is no simple addition across various entities in entangled political economy, the relationships generated among and between economic and political participants are of paramount importance for both the durability and robustness of the civil society in which they, and other actors, inhabit. Just as economic agents act competitively or collusively, depending on the incentives available to them and the institutions in existence, participants within the political order, likewise, compete and collude. Indeed, this is precisely what gives a political economy its knotted timbre: "political economy does not denote the union of separate spheres of polity and economy. Rather, it denotes an entangled network of enterprises that are constituted under different institutional arrangements that generate a continually evolving admixture of cooperation and conflict" (Wagner 2010, p. 160).

It is possible to visualise the distinction between additive and entangled political economy with the aid of network theory (Fig. 2.1). The hexagonals in the diagram depict economic (and other non-political) actors, whereas the triangles represent the political actors. Using the terminology of network theory, the actors are described as "elements," "nodes," or "vertices" of the network. The lines between the actors are referred to as "connections," "edges," or "links," suggesting the presence of some relationship between the actors. The connections in Fig. 2.1 may denote flows of commodities, incomes, or other forms of value. For the time being, assume that all actors observe the same (formal and informal) institutional rules, as represented by the same thick black lines of connections between actors.

The model of additive political economy is illustrated on the left side of Fig. 2.1, with the economy and polity each resembling formless masses. The unitary political entity enacts an intervention onto the rest of society

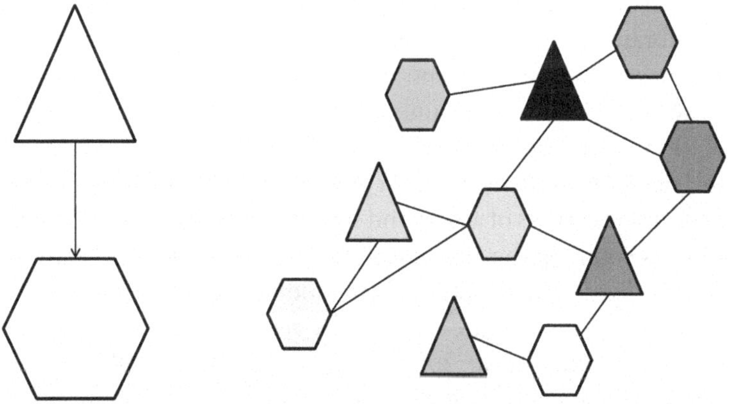

Fig. 2.1 Additive political economy (left side) versus entangled political economy (right side). Source: Wagner (2007); Author's illustrations

to achieve some public policy objective, as shown by the top-down arrow tracing from polity to non-polity. On the right of the figure is a stylised depiction of entangled political economy, bearing in mind we are illustrating a static snapshot of the necessarily evolving relationships between the non-political and the political. There are three features of entangled political economy of immediate interest:

- First, entangled political economy consists of a multitude of non-political and political elements, with different shades representing the diverse operational, technical, and other characteristics of the elements.
- Second, relationships between non-political and political actors are "open" in a sense that the connections can run in either one direction or both, thus adding a further dimension of complexity as compared against additive political economy.
- Third, the entangled political economy network is incomplete in that not every non-political agent is connected with every political agent, and vice versa. The incomplete attachments between the players give rise to structural relationships which can potentially be very complex, particularly should additional actors enter, and engage within, the network.

Forging interactions with others typically involves a great semblance of creativity. This not only encapsulates the possibility that connections between network nodes change, but that the nodes themselves can adjust and recalibrate. With the alterations of elements and links taking place, we have *evolution* in the present, with great likelihood (but not guaranteed) it would persist into the unknown future, whereas the past episodes of evolution culminate into what is generally called *history*. Acknowledging that the elements in the network, representing individuals or enterprises, are the ultimate carriers of action and source of novelty, we can decompose evolution as entailing the *variation*, *selection*, and *retention* of varied rules (i.e. generically desirable "ways of being, doing and knowing" either economically, socially, or politically) held by economic, social, and political participants (Dopfer et al. 2004; Dopfer and Potts 2008). It is these properties which condition the varying degrees of entanglement in Wagner's theoretical system.

Another fundamental point of difference between additive and entangled political economies is that there are different "levels" in which competitive and collusive actions by individuals and their enterprises occur, at least in the entangled variant. The *micro* level of interaction focuses upon individuals and individual agencies and the rules they carry; *meso* level is the analysis of individual rules and their carrier populations; and, finally, the *macro* level represents the generic coordination of all rules and all carriers (Potts 2007).

Evolutionary processes at the meso level are usually given priority by the works of Potts and colleagues, and are duly acknowledged in Wagner's research. This reflects their important insight that heterogeneous populations of individuals happen to coordinate with each other by subscribing to shared rules.[2] Sharply contrasting the micro-meso-macro perspective of entangled political economy, the formless masses within additive political economy effectively collapse the micro, meso, and macro spaces for action into one representation, and thus a rich vein of theoretical analysis is removed from the additive scene.

So far we have largely referred to interactions between economic actors and political actors. As classical liberals from Alexis de Tocqueville through to Richard Cornuelle remind us, there are other societal participants who interact and organise for altruistic and solidaristic purposes that do not fit neatly within economic and political ordering. These societal participants may operate as social entrepreneurs, donors, and philanthropists, or may agree to devise organisational structures (largely running on a non-profit basis) such as charities and mutual aid associations. Other relevant entities include hobby, recreational and other clubs and societies; interest groups and professional associations; activist organisations and social movements; and other civic bodies. Non-profit organisations and similar facets of civil society are, to a considerable extent, implicated in the knottiness of entangled political economy.

The individuals and entities composing what we call the "communal order"—representing those activities undertaken with the direct purpose of rendering mutual assistance to others in need, or to carry out acts of caring, enlightenment, and socialising—can readily be accommodated into the networking structure of an entangled political economy. The right side of Fig. 2.2 presents a meso-level perspective of entangled

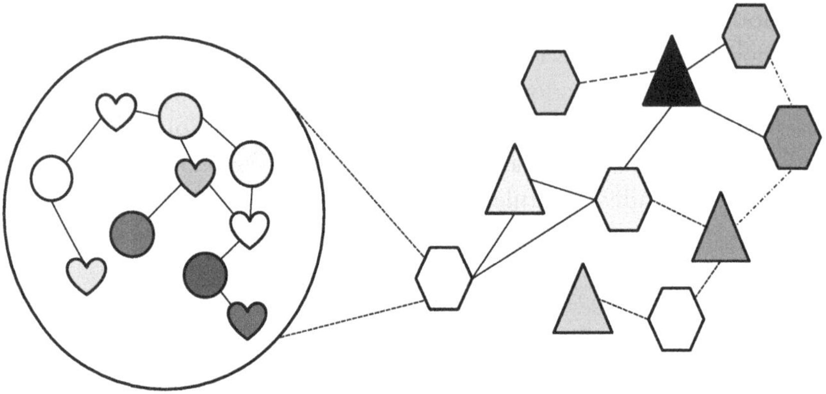

Fig. 2.2 Entangled political economy, including communal order activities. Source: Aligica and Wagner (2015); Author's illustrations

political economy, in that each element represents sub-populations of individual actors commingling in observance of shared institutional, organisational, technical, or other rules. The hexagonals represent non-political actors, and the triangles political actors.

Upon closer examination of the meso structure of one of the hexagonals, we find it actually consists of five circles (denoting for-profit, economic agents or entities) and five hearts (non-profit, communal agents or entities) interacting at the micro level. The connections within the meso population being microscopically examined can be broadened out to not only include economic or financial flows but logistical alliances, social supports, or other forms of value. The meso sub-population under close scrutiny adheres to the same institutional rule, as shown by the same thick black line of connection between the agents.

Having laid out the core properties of intertwined activity and conduct, it is appropriate to consider the relationship between individual action and the social environment in which such actions are conducted. Wagner and certain other scholars in the modern classical liberal tradition (e.g. Lewis 2000, 2012; Martin 2011) submit there is some credence to the notion that conventions, expectations, norms, and practices observed in society do influence the conduct of individuals. As Scott Beaulier and Peter Boettke have similarly indicated, "the individuals acting in the social world are deeply affected by the noneconomic institutions of power, culture, and history surrounding them" (Beaulier and Boettke 2004, p. 196). This is not to suggest, however, that the direction of causation is unilateral, running from social mores onto individual deliberation and action. There is a good case to make that there is, in fact, a bi-directional interrelation between the individual and the society in which they inhabit:

> Only individuals undertake action, but as social creatures bound up in various practices, conventions, and organizations that have emerged through preceding interactions, societal configurations feed back onto individual action. It is always possible to offer descriptive statements about macro or societal phenomena … however, any meaningful analytical statement that pertains to the macro entity denoted as society must make connections with individuals inside the society, for it is those individuals and their connections that drive societal change. (Wagner 2016a, p. 86)

It is our central claim that an evolutionary and interactionist account of societal phenomena, as provided by entangled political economy, provides a far richer depiction of the ways and means in which people coordinate and engage with each other. We proffer this claim on the basis of a comparison against the more rigid, and ultimately dissatisfying, conventional narrative grounded in additive political economy strictures.

Entangled Political Economy and Its Perspectives on Economic and Political Organisation

From the perspective of entangled political economy, the pro-social *Homo sapiens* consistently demonstrate their inclination to compete with each other, irrespective of the organisational or institutional setting in which such behaviour is filtered. This competitive process is, for better or for worse, synonymous with action within the economic order, with researchers typically limiting their discussion about those competitive processes which unfold within market settings.

Generically speaking, markets are populated by producers (sellers) and consumers (buyers) who are all seeking mutually agreeable exchanges of commodities (received by consumers) for sales revenue (received by producers). On the seller side, the production and provision of commodities reflects the hypotheses (or expectations) of suppliers as to the kind and intensity of consumer preferences, and the relative prices emergently attached to products communicate knowledge to consumers about the underlying commodity values and production costs. The markets which compose the economic order happen to come in many meso-forms because of the kinds of products sold, characteristics of market participants, legal structures, and so on (Boettke et al. 2004).

Irrespective of whether the products for sale reflect variation of existing goods and services, or replicate commodities already in existence, producers making the best conjectures about satisfying consumer demands gain a competitive advantage. Successful producers receive sufficient sales revenues and potentially enjoy profits, in comparison with their competitors. On the other hand, those producers who do not attract a large enough market share for their commodities are more likely to incur insufficient sales revenue, threatening low profitability or even an outright financial loss (Novak 2005). It is also known that buyers themselves engage in forms of competition against each other to discover the most efficacious purchases they could potentially make which, in turn, affect the economic fate of suppliers (Boettke 2012).

In the opinion of Friedrich Hayek, the "marvel" of the market process—in which competition is of great importance—is that it provides a decentralised means through which knowledge about what market participants want is signalled. Individuals engage with the market process to learn about what it is they want, what others want, and what feasible opportunities for gain are available: "which goods are scarce goods, or which things are goods, and how scarce or valuable they are—these are precisely the things which competition has to discover" (Hayek [1968] 1978, p. 181).

Arguably what is less appreciated is that competitive impulses, to some degree, also drive human behaviour within political settings. General elections enabling citizen-voters to select political candidates for representative political office, or the convening of plebiscites or referenda enabling a majority (or super-majority) of voters to decide upon specific public issues, are obvious examples of political competition. Political advertising, speeches given at public rallies, and small-talk with voters in public spaces are also employed by aspirant politicians in their quest to generate followership and secure sufficient electoral support.

As Wagner (2016a) rightly notes there are other, perhaps less obvious, forms of political competition. To be included among these are the jostling efforts of politicians, once elected, to obtain lucrative positions such as committee memberships, ministries, or even leadership status. It would be remiss of us to not mention the competitive striving amongst public sector administrative staff for more desirable offices and positions in the context of democratic political processes (Niskanen 1971).

Belying the popular image fostered by civil and other associations, whose publicly stated missions involve care and support for others, competition is also evident within the communal order. Non-profit organisations compete to receive donations, philanthropic funds, bequests, and other forms of financial revenue, and regularly attempt to solicit funds by publicising their specific causes and organising benefit appeals. Other entities within the communal order, such as interest groups and professional associations, vie against each other for affiliation and support within the broader civil society—an example of this could be seen in the quarrelling between fossil-fuel industry representatives and climate change non-government organisations in their respective efforts to garner social influence.

In an entangled political economy there is perhaps as much collaborative activity between individuals and enterprises as there is competition.[3] Firms and other enterprises organise supply chains, in attempts to more effectively manage inventory flows and harness innovative partnerships, consequently producing higher-quality goods and services for end-consumers at reasonable prices. There are oftentimes numerous instances of cooperation among political representatives over, say, certain aspects of the government's legislative agenda or, in other instances, cross-party efforts to project unity during times of local or national emergencies. Associational groups within the communal order may also form alliances or coalitions, whether loosely or tightly, over certain matters of shared interest.

Competitive and collaborative actions undertaken by individuals, or groups thereof, within an entangled political economy may fall under a more generalised umbrella concept of *entrepreneurship*. Entrepreneurial conduct need not be understood merely in its well-known economic incarnation but, in fact, as an aspect of generalised human conduct present in all societies across time and space (Boettke and Coyne 2009; Koppl 2006; Koppl and Minniti 2008). As one observer pointedly stated, "[e] ntrepreneurship is an aspect of all human action. Entrepreneurship is a human universal" (Koppl 2006, pp. 1–2).

Entrepreneurship is improvised action by people who are sufficiently mentally alert and socially adept to opportunities potentially enhancing their position, and that of others, in typically novel ways. Those opportunities could be generated either through competition against, or in collaboration with, other people. Major companies such as Apple and Samsung could be said to be exercising entrepreneurship through their competitive development of alternative "smartphone" technologies. Meanwhile, the success of the "Black Lives Matter" movement in raising public awareness about racial injustice could be seen, in a sense, as socially entrepreneurial collaborative efforts by alliances within civil society. As for political entrepreneurship, this is frequently demonstrated in the form of ingenious projections of leadership by politicians to encourage a mass followership amongst the citizenry (Wieser [1926] 1983; Mitchell 1984). Consistent with the previously mentioned insight that entrepreneurship is a universal phenomenon, we roughly map the concepts of *economic entrepreneurship*, *social entrepreneurship*, and *political entrepreneurship* onto the initial micro-level injections of novelty into the economic, communal, and political order meso trajectories of evolution, respectively.

It should be recognised that entrepreneurship represents an act of *dissensus* from, rather than consensus with, conventional ways of being, doing, and knowing (i.e. rules) (Boettke and Coyne 2008). Despite social life equipping us with opportunities to better adjust ourselves in the interest of seeking greater alignment with others, the fact is that entrepreneurship oftentimes arouses controversy and discord. Novelty often elicits a modicum of discomfort and resistance among those who bear the costs and fatigues of adjustment and readjustment. Even so, "[w]ithout the possibility of individual entrepreneurs conceiving of new ways of doing things, dissenting from existing social structures, those structures would simply reproduce themselves *ad infinitum*. Interaction may give rise to novelty, but that novelty must be recognized and acted upon by individuals to have any lasting effect" (Martin 2011, p. 141). It is through an appreciation of entrepreneurialism as a human universal that entangled political economy is afforded much of its dynamic calibre.

Entrepreneurialism may be ubiquitous, but it varies in substance, depending upon which realm of civil society they are carried out. One way in which entrepreneurial processes vary is through which "feedback mechanisms" exist to inform actors whether or not their actions are beneficial and advantageous, both to their interests and the interest of others. Scholarly proponents of the Austrian school of economics indicate that decentralised economic coordination is achieved through the emergent properties of relative prices, (clearly defined and secured) property rights, and the mechanisms of financial profits and losses. "What spurs entrepreneurship," says Peter Boettke and Christopher Coyne, "is the lure of profit, and what disciplines entrepreneurs is the penalty of loss. The property rights structure provides the incentives and establishes the issue of the residual claimant, and the price system provides economic actors with the information to act on the bases of those incentives to utilize resources effectively" (Boettke and Coyne 2009, p. 167). Each of these background features serves as an aid towards productive market entrepreneurship and efficient investments; without those feedback mechanisms there is little feasible basis to conduct appropriate economic calculations about how, where, and when to produce and exchange what goods and services for the benefit of other people.

For the largest part, individuals and associations operating within the communal order tend not to directly rely upon the "tight feedbacks" (Martin 2010) available in markets when making their decisions. Even so, it is suggested that some "looser" kinds of feedback help non-profits and other civic groups to "do well by doing good." Reputational mechanisms serve as a useful feedback, directing donors and supporters towards credible groups and associations displaying effectiveness in the fulfilment of their missions. These signals provide incentives for investment (of time, money, and degree of engagement) in worthwhile ventures of mutual assistance (Chamlee-Wright and Myers 2008; Boettke and Coyne 2009).

Political entrepreneurship—efforts to discover opportunities for political gain—similarly plays an important role in entangled political economy. However, feedbacks that condition and constrain entrepreneurship within the political scene are certainly not economic, given the absence of prices, property, and profit-and-loss: "[t]he political world does not generate … a monetary indicator in any direct fashion because political practice is organized within an institutional framework that is incapable of generating prices and transferable claims to ownership rights over cash flows" (Wagner 2016a, p. 27). Reputational mechanisms may not necessarily tighten political feedbacks by engendering desirable entrepreneurial responses, either, given the biases exerted by "rationally ignorant voters, special interest groups, and vote-seeking politicians" (Boettke and Coyne 2009, p. 185).

The dissimilarities between the kinds of entrepreneurial action are magnified once we consider the distinction between what is labelled as "dyadic" versus "triadic" exchanges (Podemska-Mikluch and Wagner 2013; Wagner 2016a, b). By way of principle, it could be said that interactions unfolding within the market sphere generally consist of mutually beneficial, value-added exchanges voluntarily undertaken between parties. These exchanges are called "dyadic" exchanges, and resemble the kinds of "win-win" economic interactions lauded by classical liberals as conducive to economic prosperity and social peace. It would also be presumed by liberals that, by and large, the same principles apply to proposals for new models of care and support within the communal order.

Entangled political economy researchers have identified triadic exchanges which "denote interactions that are beneficial to a subset of the participants implicated in the transaction while being detrimental to the remainder of those participants who contribute to financing that activity as forced carriers" (Aligica and Wagner 2015, p. 8). The phenomenon of triadic exchange appears to be most prevalent within the political order of society wherein fiscal and regulatory proposals to reallocate or redistribute resources, realigning the pattern and strength of network connections, "feature a winning subset of people gaining at the expense of others in society" (Patrick and Wagner 2015, p. 105). The prospect of securing triadic exchanges may prove especially attractive to managers of underperforming economic enterprises vulnerable to competitive challenge, who wish to avoid liquidation in market settings.

Richard Wagner's research highlights not only variations in processual form between non-political and political exchanges, but potentially extensive differences with respect to organisational substance. Although polity does not denote a singular entity, the role of legislative assemblies is accorded special attention, with Wagner himself referring to these as a primary example through which the "peculiar business" of state takes place.

A legislative assembly is a deliberative grouping of politicians who are charged with the power to initiate, modify, or repeal the legislation of the jurisdiction (national or sub-national) they are elected to represent. Legislation gives effect to fiscal and regulatory policies, and it is the authority of the members of the legislature which equips the public sector with immense powers to invoke triadic exchanges. As economic historian Robert Higgs once put it, "[b]efore the government can spend or employ, it must obtain the authority to promote a specified public purpose. If the requisite authority cannot be acquired (a legislative question) and sustained (a judicial question), then the matter is settled: no authority, no program" (Higgs 1987, pp. 29–30).

The legislature may filter enduring episodes of political interaction, but the fact remains that "[p]arliaments don't produce goods and services for customers, but rather serve as intermediaries between people who are seeking support for their enterprises and people who have the means to support those enterprises" (Wagner 2016a, p. 163). The members of society who wish to alter existing dyadic exchanges within the economic and communal orders invest time, money, and effort to persuade politicians, the latter having the potential to legislate so that dyadic exchanges are transformed into triadic.

Bureaucracies represent another important component of modern public administration, and their modes of operation have attracted the interest of several prominent classical liberal scholars during the twentieth century (Mises 1944; Tullock 1965; Niskanen 1968, 1971). Public choice theorists contend managers and other staff employed by official agencies, offices, and bureaus wield political influence through their capacity to advise government over the various implications of public policies, as well as a result of their responsibilities to design and enforce legislative edicts. Through the evolutionary cut-and-trust of political affairs there seems great potential for bureaucrats to exercise both discretion and influence. Salter (2016) suggests that an examination of bureaucratic behaviour—including the effects of bureaucratic discretion upon democratic accountability and the integrity of non-political conduct—could serve as a potentially fruitful extension of the entangled political economy research programme.

Under the entangled political economy approach, the coverage of peculiar enterprises is not limited to legislatures and bureaucracies. Richard Wagner states that certain individuals and entities (mis)apply moral and ethical norms whilst engaging within a given order of civil society, but that are more appropriately applied within other orders (Wagner 2016a, 2017; also Salter 2012). An extensive degree of entanglement between an economic enterprise seeking to obtain a fiscal or regulatory advantage, say, and a political enterprise may create a situation whereby the commercial norms of the economic enterprise become gradually displaced by political norms. The commercial ethics of industriousness, honest dealings with others, and exemplary customer service get "crowded out" by political ethics such as loyalty, obedience, and respect for hierarchy, with significant implications for the integrity of sound ordering principles within entangled political economy. By virtue of the awkward enmeshing of commercial and political moralities, the affected economic enterprise mutates into what has been labelled as a "monstrous moral hybrid."

Assume that the operation of a given hybridised economic enterprise may, for some reason, be generating unequal income and wealth outcomes. By virtue of its extensive entanglement with the political domain, the consequent inequalities generated are most assuredly deemed, from a classical liberal perspective, to be unacceptable. However, the free and open competition that would ordinarily dissipate illiberally sourced inequality is severely compromised by the political imprimatur to support the economic enterprise (as measured by the flow of subsidies, contract work, regulatory-specific rents, etc.). Accordingly, the politically supported economic enterprise, the inequality it generates, and the confounding ethical qualities embodied in its operations will win the day.

The monstrous moral hybrid problem can also pervade interactions between non-economic and political actors. A growing concern expressed by non-government organisations, charities, and other mutual-assistance bodies has been that the outsourcing of public sector welfare and social service programmes has been accompanied by stringent regulatory conditions. Those conditions are not limited to how recipients are to expend funds—they incorporate additional, politically motivated considerations not directly related to the delivery of the outsourced programmes, which can then be seen to compromise the underlying "social mission" of the recipient entities. As a result, the communal enterprise takes on more of the ethical notions commonly perceived to be associated with political action, and less of those norms considered most appropriate to the fulfilment of communally ordered mutual assistance. Other applications of monstrous moral hybridity, resulting from extreme commingling between agents motivated by varied ordering principles, may also be identified—for example, the infiltration of commercial ethical norms in political action as government engage economic agents to deliver basic public services (e.g. law, order, and justice).

Managing Tectonic Relationships in Entangled Political Economy

The upshot of the preceding discussion is that human action overlaps several domains of activity, reflecting the obvious point that we live, and cross paths, with each other. The confluence of activities of differing characters and qualities within entangled political economy presents significant opportunities for heterogeneous individuals and groups to procure gains. The forms that "structured living-togetherness" ultimately assume also pose immense challenges to the objective of ensuring that certain fundamental values, such as liberty, are maintained.

In keeping with his view that certain Italian scholars of the late nineteenth and early twentieth centuries yield social-scientific insights of contemporary relevance, Richard Wagner invokes the figure of that famed Italian economist-*cum*-sociologist Vilfredo Pareto concerning the latter's invocation of a division between "logical" and "non-logical" frames of action. Pareto considered all human action to be rational, in that people perform actions in response to desires to fulfil some objective. The key issue is the different environments, or systems of interaction, within which people act, can lead to logical or non-logical (*not* irrational) action (Wagner 2016a, 2017).

In the most general sense, logical action exudes "a direct connection between action and objective which can be rendered sensible to an external observer and which can be tested through experience" (Wagner 2016a, p. 97). As described in the previous section, supplying products through the market sphere on the *ex-ante* presumption that this would generate an adequate stream of revenue flows can be tested against actual market valuations, *ex post*. Prices are attached to the outputs on offer in the market, and this facilitates appraisals of trade-offs between quality and price. In other words, logical action is closely associated with the market domain wherein relative prices allow a direct, "scientific" comparison by observers between magnitudes and performances (Wagner 2017).

The frame of non-logical actions, on the other hand, refers to interactions in which there is a far looser sense of connection between action and outcome: "[i]n settings dominated by non-logical action, the direct link between choice and consequence vanishes, which takes with it the ability to feel good about actions through directly experiencing the consequences of those actions" (Wagner 2016a, p. 99). In the view of Candela and Wagner (2016), politics stands as a primary example of an environment in which non-logical action takes precedence (with religion being another).

Governments may be prone to provide goods for which "it is impossible to test producer claims about the qualitative aspects of the vendor's services" (Wagner 2016a, p. 30). When it comes to these so-called credence goods, it is much more difficult for consumers to discern their quality merely by inspection or by sampling. In this setting, political actors strive to elicit acceptance from those harmed in triadic exchanges in order to maintain their provision. The provision of goods that cannot be rigorously tested (and be potentially rejected) by final consumers—thus coming under the scope of rhetorical persuasion by politicians attempting to rally endorsement and sentiment behind such activities—falls squarely into the realm of non-logical action.

In reality, the distinction between logical and non-logical action is not entirely clear-cut in every instance. Patrick and Wagner (2015) submit, nonetheless, that logical and non-logical frames of human action are incommensurable, bearing significant implications for the evolutionary integrity of a political economy featuring a high degree of complex, intertwining economic (largely logical) and political (largely non-logical) interactions. One of the main features of entangled political economy is the observation that entanglement is a fact of life. Given the interdependencies which draw people together, the encountering of action variously informed by logical and non-logical action framing is likely to produce conflict and discord. The sense of turbulence when economic (and communal) and political enterprises intersect is known in the entangled political economy literature as "social tectonics." In much the same way that shifts in the San Andreas Fault reshape the Californian landscape, or the Wellington Fault alters the geographical profile of New Zealand's North Island, social tectonics may confound the fundamentals of private ordering given the smuggling of the triadic character of exchange into dyadic relations, thus leading to coercion within exchange relationships which would otherwise not transpire (Podemska-Mikluch and Wagner 2013).

The concept of "regime uncertainty," coined by Robert Higgs (1987), is viewed as one of many consequences pursuant to the infusion of political prerogative into the market arena. Regime uncertainty refers to the inability of private investors to foreshadow the extent to which future public sector actions impact the security of property rights and investment yields, adding confusion and turbulence to economic calculation. An underappreciated feature of regime uncertainty is that, from the perspective of the policymaker, a higher frequency of intervention tends to diminish the capacity to maintain clear and consistent (rule-based) policies. The constant opening of new rationales for policy intervention only succeeds in adding to the clutter of a "legacy of accumulation of legislative redress of the negative consequences of meso trajectories by the so effected who could then organise into political units" (Potts 2005).

As noted by Novak (2017), even highly discriminatory political processes regrettably acquire a begrudging tolerance among the populace, insofar as politicians successfully invoke non-logical sentiments as persuasive rationales for their economically meddlesome actions. Taxing, subsidising, or regulating economic (and social) activities may be framed by the political class as "altruistic" acts of caring about tackling certain issues, even if evidence supporting the effectiveness of public intervention is often found wanting. Special interest groups that secure politically generated rents project their own "feel good" narratives in attempts to soothe public animosity—paeans to the effect that "what is good for business is good for the country," and similar sentimentalist rationales, often resonate throughout public discourses.

The concern is that even a sense of begrudging resignation about, let alone exuberant endorsement towards, tectonic encounters can amend the relative payoffs related to interacting non-politically or politically. Consistent with Baumol's (1990) distinction between productive and unproductive entrepreneurship, continuing injections of political action into non-political orders may well incentivise actors to realign their resources towards seeking specific, and particularised, political favours and privileges at the expense of others. An implication is that "[e]ntrepreneurship pursued within the shadow of politics can … undermine liberty, not necessarily all at once but surely through accumulation" (Podemska-Mikluch and Wagner 2012, pp. 14–15).

Richard Wagner has drawn our attention, more broadly, to the issues posed by the gradual encroachment of the political into non-political life. A consequence of "sentimental expressions that resonate with people's desires to feel good about themselves and their activities" (Wagner 2016a, p. 103), non-logical action inherent within political activity can relegate profitable activity and mutual assistance to the background of societal attention and concern. It is conceivable that, as collective action continues to gradually take precedence over non-collective action, the influence of political beliefs, ideologies, sentiments, and values will keep growing in relative importance.

Discovering an acceptable degree of entanglement which does not extirpate liberty requires not only institutional renewal and innovation, but perhaps needs new and attractive "non-logical" ways of inspiring people to support extended liberties and the responsibilities inextricably associated with them (Wagner 2016a; Novak 2017). Alexander Salter (2016) similarly raises a reinvigoration of informal constraints we invariably take for granted—norms, rhetoric and attitudes, and a sense of the "moral imagination"—as warranting further consideration. The importance of informal rules underpinning economic prosperity and social harmony cannot be overstated, an issue which is afforded some attention in subsequent chapters.

Conclusion

Entangled political economy has emerged in recent years as a viable research programme intersecting the social scientific disciplines of economics, political science, sociology, law, and history. It joins the growing cohort of alternatives to political economy which attempts to rekindle an approach to theorising, tracing back to the seminal contributions of Adam Smith (Paganelli 2014) and Carl Menger (Becchio 2014). All of these theoretical expositions emphasise how fallible, yet capable, individuals, driven by a plurality of beliefs, interests, and values, manage to peacefully interact with each other and, in so doing, foster cooperative outcomes (Boettke 2012, 2016; Mitchell and Boettke 2017).

Emphasising the diversity, entrepreneurialism, and vibrancy that are readily detectable in any society, the foundations of entangled political economy stand in stark contrast to the mainstream economic consensus—theoretically reliant upon the fictionally representative agent rather than factually divergent agents; the predominance of the rigid stasis of equilibrium instead of the fluid dynamism of evolution; and prioritising simple instead of complex representations of human conduct.

The sense of entanglement which permeates society is largely inescapable, and should not reflexively be perceived as an automatic problem to be resolved in every circumstance in which it reveals itself. The alternative to entanglement is disentanglement which, in many cases, would undesirably correspond with the solitary, poor, nasty, brutish, short existence of autarky. An accommodation of a multiplex of dispositions, norms, priorities, and standards is the very hallmark of social coordination, with the proviso that the multiplicity of values is subject to change. By the same token, new proposals about how to live will remain endlessly contested, and this contestability can bring about conflict and discord. Many of these flashpoints can be settled to the extent that changes are mutually consented to, and that the agents propounding change continue to respect the inherent right of others to exercise their freedoms in ways they so choose.

Scholars versed in entangled political economy have noted the tendency of individuals and groups to emergently commingle with each other in non-uniform ways. In other words, it is entirely possible for interactions to give rise to economic inequalities. It is also noted that the incomplete networks of entangled political economy may be shaped by the phenomenon of social inequality, and that this can feed into unequal income and wealth distributions about which we have concern. From a theoretical vantage point, we are interested in rigorously applying the framework of entangled political economy to understand and trace the causes and consequences of inequality. This task commences in the next chapter.

Notes

1. Entangled political economy has also been referred to as commingled, conjunctive, intertwined, knotted, or non-separable political economy.
2. It is at the meso level that Potts and other evolutionary economists map what they refer to as meso-evolutionary trajectories 1, 2, and 3 onto variation, selection, and retention decisions.
3. Going one step further, it is quite conceivable that collaborative efforts between individuals and their agencies could, in fact, transform into acts of collusion between the interacting parties. It may generally be said that collaboration represents efforts to associate without limiting the potential for newcomers to join, and without intending to attain privileges at the expense of others, whereas collusion tends to close networked associations and is intended to obtain advantages at the cost of others. Although the difference between collaboration and collusion could vary, and subtly, depending upon the circumstances, the prospect of collusion in social affairs is generally considered to be problematic, for reasons as discussed later in this chapter and in subsequent chapters.

References

Aligica, Paul Dragos, and Richard E. Wagner. 2015. Economic Coordination in Environments with Incomplete Pricing. George Mason University, Department of Economics, *Working Paper No. 15-49*, November 5. Accessed September 4, 2017. https://papers.ssrn.com/sol3/papers.cfm?abstract_id=2686387

Baumol, William J. 1990. Entrepreneurship: Productive, Unproductive, and Destructive. *Journal of Political Economy* 98 (5, Part 1): 893–921.

Beaulier, Scott A., and Peter J. Boettke. 2004. The Really Real in Economics. In *Transforming Economics: Perspectives of the Critical Realist Project*, ed. Paul A. Lewis, 187–201. London, UK: Routledge.

Becchio, Giandomenica. 2014. Carl Menger on States as Orders, Not Organizations: Entangled Economy into a Neo-Mengerian Approach. *Advances in Austrian Economics* 18: 55–66.

Boettke, Peter J. 1997. Where Did Economics Go Wrong? Modern Economics as a Flight from Reality. *Critical Review* 11 (1): 11–64.

———. 2012. *Living Economics: Yesterday, Today, and Tomorrow*. Oakland, CA: Independent Institute.

———. 2016. *Mainline Economics: Six Nobel Lectures in the Tradition of Adam Smith*. Fairfax, VA: Mercatus Center.

Boettke, Peter J., and Christopher J. Coyne. 2008. The Political Economy of the Philanthropic Enterprise. In *Non-Market Entrepreneurship: Interdisciplinary Approaches*, ed. Gordon E. Shockley, Peter M. Frank, and Roger R. Stough, 71–88. Cheltenham, UK: Edward Elgar.

———. 2009. Context Matters: Institutions and Entrepreneurship. *Foundations and Trends in Entrepreneurship* 5 (3): 135–209.

Boettke, Peter J., Christopher J. Coyne, and Peter T. Leeson. 2004. The Many Faces of the Market. *Journal des Economistes et des Etudes Humaines* 14 (2): 71–86.

Buchanan, James M. (1979) 1999. Politics Without Romance: A Sketch of Positive Public Choice Theory and Its Normative Implications. In *Collected Works of James M. Buchanan*, vol. 1, 45–59. Indianapolis, IN: Liberty Fund.

Candela, Rosolino A., and Richard E. Wagner. 2016. Vilfredo Pareto's Theory of Action: An Alternative to Behavioral Economics. George Mason University, Department of Economics, *Working Paper No. 16-35*, September 20. Accessed September 15, 2017. https://papers.ssrn.com/sol3/papers.cfm?abstract_id=2841529

Chamlee-Wright, Emily, and Justus A. Myers. 2008. Discovery and Social Learning in Non-Priced Environments: An Austrian View of Social Network Theory. *Review of Austrian Economics* 21: 151–166.

DiLorenzo, Thomas J. 1988. Competition and Political Entrepreneurship: Austrian Insights into Public-Choice Theory. *Review of Austrian Economics* 2 (1): 59–71.

Dopfer, Kurt, and Jason Potts. 2008. *The General Theory of Economic Evolution*. London, UK: Routledge.

Dopfer, Kurt, John Foster, and Jason Potts. 2004. Micro-Meso-Macro. *Journal of Evolutionary Economics* 14 (3): 263–279.

Duflo, Esther. 2017. Richard T. Ely Lecture: The Economist as Plumber. *American Economic Review* 107 (5): 1–26.

Hayek, Friedrich A. (1968) 1978. Competition as a Discovery Procedure. In *New Studies in Philosophy, Politics, Economics, and the History of Ideas*, 179–190. London, UK: Routledge and Kegan Paul.

Higgs, Robert. 1987. *Crisis and Leviathan: Critical Episodes in the Growth of American Government*. Oxford, UK: Oxford University Press.

Koppl, Roger. 2006. Entrepreneurial Behavior as a Human Universal. In *Entrepreneurship: The Engine of Growth—Volume 1: People*, ed. Maria Minniti, 1–20. Westport, CT: Greenwood Publishing.

Koppl, Roger, and Maria Minniti. 2008. Entrepreneurship and Human Action. In *Non-Market Entrepreneurship: Interdisciplinary Approaches*, ed. Gordon E. Shockley, Peter M. Frank, and Roger R. Stough, 10–27. Cheltenham, UK: Edward Elgar.

Lewis, Paul A. 2000. Realism, Causality and the Problem of Social Structure. *Journal for the Theory of Social Behaviour* 30 (3): 249–268.

———. 2012. Emergent Properties in the Work of Friedrich Hayek. *Journal of Economic Behavior and Organization* 82: 368–378.

Martin, Adam. 2010. Emergent Politics and the Power of Ideas. *Studies in Emergent Order* 3: 212–245.

———. 2011. The Catallactic Point of View. *Studies in Emergent Order* 4: 133–148.

von Mises, Ludwig. 1944. *Bureaucracy*. New Haven, CT: Yale University Press.

Mitchell, William C. 1984. Schumpeter and Public Choice, Part I: Precursor to Public Choice? *Public Choice* 42 (1): 73–88.

Mitchell, Matthew D., and Peter J. Boettke. 2017. *Applied Mainline Economics: Bridging the Gap Between Theory and Public Policy*. Fairfax, VA: Mercatus Center.

Niskanen, William A. 1968. Nonmarket Decision Making: The Peculiar Economics of Bureaucracy. *The American Economic Review* 58 (2): 293–305.

Niskanen, William A., Jr. 1971. *Bureaucracy and Representative Government*. Chicago, IL: Aldine-Atherton.

Novak, Mikayla. 2005. Sensory Order and Economic Order: The Links Between Human Cognition and Economic Freedom in Hayek's Thought. The Centre for Independent Studies, *Occasional Paper No. 101*. St. Leonards, NSW: CIS.

———. 2017. Review of Richard E. Wagner, *Politics as a Peculiar Business: Insights from a Theory of Entangled Political Economy*. *Cato Journal* 37 (1): 179–184.

Paganelli, Maria Pia. 2014. Adam Smith and Entangled Political Economy. *Advances in Austrian Economics* 14: 37–54.

Patrick, Meg, and Richard E. Wagner. 2015. From Mixed Economy to Entangled Political Economy: A Paretian Social-Theoretic Orientation. *Public Choice* 164: 103–116.

Podemska-Mikluch, Marta, and Richard E. Wagner. 2012. Entangled Political Economy and the Two Faces of Entrepreneurship. George Mason University, Department of Economics, *Working Paper No. 12-26*, July 16. Accessed September 15, 2017. https://papers.ssrn.com/sol3/papers.cfm?abstract_id=2084487

———. 2013. Dyads, Triads, and the Theory of Exchange: Between Liberty and Coercion. *Review of Austrian Economics* 26: 171–182.

Potts, Jason. 2000. *The New Evolutionary Microeconomics: Complexity, Competence and Adaptive Behaviour*. Cheltenham, UK: Edward Elgar.

———. 2005. Politics Is Just Evolutionary Failure Socialised. *Oysterium blog*, December 12. Accessed September 15, 2017. http://oysterium.blogspot.com.au/2005/12/politics-is-just-evolutionary-failure.html

———. 2007. Exchange and Evolution. *Review of Austrian Economics* 20: 123–135.

Salter, Alexander William. 2012. A Theory of the Dynamics of Entangled Political Economy with Application to the Federal Reserve. *Journal of Public Finance and Public Choice* 30 (1–3): 77–102.

———. 2016. Review of Richard E. Wagner, *Politics as a Peculiar Business: Insights from a Theory of Entangled Political Economy*. *Public Choice* 167: 291–293.

Tullock, Gordon. 1965. *The Politics of Bureaucracy*. Washington, DC: Public Affairs Press.

Wagner, Richard E. 2007. *Fiscal Sociology and the Theory of Public Finance*. Cheltenham, UK: Edward Elgar.

———. 2010. *Mind, Society, and Human Action: Time and Knowledge in a Theory of Social Economy*. London, UK: Routledge.
———. 2014. Entangled Political Economy: A Keynote Address. *Advances in Austrian Economics* 18: 15–36.
———. 2016a. *Politics as a Peculiar Business: Insights from a Theory of Entangled Political Economy*. Cheltenham, UK: Edward Elgar.
———. 2016b. The Peculiar Business of Politics. *Cato Journal* 35 (3): 535–556.
———. 2017. *James M. Buchanan and Liberal Political Economy: A Rational Reconstruction*. Lanham, MD: Lexington Books.
von Wieser, Friedrich. (1926) 1983. *The Law of Power*. Translated by W. E. Kuhn. Lincoln, NE: University of Nebraska-Lincoln.
Wohlgemuth, Michael. 1995. Economic and Political Competition in Neoclassical and Evolutionary Perspective. *Constitutional Political Economy* 6: 71–96.
———. 2002. Evolutionary Approaches to Politics. *Kyklos* 55 (2): 223–246.

3

Explaining Inequality in an Entangled Political Economy

Introduction

A concern with efficiency has been a hallmark of mainstream political economy. According to the mainstream view, in an economy composed of rational economic agents, and in which no market imperfections existed, it would be impossible to reallocate resources to make an individual better off without making another worse off. The "economic problem," as it were, is to ensure that the market operates efficiently. During the twentieth century, this framing was increasingly complemented by macroeconomic questions concerning how to grow an economy, and in so doing stave off the underutilisation of labour and capital without stoking economy-wide price increases.

Distributional matters were noted but, by the same token, appeared to be largely treated by mainstream political economists as a niche concern at best, or, at worst, as a form of "non-economic" inquiry outside the realm of economic consideration.[1] Economist Agnar Sandmo speculated that "the study of income distribution is so tied up with normative issues of equity and justice that many economists, keen to pursue a value-free version of their subject, have tended to shy away from it" (Sandmo 2015,

M. Novak, *Inequality*, Palgrave Studies in Classical Liberalism,
https://doi.org/10.1007/978-3-319-89417-1_3

p. 5). Of course, if we assume away heterogeneity by taking a representative agent as occupying the entire field of economic activity, then it is nigh on impossible to conceive of distributional issues materialising within this framework.

Entangled political economy has emerged as a viable alternative to mainstream economic theorising, portraying knotted and intertwined, not estranged and separated, relationships between economic, social, and political actors. In an entangled world, human action is interpreted within the prism of a *network* of alterable human actions within civil society. Inequality also matters in this framework—in particular, inequalities of income and wealth culminating from human action assume a *complex* and *emergent* character. Economic intuitions embracing networking, complexity, and emergence tend to lean towards a characterisation of inequality as a pervasive, if not "natural," aspect of living, informed by both the hierarchical and bonding nature of connections between actors across perforated economic, communal, and political spheres (Foster 2005).

Inequality has truly emerged as a focal point of discussion in most developed countries, with many individuals and groups calling for various measures to redress skewed distributions of income and wealth. This development can no longer be ignored, but redressing inequality is easier said than done, given the pervasiveness of the phenomenon. Furthermore, it is not evident that inequality is actually harmful in every circumstance. Human actions that are reflective of voluntary choices are typically both beneficial and "liberty-consistent," even if they bring about inequality as a side effect. It is unclear that inequality in this context should be repelled. However, as noted previously, inequality may also malignly emerge as the consequence of harmful actions that constrain liberties (Watson 2015; Geloso and Horwitz 2017), and it is against this specific background that inequality should be redressed.

This chapter illustrates how entangled political economy serves as a novel platform to study inequality issues. In the next section we explore how the key principles of entangled political economy can be used to illustrate the presence of economic inequality within society. Grounded in an appreciation that entangled political economy incorporates both economic and non-economic action, we then assess the complex relationship between economic, social, and political inequalities. This discussion is followed by an assessment of the conditions under which inequality affects the resilience and robustness of entangled political economy. This chapter concludes by reprising the ways and means in which entangled political economy provides rich insights about inequality.

Inequality and Entangled Political Economy: Positive Aspects

Acknowledging the structured complexity of network interactions, emerging within and across overlapping economic, communal, and political orders of civil society, provides us with the basic ingredients of Richard Wagner's conception of entangled political economy. These ingredients can then be used to theorise about inequality, conceiving the unequal distributions of income and wealth as by-products of behaviour and interaction among society's members.

Improvisational efforts of entrepreneurial conduct, in which heterogeneous actors with different drives creatively seek out opportunities to exact gains in competition or collaboration with others, both inform and pervade the human interactions that emerge. In an economic sense, "novelty will be continually injected into human population systems. Much of that novelty will take the form of inventions that lead to new businesses and products. Some of these inventions will prove commercially successful while others will be failures. Either way, they will generate changes in the system's structure" (Wagner 2016, p. 73). As outlined in the previous chapter, it is possible to envisage similar entrepreneurial initiatives and feedback mechanisms shaping political and social conduct.

The overall pattern of interactions between people resembles a network reflecting, as Scottish Enlightenment philosopher Adam Ferguson famously exclaimed, "the result of human action, but not the execution of any human design." The interconnection between people with divergent mental models—all with the capability of projecting paradigmatic change onto the world about them, yet with the imprint of social expectations, customs, and traditions somewhat conditioning their perceptions—creates an astonishing degree of complexity (Foster 2005). This contrasts theoretical efforts to render the economy or society as possessing simplistic, machine-like qualities. Complexity means that network structures are not entirely reducible to individual action. By the same token, it is conceivable to comprehend meso-level social structures to the extent actions by certain groups of participants are impacted by similar beliefs, interests, motivations, sentiments, and values.

Departing from the implicit mainstream condition of network completeness, linking every actor directly, entangled political economy illustrates that it is the connections between people *which are not made* that yields an incomplete structure of economic-political-social relations. It is entirely possible that economic agents become entangled with political agents, and political agents with members of civic associations and other communal enterprises, and so on. Nonetheless, the existence of incomplete connections generically implies that entanglement is imperfect. Therefore, "networked patterns of relationships of variable density" (Wagner 2010, p. 110) between actors—with the connections they create represented by income flows (which, to some extent, accumulate into wealth stocks over time)—presuppose the existence of economic inequality to a certain extent.

It is the convention for modern policymakers to refer to fiscal and regulatory measures as imposing directly upon statistical artifices as gross domestic product, the unemployment rate, the rate of price inflation, and so on. This appears to reflect the mainstream economic conception of complex economic and political orders as macro-level phenomena, often reduced to statistical aggregates apparently with a life of their own but lacking reference to the underpinning micro- and meso-level activities that compose the macro (Dopfer et al. 2004; Potts and Morrison 2007; Dopfer and Potts 2008). In several recent works, Richard Wagner (2012a, b, 2016) has made a remedial distinction between the "action level" and "system level" of observation. It is suggested that economic action (and political and social actions, for that matter) only takes place on the action level (situated either on a micro or meso plane of activities), and that the system level cannot be an object of action in itself.

Wagner (2012a) characterises the macro economy as something of an "ecosystem" of micro- and meso-level plans. Embracing this notion, we may interpret inequality measures (e.g. Gini coefficient) as a synthetic and artificial system-level measure which, in reality, cannot be divorced from changes to the ecology of incomplete interactions within the networked webs of entangled political economy. Indeed, "[a] distribution of income or wealth is not something that someone chooses. To the contrary, it is a variable that emerges through interactions among people throughout a society" (Wagner 2017, p. 168; also Higgs 2014).

Figure 3.1 illustrates the distinction between action and system levels when it comes to the conceptualisation and analysis of economic inequality. At the action level of society (bottom of diagram) we have the entangled, yet incomplete, relationships between non-political (represented by hexagons) and political (represented by triangles) agents at a meso level. The income-flow connections within the network are patterned differently, indicating support by sub-populations of agents for varying meso rules. The system level of society (top of diagram) is depicted in terms of the inequality measure and its movements. At the risk of dramatically simplifying the dynamic adjustments of inequality, we specify two discrete time periods (t and $t + 1$) during which inequality has worsened by

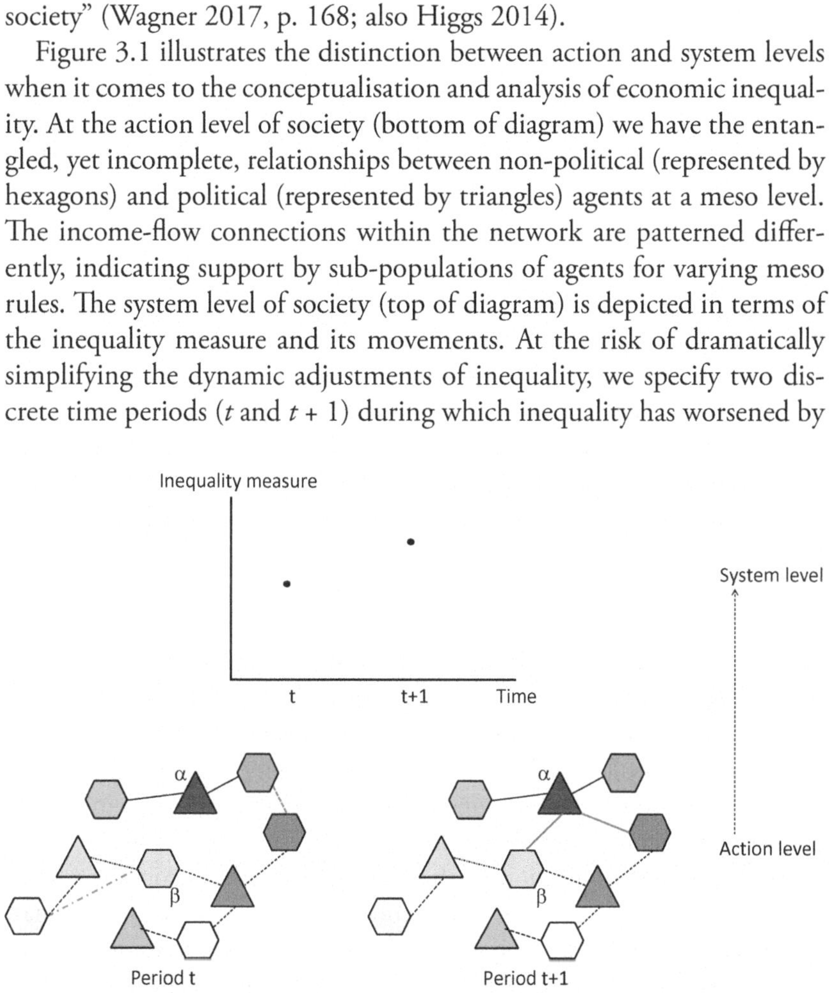

Fig. 3.1 Inequality statistical measurement as system-level reflection of action-level inequalities. Source: Wagner (2016); Author's illustrations

virtue of an even greater concentration of income. This development is represented by the two new income-flow connections favouring a political entity in $t + 1$, as marked in red, and the loss of two connections between non-political entities (marked blue) that existed in t.

In the parlance of network theory, the degree of an element refers to the number of connections it has to other elements.[2] In Fig. 3.1, most elements have connections of one or two degrees as at t. By the end of $t + 1$, income flows have concentrated; this is reflected by the fact that one meso cohort of political actors (denoted by α) has developed a hub with a connection of four degrees. A skew in the degree distribution, referred to mathematically as a non-Gaussian (i.e. non-normal) distribution, indicates there are disparities in the connective structure—for our purposes, an inequality of income earnings. The action-level scenario outlined here, illustrated as exuding change within the meso level of society, suggests the formation of a more concentrated network centred upon political action. Additional actors are subscribing to the (enforced) meso rule embraced by political actors α. This worsening of concentration, for our purpose, is reflected in an increase in the inequality measure.

The point of this exercise is to reinforce the notion that inequality is an emergent phenomenon, and that it is the by-product of decentralised action. The possibility of inequality-as-emergence is not necessarily countenanced in great detail by the atheoretical, macro-level statistical representations used in mainstream political economy. According to Wagner, "macro-level explanation in political economy is a form of shell game, in that it diverts people's attention by getting to look where the action is not" (Wagner 2016, p. 64). A consideration of the action level of activity also leads us to recognise that a similar outcome—in terms of degree distribution—could well occur under many other connective combinations (for example, non-political meso actors β generating new connections as a result of innovation).

An important implication of the entangled political economy framework for inequality analysis is that inequality is pervasive, because human beings have a tendency to maintain and create network connections in partial and non-encompassing ways. The reasons for this are varied, such as practical limitations upon the establishment of friendships and alliances, the "tyranny" of geographical distance, and our tendencies towards assortative mixing. It is not beyond the realm of possibility that decentralised exchange actions by individuals may well contribute towards the emergence of a network structure which is synonymous with a high degree of economic inequality.

The work of scholars associated with the "Brisbane Club" of evolutionary economics provides an inequality-as-emergence narrative fitting neatly with entangled political economy (Foster 2005; Markey-Towler 2012, 2016; Markey-Towler and Foster 2013a, b).[3] Assuming that the connections represent the flow of income between parties, inequality may be observed via an emergent process in which a relatively large number of network (actor-)elements possess a small number of connections, yet a relatively small number of elements maintain a large number of connections. In other words, the network structure of entangled political economy becomes concentrated about certain elements, be they non-political or political enterprises.

From the vantage point of network theory, extreme inequality is perhaps most synonymous with what is known as a "scale-free" network. Connective activities under this type of scenario tend to be concentrated about the relatively few centralised elements in such a network. In some limiting circumstances, the extent of centralisation within a scale-free network could become so great that all connections are mediated by one monopolistic "hub." In that case, the network takes on the graphical appearance of a "star" shape. Random networks, by contrast, typically exhibit a low level of clustering between elements, small differences in degree among the elements, and short distances of connections between the elements (Bonacich 2004).

Vilfredo Pareto's intellectual contributions extended to his late nineteenth-century studies of the income distribution of selected European countries. With the aid of the taxation record of certain jurisdictions, such as Britain, France, and Prussia, he found a reasonable degree of consistency in terms of a skewed distribution of income. Roughly speaking, 80 per cent of income was being earned by 20 per cent of the population. Although the precision and prevalence of Pareto's findings have been contested over the years, there are some studies alluding to the existence of such highly skewed income distributions (summarised by the likes of Gabaix 2009, 2016; Jones 2015). This so-called Paretian power law is generally commensurable with the highly skewed degree distribution found in scale-free networks, implying that incomplete network connections embody the very notion of inequality.

In reality, network structures will vary greatly with respect to the number of elements which exist within the system, the number of connections attached to each element, and the extent of degree distribution, as well as the clustering of elements and the degree to which new elements affiliate with existing elements (Potts et al. 2008). It would be fair and reasonable to suggest that most networks are intermediately situated between the extremes of the random network and the scale-free network (certainly, those rare cases of networks containing a single, monopolistic hub). An entangled political economy contains network structures which are "not necessarily regular, but may contain hubs, weak and strong connections, and close and distant connections" (Ibid., p. 172); thus, economic inequality seems to arise quite readily within such a system of human interaction.

Network theorists have developed numerous explanations for the development of networks characterised by invariant scale, and these explanations may serve as a basis for skewed distributional outcomes. Although the theories underpinning scale-free networks do vary, they share the general notion that new elements will tend to affiliate with existing elements possessing greater connections. At the risk of simplification, there are two classes of scale-free network theories—the scale-free network may be influenced by "preferential attachment" or "fitness" considerations.[4]

Physicists Alain-Lászió Barabási and Réka Albert developed a now-famous model of networking behaviour which accommodates both growth of a scale-free network (providing for *evolution*) and the incompleteness of that network (providing for *structure*) (Albert and Barabási 2002; Barabási and Albert 1999). For reasons that will soon become clear, the Barabási-Albert model is also known as the "rich get richer," or cumulative advantage, model. Starting with a random network with a fixed number of elements, new elements are progressively added to the network in a certain way such that a scale-free network ultimately emerges. The new elements develop non-random connections, with old, incumbent elements possessing a greater number of connections more likely to attract more connections, compared against those with fewer connections. In other words, preferential attachment dictates that the higher the degree of an incumbent element, the higher the probability it will attract a new connection. In a summary of the scale-free network literature, Caldarelli and Catanzano suggest in these cases "a hierarchy of different nodes emerges, with a large variety in their degrees, ranging from the least connected ones to those that have accumulated many links, i.e. the hubs. The resulting network is heterogeneous, with a power-law degree distribution" (Caldarelli and Catanzaro 2012, p. 71).

The distinctive contribution of Barabási and Albert was to suggest the acquisition of new connections within a scale-free network is a function of how many connections an element already had. To some extent, however, their model has provoked criticism. In response, Bianconi and Barabási (2001a, b) develop a scale-free network model in which the "fit get richer." This suggests that cumulative advantage could be moderated by the entry of new elements with intrinsically attractive features that enable them to develop a disproportionate number of connections with others. Similar fitness models have been developed by the likes of Caldarelli et al. (2002), Borgs et al. (2007), and Ghadge et al. (2010). As noted by a group of researchers, "[v]ery fit nodes can thus attract new edges despite a moderate value of their degree and this new 'fittest-get-richer' process is thus superimposed on the degree-driven attachment mechanism" (Barrat et al. 2008, p. 67). Additional mechanisms suggest that network growth takes place purely as a result of copying element or connection characteristics which are perceived to be highly functional in an evolutionary environment (Caldarelli 2013; Potts 2013). In general terms, elements with better fitness (or attractiveness or competitiveness) attributes can acquire additional connections relative to elements with lesser fitness.

Irrespective of which mechanism is seen as most appropriate, the networks described here will tend to display features of interactive concentration. The underlying intuition for this is that "people are not random in making connections—people have agendas (aspirations and preferences) in making connections. We do not have random conversations nor do we enter into binding contracts with random individuals" (Foster 2005, p. 887). By the same token, it is important to recall that the networked structures of an entangled political economy evolve. The Austrian economist Ludwig Lachmann vividly depicts this sense of dynamism as it pertains to distributional issues: "[t]he owners of wealth, we might say … , are like guests at a hotel or the passengers in a train: They are always there but are never for long the same people" (Lachmann [1956] 2008, p. 180).

A number of researchers have found some evidence of turnover within the ranks of the wealthy in actually-existing markets (Arnott et al. 2015; Hirschl and Rank 2015; Rallo 2017). In more recent times, this churning has been evidenced in nascent cryptocurrency markets, especially during the rapid phase of income accumulation by prominent traders in this space during late 2017 (Popper 2017; Doherty 2018). Alternative research focuses upon the extent of upward mobility exercised by low- and middle-income earners, with some findings suggesting considerable room for improvement on that score (Blanden 2013; Corak 2013; Mendolia and Siminski 2016). Some individuals may increase their income and wealth, in a relative sense, whereas others (even the rich) see their economic advantages diminished—the fundamental point is that inequality is a dynamic, not static, matter.

Inequality Drivers: Insights from Economics, Sociology, and Political Science

Economic inequality is the by-product of ongoing decisions made by actors situated within, and engaging across, the economic, communal, and political orders to seek out relationships that will yield gains along various dimensions. When heterogeneous individuals and their enterprises engage with others, it is necessarily performed in partial and incomplete ways, and this leads to structural relationships exuding inequalities in the flow of incomes and revenue, and, subsequently, the stock of wealth. The previous section illustrated how concentrated networks can arise and perpetuate, embodying the economic inequality that is the subject matter of this book. Given our emphasis upon understanding inequality from social-scientific perspectives, preferential attachment and fitness propensities within scale-free networks need interpreting from a variety of disciplines—such as economics, sociology, and political science—and it is this task to which we now turn.

Contemporary economic literature has tended to focus, though not exclusively, on several market-driven explanations of inequality, one of which is the suggestion that highly educated and skilled individuals will earn a substantial wage premium. In some cases, whereby the skills possessed by individuals are unique or in extremely high demand, there is the potential for the "superstar effect" to take hold, as reflected in very substantial wage premiums (Rosen 1981; Frank and Cook 1996; Lucifora and Simmons 2003; Kaplan and Rauh 2010). In contrast, people with relatively few experiences and with low levels of knowledge and skills will tend to attract smaller income streams through their (presumably less dense) economic networks over time.

As a result of economic contributions by Jacob Mincer, Theodore Shultz, Gary Becker, James Heckman, and others, there is now a widespread appreciation that education and training experiences and skills development—commonly referred to as "human capital"—facilitate productive economic activity. Human capital is itself not a flow variable in a set of connections between people, nor is it an element in a network. It is, rather, embodied knowledge whose application enables connectivity within the labour market, in turn playing an important role in yielding income flows to the person possessing the embodied knowledge (Cañibano and Potts 2016). Investment in human capital tends to increase the productivity of workers by enabling them to work more efficiently (including through their capable use of non-human capital such as machinery and equipment), and to think and act more creatively, encouraging further technological changes and process innovations. These effects raise the aggregate level of goods and services produced, for a given amount of labour input, and, as will be discussed later, improve the relative earnings potential of educated individuals.[5]

From an economic perspective, human capital is a significant factor underpinning the observed dispersion in wages and salaries within developed countries. In their book *The Race Between Education and Technology*, Claudia Goldin and Lawrence Katz (2008) argued that skills-biased technological change increases the demand for skilled labour. A slowdown in the relative supply of college workers in the U.S. labour market in about 1980, according to the authors, informs the strong increase in the college wage premium for skill from 1980 to 2005.

Inequality theorists generally recognise the effects of human capital accumulation upon the dispersion of incomes, working through economic channels in which technological changes intersect with skills. Others point to substantial earnings increases afforded to chief executive officers (CEOs) and other senior managers of large corporations as a key driver of economic disparities. It is suggested executives connect with company directors and other influential figures internally within the firm (itself a bundle of network connections) to redistribute salaries to themselves, in a form of "private rent-seeking" detrimental to the interests of shareholders and the general public alike (Hillman 2013; Piketty 2014; Creighton 2017). There are alternative explanations for rising executive remuneration. One of these is that executive remuneration is largely market-determined, and, thus, is competitively set by firms attempting to attract the best managerial talent available (Frydman and Saks 2010; Murphy 2013). Similar theories of executive remuneration relate CEO pay to firm size (Gabaix and Landier 2008) and globalisation (Grubel 2015), among other factors.

Individuals can also reap substantial, and unevenly distributed, incomes by applying their entrepreneurial flair and creativity in an attempt to realise opportunities. The successful application of entrepreneurship within the economic order is likely to generate monopoly profits and, not coincidentally, greater inequality. From a network perspective, the successful introduction of novel ideas within the economy encourages new connections to attach to the entrepreneur, perhaps allowing that entrepreneur to gain business at a rate faster than their rivals (Markey-Towler and Foster 2013b). In relation to these kinds of theoretical accounts monopoly is, actually, a regular feature of meso-level evolutionary process:

> the origination of the rule population … is characterized by a particular market structure: namely monopoly. But this is a natural and normal form of monopoly that is a consequence of the entrepreneur creating or opening up a new market about a new generic rule and then being the first to

> occupy it. This is very different from a monopoly that is the result of a micro unit driving out all other carriers, and so being the last to occupy it. If it is possible for others to adopt the generic rule, and so challenge with improvements to the rule or its operational form, then there need be no welfare concern. Instead, this is generally the precursor to competitive rivalry. (Dopfer and Potts 2008, p. 47)

There is no inconsistency between temporal monopoly profit, generated as a result of entrepreneurial action, and the classical liberal insistence that market processes are expected to contain income and wealth concentrations in the long run. The origination of entrepreneurial activity may generate novelties that, indeed, create unequal rewards during the meso-adoption phase. The subsequent retention phase of meso evolution, though, is never completely settled, as sub-populations of wealthy individuals incessantly get churned and displaced as the result of market dynamism. A free and open economic order should, generally speaking, coincide with a high degree of turnover of otherwise ossified hubs and connections (Foster 2005).

The historical record suggests political enterprises are, in fact, amongst the oldest of human organisational arrangements situated within an entangled political economy (Scott 2017). Political action has been prevalent in all societies from antiquity, and so it stands to reason that political actors and the organisations they create and maintain—including government itself—are deeply implicated in economic inequalities. This is particularly the case if choice and effort are winnowed through politics, and not through markets or any other realm of civil society which is centred upon dyadic, voluntary exchanges.

From a network perspective, "there are different kinds of connections, and these do different kinds of work within a system of entangled political economy. Some connections are forged voluntarily, others are forged forcibly" (Wagner 2016, p. 74). Recalling the insights expressed in the previous chapter, political exchanges are invariably characterised by triadic relations in that two immediate parties to the exchange are involved in transferring fiscal and regulatory favours (in return for commitments of political support, future job-creation, and other forms economic activity, etc.) whilst third parties bear the losses arising from new or refashioned interventions.

Beinhocker (2013) remarks that in truly free and competitive markets there arc no economic rents (defined as unearned monetary incomes, or non-monetary privileges, or other benefits), only market returns. In network environments in which hubs are disproportionately represented by legislators and bureaucrats, there is the greater likelihood that political recognition of rent-seeking activities undertaken by private individuals, firms, and other groups (and even non-profit organisations and other associations within the communal order) would aggravate income and wealth inequalities.

The receipt of particularised fiscal and regulatory advantages through the political process is likely to have significant implications for the successful functioning of the economic order. According to Brendan Markey-Towler, "dominant firms will be highly profitable and able to engage in rent seeking behaviour, locking the new entrant out of the market. … This will intensity natural preferential attachment arising by reducing the ability of new entrants to the market system to attract business from the dominant firms" (Markey-Towler 2012, p. 75). Our particular emphasis is upon the possibility that rent-seeking efforts may exacerbate inequality, to the extent that public policy changes enable the sales revenues and profit margins of incumbents to be protected against dissipation via entrepreneurship and competition (Aligica and Tarko 2015).

We now consider the rich array of non-economic explanations for income and wealth distributional outcomes. In the voluminous social network literature, it is emphasised that certain behaviours, of anthropological, psychological, and sociological dimensions, can provide a given network a semblance of structure that persists over the course of time.

One of the potential non-economic drivers of inequality is the concept of "homophily," a form of biased connective sorting within networks reflecting people's preferences to form connections with others who are similar to themselves (Centola 2015; McCulloh et al. 2013; DiMaggio and Garip 2012). The effects of homophily can become apparent within a network structure through the aegis of opportunity or choice (Jackson 2008), although there is a sense of overlap between these two underpinning factors. In the case of the former, school children and white-collar workers will tend to regularly interact with people of similar backgrounds because of the environment in which they are situated (that is, a school or an office).[6] Homophily also results from choice-acts. In either case, be it opportunity or choice, it is possible that homophily "may generate pressure for greater inequality given the presence of network effects" (DiMaggio and Garip 2012, p. 98).

The inclination to associate with, or disassociate from, others is generically informed by judgements that individuals make about the merit and worthiness of those surrounding them. Scholars such as Roger Gould (2002) and Joseph Henrich and Francisco Gil-White (2001) have developed status-laden theories illustrating that freely conferred esteem and prestige emerges as a result of social processes, reflecting individual valuations about the credence, quality, or usefulness embodied in other people and their ideas. Prestigious, high-status individuals within a social network can influence others, even well beyond that dictated by their level of knowledge and expertise, potentially contributing to the inequitable bunching of elements and connections within a network. The concept of a "Blau-space," named after sociologist Peter Blau, illustrates that networks can stratify into concentrated sub-networks in which homophilous actors tend to engage only with similar others (McPherson 1983, 2004).

Another way to think about the implications of social distinction and rank is to consider Hartley and Potts' concept of "universal adversarialism." In line with the observed proclivity of *Homo sapiens* as a high-trusting, instinctually cooperating, and pro-socialising animal, individuals tend to associate with others in groups sharing similar rules. The promulgation of narratives and stories (or "demes") serves to fortify group loyalty. People cooperate within their chosen social groups, and they can also display animosity, discrimination, and even violence against other, somehow unfavoured groups of people (so-called "out-groups"). It is against this background of "us" versus "them" that "social and cultural *dynamics* work along the *boundaries* of groups and through the creation of *changed* groups and new groups. Importantly, this process also works through group *conflict*" (Hartley and Potts 2014, p. 79).

Our tendencies to create rules assigning certain people as part of an "in-group" identity, but banishing all others to the out-group to varying degrees, pose as a potential driver of social inequality. In some circumstances, this phenomenon could feed into income and wealth disparities. Out-groups whose members are discriminated against socially may suffer constraints in terms of forming value-added connections with in-group members (Novak 2016; Boettke and Candela 2017). The key to dispel inequality in this context is to reverse such trends, to the extent they occur within the network space.

The pervasiveness of entangled structures between non-political and political actors also almost certainly guarantees that there will be some confluence between economic and political inequalities. For expediency, we define political inequality as systematic differences in the distribution of political influence amongst the population. A dimension of political influence is wealth itself: "[a]lthough the rich don't have more votes than the poor, they have more money to spend on lobbying, campaign contributions, and so on. As a result, the rich enjoy greater *substantive* political power even when formal political power is equalized" (Freiman 2018, p. 304). Aside from access to decision-makers, political inequality is shaped by the degree of accountability of politicians, bureaucrats, and other political agents towards citizen-voters and the civil-societal organisations representing them; the level of political recognition of the concerns expressed by individuals and non-political organisations; and resourcing of the institutions which give effect to, and constrain, the exercise of political power.

It has been observed from an entangled political economy standpoint that, "[a] graph of legislator-constituent interactions will have power-law features where the preponderance of people has no direct connection, and with nearly all connection occupied by a few, moreover, that have multiple sources of power and influence behind them" (Wagner 2016, p. 162). This insight is consistent with the classical liberal theme of a broad distinction between those people who politically rule and those people who are politically ruled. The asymmetric distribution of coercive, forceful political power forever poses as a threat to the exercise of individual freedoms and liberties if not appropriately restrained.

Classical liberals have long made a distinction between, essentially, the political and economic classes within society. In an entangled political economy approach, the political-economic class demarcation becomes distinctly more blurred. The potential for economic actions to mutate into the "monstrous moral hybrid" form, by virtue of embracing the underlying ordering features maintained by individuals and enterprises operating within other orders of civil society, threatens to become a reality (Salter 2012; Wagner 2016, 2017). Political agents participate in the affairs of others by propounding triadic exchange novelties, whilst at the very same time non-political agents vigorously compete against their compatriots in their wish to collaborate with the offices of the state to exact alternative triadic exchanges. An intermingling of operational practices and ethical standards may become the norm under this scenario.

The consequences that differential access bring to bear within the democratic political system—a system which in principle is meant to ensure that the public interests and values of each and all are acknowledged, and receive their due consideration, politically—have been the subject of extensive investigation. Brown and Huang (2017) have found that corporate executives' meetings with policymakers are associated with positive (yet abnormal) stock returns, and that firms tend to receive more government contracts and receive regulatory relief after such meetings. Another recent paper (Blau 2017) reports that firms with political connections have better access to debt and government-sponsored bailouts, lower corporate tax liabilities, and a lower likelihood of being detected for fraud, and that connections with political agents and their enterprises also tend to increase firm value. Studies by the likes of Brezis and Cariolle (2017) and, as mentioned previously, Canayaz et al. (2016) find a "revolving door" relationship in which government officials, who subsequently work for major firms, increase firm profits and value. These sorts of findings appear to bear all the hallmarks of monstrous moral hybridity, or at the very least the blurring of ordering principles within society.

Although entanglement cannot be completely exhumed from human existence, we do not enter a plea for indifference when it comes to the degree and quality of actually-existing entanglements. Brink Lindsey and Steven Teles remind us that "[i]n the ideal democracy, the mechanisms of government are devised so that the clash of contending opinions and interests is converted into policies that serve the common good" (Lindsey and Teles 2017, pp. 17–18). The exercise of concentrated political power is likely to counter such mechanisms and, in so doing, egregiously amplify economic inequalities of an inappropriate kind. The proclivity of political actors in an entangled political economy to mould and shape the operations of the economic order—with respect to prices, quantities, or income structures and flows (Dopfer and Potts 2008)—is, from a classical liberal perspective, seen as a sign of inherent weakness of political character rather than strength.

Inequality, Scale, and Turbulence in Entangled Political Economy

Throughout his recent work Richard Wagner has placed great weight upon the implications of differences in network structure within entangled political economy. Wagner suggests the difference between a tiny micro-business serving local customers and a sprawling multinational corporation serving customers globally is, in a certain respect, muted. Irrespective of size attributes, a given firm will, just like other firms, be bound by the conventions of private property and competition such that they are "forced systemically to serve consumer desires" (Wagner 2016, p. 28).

From a network-theoretic viewpoint, the competitive, decentralised market arrangements which promulgate dyadic exchanges seem to roughly approximate random and scalable network structures, wherein "the size of a network is pretty much irrelevant because there is no significant change in network qualities as networks become larger" (Ibid., p. 75). To put this in another way, because market-based enterprises are inherently scalable, this means that a large firm with 5000 employees is merely that same firm with 50 employees (albeit multiplied by a factor of 100).

Contrasting the scalability of economic enterprise, actions undertaken by those involved in the political realm appear to predominantly take on non-random, scale-free attributes. From Wagner's perspective, "if economic relationships are scalable while political relationships are not, a system of entangled political economy might feature a form of increasing returns to political power within society" (Ibid., p. 76), with the threat that oligarchic political arrangements—illustrated by the political executive dominating the operation of a parliament, and centralisation of political influence within federal systems of government—might unfold as the prevailing feature of entangled political economy.

At the heart of the difference between the effect of economic and political enterprises on network scale is, as discussed previously, that free and open competition would be expected to fracture concentrations of private power and, consequently, dissipate any inequalities associated with economic concentration. In this idealised situation, income and wealth disparities would reflect "choice-and-effort" dyadic exchanges generated within the economic order. The "turnover of dominant hubs … will be an indication that competitive networks are emerging and realigning the distribution of value" (Foster 2005, p. 888).

It is much more difficult to envisage similar principles applying to the political order, even under democratic regimes typified by extensive public discourse, universal voting franchise, and electoral competition for political office. The successful application of agenda-setting techniques by political actors—including the use of moral suasion to induce mass acquiescence (if not acceptance) regarding triadic exchange arrangements—surely undermines the ability of the "voice" mechanism (i.e. voting, petitioning and protesting) to curtail the accumulation of political power (Hirschman 1970). The effectiveness of the alternative, external "exit" mechanism (i.e. relocating across political borders) to render politicians and bureaucrats more accountable may be undermined by, amongst other things, the limited array of policy offerings in other jurisdictions. There is the potential for individuals to undergo a kind of "internal exit"—via participation in the "shadow economy" or, more recently, engaging with blockchain applications such as cryptocurrencies (MacDonald 2015). However, the capacity to entertain this option is usually subject to stringent political constraints. Relative to the situation found within an economic domain allowing for an extensive exercise of liberty, activities within the political order (even under democratic regimes) seem less likely to correspond with a dissipation of inequalities. If anything, a tendency towards monocentricity within the political order would seem to *encourage* the development of unequal income and wealth outcomes.

It appears that, once again, we have arrived at a situation encountered on numerous occasions in this book: entanglement is prevalent throughout the facets of human existence, and inequality is a largely inescapable consequence of such entanglement. However, not all is lost in the quest to ensure that "bad-sourced" or "liberty-inconsistent" inequalities are restrained. Although entanglement is omnipresent, it is also clear that certain guises of entanglement are, from the classical liberal viewpoint, preferable than others. As will be discussed later in this book, patterns of entanglement which are ordered by rules and which keep the incidence of social tectonics within reasonable limits would appear to be conducive to the promotion of the liberal order.

Containing social tectonics would ultimately entail limiting the scale and scope of political action. Proposals to circumscribe governmental activity elicit adverse reactions along many fronts—for instance, rolling back the state is often alleged to induce chaos and turbulence because economic entrepreneurs are given greater avenues to "fail" from the perspective of mainstream economics. However, a contrasting position—that liberty *calms* turbulence as people enjoy open opportunities to discover what each want and need, and explore avenues to reconcile disagreements (or, at least, arrive at a détente of shared understanding)—can be just as validly argued (Wagner 2012c). Far from a highly adaptive and flexible network structure routinely exhibiting concentrations of influence and power, "[g]reater preferential attachment and income inequality will typically prolong the 'stagnation' phase of evolution in economic systems which precedes the advent of a new innovation and the beginning of a new phase of growth through evolution" (Markey-Towler 2014, p. 12).

Conclusion

Entangled political economy is an ideal framework to study economic inequality because the distribution of income and wealth is, ultimately, relational and dynamic in its nature. Inequality is commonplace throughout society as heterogeneous agents interact with each other across the associational, commercial, and political divides, developing relationships embodying structures that bear the hallmark of unequal distributional patterns.

Some inequalities arise as a consequence of the operation of markets, in which selling individuals with astonishingly divergent knowledge, skills, and talents comingle to offer goods and services to buyers with astonishingly divergent preferences and tastes. Voluntary activities undertaken in the pursuit of mutual gains may give rise to "good inequalities," in the sense that the underlying activities, let alone the resultant dispersion of income and wealth, do not necessarily hamper the ability of others to copy or modify them. Other inequalities, however, can emerge as the result of successful efforts by special interests to lobby and pressure governments to reallocate and redistribute economic resources so that they can enjoy advantages and benefits at the expense of all others. These are labelled "bad inequalities," and are best avoided in the interests of promoting market-tested betterment and a flourishing society.

We are also aware that cultural, social, and political attitudes, norms, and values will play a not-insignificant role in shaping income and wealth distributions. Entangled political economy is, in the final analysis, a theory of social action, and therefore these additional considerations cannot be ignored. We acknowledge the liberty-consistent avenues for inequality that can arise socially, say, when people form friendships and relationships with like-minded people. Largely unavoidable demographic changes also fit into this broader social picture. On the other hand, discriminatory social exclusions should arouse suspicions from classical liberal principles. This chapter also refers to the relationship between political and economic inequality, illustrating that the rent-seeking which alters economic distribution is also grounded in a loosening of standards enshrining democratic political equality for all.

The challenge which lies ahead is to redress the negative impacts of economic inequality, whilst not overriding some of the more positive aspects of the phenomenon spurring incentives for productive entrepreneurship and dynamic innovation. It is necessary, therefore, to gain an appreciation of key public policies exacerbating economic inequalities, and generating significant harms in the process—such as reduced opportunities for economic mobility and social advancement, and the persistence of political domination by the few over the many.

Notes

1. Although mainstream economics versed in general competitive equilibrium analysis may have largely eschewed income distribution theory and analysis, there have been numerous non-mainstream, heterodox economic efforts—drawing upon institutionalist, Marxian, radical political economy, and other perspectives—studying the causes and consequences of inequality during the twentieth century.
2. Given that the network illustrated in the figure is undirected, we need not consider the in-degree (the number of incoming connections) or out-degree (number of outgoing connections) applicable to any given node.
3. The "Brisbane Club" describes a certain grouping of economists either currently or previously affiliated with The University of Queensland (UQ), or who have collaborated with certain UQ scholars. The members of the Brisbane Club each share an intellectual specialisation in evolutionary economics. The key figures include (but is not limited to) John Foster, Jason Potts, Stan Metcalfe, Kurt Dopfer, Ulrich Witt, and Giovanni Dosi, and their students such as Trent MacDonald and Brendan Markey-Towler.
4. It should be acknowledged that researchers have also attempted to devise more realistic dynamic network properties incorporating elements of preferential attachment and fitness.
5. Greater endowments of human capital are beneficial for reasons other than boosting individual productivity. The presence of educated labourers in the workplace, for example, may improve the productivity of other workers, producing even more products than would otherwise be the case. Such "spillover" effects of human capital investment also manifest themselves in the social realm, with an educated community contributing towards reduced crime rates and healthier lifestyles.
6. The effect of homophily may be ameliorated to some extent if systems of education and workplace relations, aiming to promote a diverse mix of students and workers, respectively, are enacted.

References

Albert, Réka, and Alain-Lászió Barabási. 2002. Statistical Mechanics of Complex Networks. *Reviews of Modern Physics* 74: 47–97.

Aligica, Paul Dragos, and Vlad Tarko. 2015. Crony Capitalism. *CESifo DICE Report: Journal for Institutional Comparisons* 13 (3): 27–32.

Arnott, Robert, William Bernstein, and Lillian Wu. 2015. The Myth of Dynastic Wealth: The Rich Get Poorer. *Cato Journal* 35 (3): 447–485.

Barabási, Albert-Lászió, and Réka Albert. 1999. Emergence of Scaling in Random Networks. *Science* 286 (Oct.): 509–512.

Barrat, Alain, Marc Barthélemy, and Alessandro Vespignani. 2008. *Dynamical Processes on Complex Networks*. Oxford, UK: Oxford University Press.

Beinhocker, Eric. 2013. A Truer Form of Capitalism. *Democracy: A Journal of Ideas* 29: 22–28.

Bianconi, Ginestra, and Albert-Lászió Barabási. 2001a. Bose-Einstein Condensation in Complex Networks. *Physical Review Letters* 86 (24): 5632–5635.

———. 2001b. Competition and Multiscaling in Evolving Networks. *Europhysics Letters* 54 (4): 436–442.

Blanden, Jo. 2013. Cross-Country Rankings in Intergenerational Mobility: A Comparison of Approaches from Economics and Sociology. *Journal of Economic Surveys* 27 (1): 38–73.

Blau, Benjamin M. 2017. Lobbying, Political Connections and Emergency Lending by the Federal Reserve. *Public Choice* 172 (3–4): 333–358.

Boettke, Peter J., and Rosolino A. Candela. 2017. The Liberty of Progress: Increasing Returns, Institutions, and Entrepreneurship. *Social Philosophy and Policy* 34 (2): 136–163.

Bonacich, Phillip. 2004. The Invasion of the Physicists. *Social Networks* 26: 285–288.

Borgs, Christian, Jennifer Chayes, Constantinos Daskalakis, and Sebestien Roch. 2007. First to Market is Not Everything: An Analysis of Preferential Attachment with Fitness. In *STOC '07: Proceedings of the Thirty-Ninth Annual ACM Symposium on Theory of Computing*, 135–144. New York, NY: ACM Press.

Brezis, Elise S., and Joel Cariolle. 2017. The Revolving Door: State Connections and Inequality of Influence in the US Banking Sector, August 24. Accessed September 29, 2017. https://papers.ssrn.com/sol3/papers.cfm?abstract_id=3025559

Brown, Jeffrey R., and Jiekun Huang. 2017. All the President's Friends: Political Access and Firm Value. National Bureau of Economic Research, *Working Paper No. 23356*, April. Accessed September 4, 2017. http://www.nber.org/papers/w23356

Caldarelli, Guido. 2013. *Scale-Free Networks: Complex Webs in Nature and Technology*. Oxford, UK: Oxford University Press.

Caldarelli, Guido, A. Capocci, P. De Los Rios, and M.A. Muñoz. 2002. Scale-Free Networks from Varying Vertex Intrinsic Fitness. *Physical Review Letters* 89 (25): 258702.

Caldarelli, Guido, and Michele Catanzaro. 2012. *Networks: A Very Short Introduction*. Oxford, UK: Oxford University Press.

Canayaz, Mehmet İhsan, Jose Vincente Martinez, and Han N. Ozsoylev. 2016. Is the Revolving Door of Washington a Back Door to Government Contracts and Excess Stock Market Returns? December 20. Accessed August 31, 2017. https://papers.ssrn.com/sol3/papers.cfm?abstract_id=2596520

Cañibano, Carolina, and Jason Potts. 2016. Toward an Evolutionary Theory of Human Capital, June 29. Accessed September 27, 2017. https://papers.ssrn.com/sol3/papers.cfm?abstract_id=2802236

Centola, Damon. 2015. The Social Origins of Networks and Diffusion. *American Journal of Sociology* 120 (5): 1295–1338.

Corak, Miles. 2013. Income Inequality, Equality of Opportunity, and Intergenerational Mobility. *Journal of Economic Perspectives* 27 (3): 79–102.

Creighton, Adam. 2017. CEO Pay—It's Not Like They're Sports Stars. *The Australian*, February 27.

DiMaggio, Paul, and Filiz Garip. 2012. Network Effects and Social Inequality. *Annual Review of Sociology* 38: 93–118.

Doherty, Brian. 2018. In Search of the Elusive Bitcoin Billionaire. *Reason*, January. Accessed January 29, 2018. http://reason.com/archives/2017/11/28/in-search-of-the-elusive-bitco

Dopfer, Kurt, and Jason Potts. 2008. *The General Theory of Economic Evolution*. London, UK: Routledge.

Dopfer, Kurt, John Foster, and Jason Potts. 2004. Micro-meso-macro. *Journal of Evolutionary Economics* 14 (3): 263–279.

Foster, John. 2005. From Simplistic to Complex Systems in Economics. *Cambridge Journal of Economics* 29: 873–892.

Frank, Robert H., and Philip J. Cook. 1996. *Winner-Take-All Society: Why the Few at the Top Get So Much More Than the Rest of Us*. New York, NY: Penguin Books.

Freiman, Christopher. 2018. Ideal Theory. In *The Routledge Handbook of Libertarianism*, ed. Jason Brennan, Bas van der Vossen, and David Schmidtz, 301–311. New York, NY: Routledge.

Frydman, Carola, and Raven E. Saks. 2010. Executive Compensation: A New View from a Long-Term Perspective, 1936–2005. *The Review of Financial Studies* 23 (5): 2099–2138.

Gabaix, Xavier. 2009. Power Laws in Economics and Finance. *Annual Review of Economics* 1: 255–293.

———. 2016. Power Laws in Economics: An Introduction. *Journal of Economic Perspectives* 30 (1): 185–206.

Gabaix, Xavier, and Augustin Landier. 2008. Why Has CEO Pay Increased So Much? *The Quarterly Journal of Economics* 123 (1): 49–100.
Geloso, Vincent, and Steven Horwitz. 2017. Inequality: First, Do No Harm. *The Independent Review* 22 (1): 121–134.
Ghadge, Shilpa, Timothy Killingback, Bala Sundaram, and Duc A. Tran. 2010. A Statistical Construction of Power-Law Networks. *International Journal of Parallel, Emergent and Distributed Systems* 25 (3): 223–235.
Goldin, Claudia, and Lawrence F. Katz. 2008. *The Race Between Education and Technology*. Cambridge, MA: Belknap Press of Harvard University Press.
Gould, Roger V. 2002. The Origins of Status Hierarchies: A Formal Theory and Empirical Test. *American Journal of Sociology* 107 (5): 1143–1178.
Grubel, Herbert. 2015. What Piketty Misses. In *The Central Contradiction of Capitalism? A Collection of Essays on Capital in the Twenty-First Century*, ed. Geoffrey Wood and Steve Hughes, 19–22. London, UK: Policy Exchange.
Hartley, John, and Jason Potts. 2014. *Cultural Science: A Natural History of Stories, Demes, Knowledge and Innovation*. London, UK: Bloomsbury.
Henrich, Joseph, and Francisco J. Gil-White. 2001. The Evolution of Prestige: Freely Conferred Deference as a Mechanism for Enhancing the Benefits of Cultural Transmission. *Evolution and Human Behavior* 22: 165–196.
Higgs, Robert. 2014. Inequality Is a Statistical Artifact. Independent Institute, *Beacon blog*, December 1. Accessed September 21, 2017. http://blog.independent.org/2014/12/01/income-inequality-is-a-statistical-artifact/
Hillman, Arye L. 2013. Rent Seeking. In *The Elgar Companion to Public Choice*, ed. William F. Shughart II, Laura Razzolini, and Michael Reksulak, 2nd ed., 307–330. Cheltenham, UK: Edward Elgar.
Hirschl, Thomas A., and Mark R. Rank. 2015. The Life Course Dynamics of Affluence. *PLoS One* 10 (1): e0116370. Accessed January 29, 2018. https://doi.org/10.1371/journal.pone.0116370.
Hirschman, Albert O. 1970. *Exit, Voice, and Loyalty: Responses to Decline in Firms, Organizations, and States*. Cambridge, MA: Harvard University Press.
Jackson, Matthew O. 2008. *Social and Economic Networks*. Princeton, NJ: Princeton University Press.
Jones, Charles I. 2015. Pareto and Piketty: The Macroeconomics of Top Income and Wealth Inequality. *Journal of Economic Perspectives* 29 (1): 29–46.
Kaplan, Steven N., and Joshua Rauh. 2010. Wall Street and Main Street: What Contributes to the Rise in the Highest Incomes? *The Review of Financial Studies* 23 (3): 1004–1050.
Lachmann, Ludwig. (1956) 2008. The Market Economy and the Distribution of Wealth. In *On Freedom and Free Enterprise: Essays in Honor of Ludwig von*

Mises, ed. Mary Sennholz, 175–187. Auburb, AL: Ludwig von Mises Institute.

Lindsey, Brink, and Steven M. Teles. 2017. *The Captured Economy: How the Powerful Enrich Themselves, Slow Down Growth, and Increase Inequality*. Oxford, UK: Oxford University Press.

Lucifora, Claudio, and Rob Simmons. 2003. Superstar Effects in Sport: Evidence from Italian Soccer. *Journal of Sports Economics* 4 (1): 35–55.

MacDonald, Trent J. 2015. Theory of Unbundled and Non-Territorial Governance. Doctoral thesis, RMIT University.

Markey-Towler, Brendan. 2012. The Theory of Income Distribution: An Exploration of the Theory of Allocation with a New Proposal Based on Systems Science. Bachelor of Economics Honours thesis, University of Queensland.

———. 2014. A Discussion on Inequality and the Economy. Australian Senate Standing Committee on Community Affairs, Inquiry on the Extent of Income Inequality in Australia, *Submission No. 56*. Accessed September 15, 2017. https://www.aph.gov.au/DocumentStore.ashx?id=edb531fa-2333-4bd8-b723-a31bbcd65eb0&subId=300763

———. 2016. Foundations for Economic Analysis: The Architecture of Socioeconomic Complexity. Doctoral thesis, University of Queensland.

Markey-Towler, Brendan, and John Foster. 2013a. Understanding the Causes of Income Inequality in Complex Economic Systems. University of Queensland, *School of Economics Discussion Paper No. 478*. Accessed September 21, 2017. https://economics.uq.edu.au/478-understanding-causes-income-inequality-complex-economic-systems

———. 2013b. Why Economic Theory has Little to Say About the Causes and Effects of Inequality. University of Queensland, *School of Economics Discussion Paper No. 476*. Accessed September 21, 2017. https://economics.uq.edu.au/476-why-economic-theory-has-little-say-about-causes-and-effects-inequality

McCulloh, Ian A., Helen L. Armstrong, and Anthony N. Johnson. 2013. *Social Network Analysis with Applications*. Hoboken, NJ: Wiley & Sons.

McPherson, Miller. 1983. Ecology of Affiliation. *American Sociological Review* 48: 519–532.

———. 2004. A Blau Space Primer: Prolegomenon to an Ecology of Affiliation. *Industrial and Corporate Change* 13 (1): 263–280.

Mendolia, Silvia, and Peter Siminski. 2016. New Estimates of Intergenerational Mobility in Australia. *Economic Record* 92 (298): 361–373.

Murphy, Kevin J. 2013. Executive Compensation: Where We Are, and How We Got There. In *Handbook of the Economics of Finance*, ed. George

Constantinides, Milton Harris, and René Stulz, vol. 2A. Amsterdam, Netherlands: Elsevier.

Novak, Mikayla. 2016. Deirdre McCloskey, Kirznerian Growth and the Role of Social Networks: Comment. *Economic Affairs* 36 (2): 217–220.

Piketty, Thomas. 2014. *Capital in the Twenty-First Century: The Dynamics of Inequality, Wealth, and Growth*. Translated by Arthur Goldhammer. Cambridge, MA: The Belknap Press of Harvard University Press.

Popper, Nathaniel. 2017. How the Winklevoss Twins Found Vindication in a Bitcoin Fortune. *The New York Times*, December 19. Accessed January 29, 2018. https://www.nytimes.com/2017/12/19/technology/bitcoin-winklevoss-twins.html?_r=0

Potts, Jason. 2013. Rules of Spontaneous Order. *Cosmos + Taxis* 1 (1): 30–41.

Potts, Jason, and Kate Morrison. 2007. Meso Comes to Markets: Comment on 'Markets Come to Bits'. *Journal of Economic Behavior & Organization* 63 (2): 307–312.

Potts, Jason, Stuart Cunningham, John Hartley, and Paul Ormerod. 2008. Social Network Markets: A New Definition of the Creative Industries. *Journal of Cultural Economics* 32: 167–185.

Rallo, Juan Ramón. 2017. Where are the "Super Rich" of 1987? In *Anti-Piketty: Capital for the 21st Century*, ed. Jean-Philippe Delsol, Nicolas Lecaussin, and Emmanuel Martin, 31–35. Washington, DC: Cato Institute.

Rosen, Sherwin. 1981. The Economics of Superstars. *American Economic Review* 71 (5): 845–858.

Salter, Alexander William. 2012. A Theory of the Dynamics of Entangled Political Economy with Application to the Federal Reserve. *Journal of Public Finance and Public Choice* 30 (1–3): 77–102.

Sandmo, Agnar. 2015. The Principal Problem in Political Economy: Income Distribution in the History of Economic Thought. In *Handbook of Income Distribution*, ed. A.B. Atkinson and F. Bourguignon, vol. 2A, 3–66. Amsterdam, Netherlands: Elsevier.

Scott, James C. 2017. *Against the Grain: A Deep History of the Earliest States*. New Haven, CT: Yale University Press.

Wagner, Richard E. 2010. *Mind, Society, and Human Action: Time and Knowledge in a Theory of Social Economy*. London, UK: Routledge.

———. 2012a. *Deficits, Debt, and Democracy: Wrestling with Tragedy on the Fiscal Commons*. Cheltenham, UK: Edward Elgar.

———. 2012b. Rationality, Political Economy, and Fiscal Responsibility: Wrestling with Tragedy on the Fiscal Commons. *Constitutional Political Economy* 23: 261–277.

———. 2012c. Viennese Kaleidics: Why It's Liberty More Than Policy That Calms Turbulence. *Review of Austrian Economics* 25 (4): 283–297.

———. 2016. *Politics as a Peculiar Business: Insights from a Theory of Entangled Political Economy*. Cheltenham, UK: Edward Elgar.

———. 2017. *James M. Buchanan and Liberal Political Economy: A Rational Reconstruction*. Lanham, MD: Lexington Books.

Watson, William. 2015. *The Inequality Trap: Fighting Capitalism Instead of Poverty*. Toronto, Canada: University of Toronto Press.

Part II

Case Studies

4

Taxation and Expenditure Policies

Introduction

The imposition of taxation, and the disbursement of tax (and other) revenue in the form of expenditure programmes, are central forms of political action in modern societies. These activities are undertaken by government to achieve various policy objectives, with redistribution nominated as a primary reason for much of the taxing and spending. There is little doubt that the desire by policymakers to alter the distribution of income and wealth has also affected the overall growth in fiscal activity amongst developed countries.

There are numerous theoretical rationales supporting fiscal policy. The concept of "diminishing marginal utility" suggests money redistributed to the poor would increase their satisfaction, and, under certain conditions, raise the overall utility of the members of society. An "insurance" rationale is also present in the literature, stating that certain fiscal transfer programmes enable people at risk of ill-health, disability, or unemployment to be financially quarantined from such risks. Some works in public choice theory submit that redistributive fiscal policy would be supported

M. Novak, *Inequality*, Palgrave Studies in Classical Liberalism,
https://doi.org/10.1007/978-3-319-89417-1_4

within a polity that reflected the preferences of a utility-maximising median voter (Meltzer and Richard 1981).

Mainstream political economy is underpinned by a separation between economy and polity. This implies that political agents impose upon the economy, as if from a great distance, to alter distributional outcomes. Entangled political economy, by contrast, suggests policy is an emergent process formulated by political agents. The political agents cohabit a society populated by agents operating mainly within the economic and communal orders. Government is treated as a network of relationships and a process of interaction, and so it is plausible that policy emanating from their networks—including redistributive policies which rely upon taxation and expenditure—exhibits similar catallactic features.

According to entangled political economy theory, it is *not* guaranteed that taxation and expenditure would reduce disparities of income and wealth in society. Emergent policy provides much room for negotiation and contestability in fiscal policy by disparate actors, and this might lead to upward, pro-rich redistribution rather than pro-poor redistribution in the downward direction. These insights are reflected in the statement that "[a]lthough it is typically taken for granted that redistribution entails programmes that reduce the degree of inequality, redistribution simply refers to transfers among people" (Wagner 1989, p. 68). The possibility that taxing and spending may perform poorly from a redistributive standpoint is magnified by the frequency with which political agents impose tax, and expend funds, on a highly discriminatory basis.

This chapter provides an appraisal of certain taxation and expenditure policies in reducing inequality, from an entangled political economy perspective.[1] The next section discusses key insights into taxation theory and policy, emphasising the importance of human participation in the negotiated development of tax settings. The discussion about taxation is followed by an assessment of government expenditure policies in an entangled political economy. We then refer to implications which arise from spending by political agents in highly centralised systems of governance. Finally, this chapter provides a range of concluding remarks with respect to the contribution of fiscal policies towards the attenuation, or otherwise, of income and wealth disparities.

The Entangled Political Economy Vision of Taxation

The orthodox economic depiction of taxation theory rests upon several criteria to determine if a given tax system is "good" or not. Utilising taxation as an instrument to ameliorate an unequal distribution of income or wealth is just one social problem to be purportedly solved through the enlightened application of policy. It is in this context that mainstream economists have devised several equity justifications in respect of, for example, a progressive income tax structure.

The economist Francis Edgeworth suggested that, in order to help raise a given level of revenue to finance public goods and services, the income tax should be designed in order to impose the "least aggregate sacrifice" of utility aggregated over the entire community. Given the concept of diminishing marginal utility—an additional dollar in the hand of a rich person provides less satisfaction to them than would an additional dollar for a poor person—the most appropriate way to minimise aggregate utility sacrifice is to impose differential income tax rates. In short, a government abiding by this principle would design a progressive tax rate structure (Buchanan and Congleton [1998] 2003).

Under the basic Edgeworthian theoretical system for progressive income tax, the state would compulsorily acquire revenue from members of the population within the top echelons of the income distribution until its revenue-raising objective is satisfied. However, as Richard Wagner (2017) asks: why would somebody in those circumstances seek additional hours of work if the lion's share of their income is to be taxed away? Conceding that individuals need economic incentives to spur them to productive action, Edgeworth refined his basic framework to prevent the possibility of a 100 per cent tax rate upon well-off income-earners.

Edgeworth's intellectual contributions later gave way to the intellectual enterprise of "optimal tax theory" (Mirrlees 1971; Diamond and Mirrlees 1971; Diamond 1998; Mankiw et al. 2009). In essence, this literature accepts the existence of a trade-off between equity and efficiency in the design of taxation. Redistribution is supported on the presumption of declining marginal utility, but the extent of redistribution has to be limited because the incentive to earn diminishes as marginal tax rates increase (Wagner 2007). An income tax rate set at zero per cent obviously collects no revenue, whereas an income tax rate set at 100 per cent completely extinguishes the incentive of workers to supply labour; thus, an "optimal" rate of taxation imposed by a policymaker would rest someplace between these extremes.

The setting of tax rates is undertaken against the background of tax structure determination. Wagner (1989) reminds us that flat (proportional rate) income taxation also performs a redistributive function, given that the tax liability borne by a rich person will be greater than that faced by a poor person (even if no tax-free thresholds apply). For instance, a hypothetical 25 per cent flat tax on someone earning $1 million per annum would yield $250,000 to the government but only $12,500 for a person earning $50,000 per annum. As Hayek and certain other classical liberals remarked, a concern with Edgeworthian progressive income taxation is that it is predicated upon a strong, yet fundamentally arbitrary, "taste" for redistribution which correspondingly disfavours wealth creation:

> Unlike proportionality, progression provides no principle which tells us what the relative burden of different persons ought to be. It is no more than a rejection of proportionality in favor of a discrimination against the wealthy without any criterion for limiting the extent of this discrimination. (Hayek [1960] 2006, p. 272)

The orthodox treatment of taxation is predicated upon an additive political economy, wherein a benevolent and enlightened unitary state imposes tax policy to realise redistributive objectives. In contrast, the entangled approach to political economy that Wagner has explored in depth describes the phenomenon of taxation as an emergent one, a "product of interaction within some framework of rules that govern relationships among those who participate in making decisions about taxation" (Hebert and Wagner 2013, p. 169). An important consideration is that participation in tax policy deliberations often assumes an entrepreneurial character. Amongst the most important "tax entrepreneurs" are arguably the senior members of the government, collaborating with other members of the "peculiar" parliamentary bazaar. The parliamentarians bear the fatigues of sifting through proposals to introduce new and modified forms of triadic tax arrangements, and negotiate with a multiplicity of contending interests to secure political acquiescence—especially from amongst those who are more likely to lose out from the tax process.

Ignored by researchers specialising in mainstream tax economics is that the act of taxing is a primary example of "parasitical attachment" by political enterprises onto economic enterprises, and individuals and their transactions (Wagner 2012a, b). An implication of such practice is that "[t]his parasitical quality reflects recognition that the state does not have the entrepreneurial tools necessary to generate a self-supporting stream of revenue. There is no transferable ownership for public enterprises, so there can be no market valuation of those enterprises" (Wagner 2015, p. 457). Taxation represents parasitical attachment to economic activity in various ways. An income tax, say, attaches to the value of incomes generated by individuals and by corporations, whereas a sales tax is attached to the value of sales generated by individuals and agencies within the economy, and so on.

Market relationships rest upon the principles of alienable property, contract, and voluntary exchanges, which are qualities distinctly lacking within political relationships predominated by "forced exchanges." Whereas "taxation is the way politicians transform money into power" (Wagner 2012a, p. 130), the type of taxation imposed and the associated budgetary and legislative processes nevertheless "modifies the character of economic processes from that portrayed in the pure theory of markets" (Wagner 2014, p. 26). Political activity cannot generate valuations for political enterprises, but, by the same token, parasitical attachments to economic calculations both use and degrade market prices (which, in highly competitive situations, tend to correspond more closely with marginal production costs) arising through economic interaction.

Richard Wagner's fiscal sociology draws attention to techniques employed by political actors to counter resistance against paying taxation. In addition to the promulgation of political rhetoric, manufacturing anything ranging from begrudging acquiescence to willing embrace by the public to pay their tax liabilities (Wagner 2018), certain taxation properties conjure the "fiscal illusion" that people conceive they are paying less in tax than they actually are. As Hayek once put it, "the whole practice of public finance has been developed in an endeavour to outwit the taxpayer and to induce him to pay more than he is aware of" (Hayek [1979] 2013, p. 392).

The lack of income tax-scale adjustment to accommodate price inflation, or the growth in wages and salaries, induces a phenomenon known as "bracket creep" whereby people find themselves paying a greater amount of tax often as they enter a higher rate along the progressive tax structure. According to one account of this fiscal technique, "[t]he most effective way for politicians to avoid making decisions regarding taxes is to have a taxation system that delivers real increases in revenue automatically. Vote losses are minimised by the fact that increased real financing is achieved without active decisions having to be made. … A progressive income tax, for example, will deliver increased real revenue as the result of bracket creep due to macroeconomic growth" (Blount 2001, p. 348).

Another element of an illusory tax system is the tax withholding regime. Under these arrangements, employers are obligated to withhold tax from the gross salaries of their employees, and directly transfer the tax liabilities to the government. Tax withholding may be described as a form of fiscal illusion at work, given that "[t]he individual who does not have possession of income before paying it out cannot 'sense' the real cost of public services in a manner comparable to that experienced in a genuine act of outpayment" (Buchanan [1967] 1999a, p. 138).

It is difficult to isolate the effects of fiscal illusion upon the effectiveness of progressive income taxation to redistribute income. What can be said with a reasonable amount of confidence, however, is that the operation of progressive income taxes today engenders a modicum of fiscal discrimination amongst members of the taxpaying public. The concern is that "[o]nce a government acquires the power to reward or punish particular types of activity, the power to tax becomes limited only by the pragmatic exercise of political power" (Wagner 2012a, p. 130). This opens up opportunities for non-political actors to pressure legislators and bureaucrats to design more favourable taxing arrangements, or to resist unfavourable proposals.

A potential response to pressure to lighten the tax burden is for political actors to target relatively small population segments for a greater share of tax liability. Several key figures in the contemporary inequality debate have been calling upon governments to increase the severity of estate and inheritance taxes, for example, ensuring a redistribution of wealth from those well-off to those less well-off. Thomas Piketty outlined his concern that concentrations of inherited wealth would become predominant, particularly as the populations of developed economies age and their economies grow more slowly:

> inherited wealth grows faster than output and income. People with inherited wealth need save only a portion of their income from capital to see that capital grow more quickly than the economy as a whole. Under such conditions, it is almost inevitable that inherited wealth will dominate wealth amassed from a lifetime's labor by a wide margin, and the concentration of capital will attain extremely high levels—levels potentially incompatible with meritocratic values and principles of social justice fundamental to modern democratic societies. (Piketty 2014, p. 26)

Joseph Stiglitz (2012) has, in a similar vein to Piketty, suggested that estate taxes should be increased to prevent the emergence of oligarchic families skewing the distribution of wealth.

These propositions have, perhaps surprisingly, received support from some classical liberals over the years. Buchanan (1983) contended that the option for a person to bequeath their money and non-financial assets would encourage a rent-seeking process in which potential heirs would spend time, effort, and even resources in an attempt to win the approval, and ultimately the inheritance, of the would-be donor. For Buchanan, these efforts were seen as potentially wasteful from a societal point of view. To avoid social waste, he insisted that wealth inequalities which arise from the accident of birth should be rectified by heavy inheritance tax, even levied at 100 per cent. Deirdre McCloskey (2006) also expressed support for steep inheritance taxes.

Despite the anti-inequality rationale for taxes on estates and inheritances, the effectiveness of such a policy is contingent upon a range of factors. These include the appetites of potential donors to give away their estates or not, to whom (their relatives or, say, to some philanthropic or charitable cause), and the use of certain tax-planning strategies in an effort to avoid taxation (Schmalbeck 2001; Scholes et al. 2002). It should be recognised that the revenue from these taxes is received by the state, whose subsequent expenditure activities may either reinforce or offset (at least in part) the implicitly equalising effects of the tax. Critics of estate and inheritance taxes also point to the potential disincentive effects associated with these forms of taxation for savings and capital accumulation (Landsburg 2011; Novak 2015; Watkins and Brook 2016).

Consistent with the fiscal insights of entangled political economy, scholars whose work intersects public finance, psychology, and sociology have observed that public perceptions about the appropriateness of taxation depend upon the way in which rationalisations for such exactions are framed (Beckert 2008; Hill 2010; Norton and Ariely 2011). On the one hand, the detractors of estate and inheritance taxes frequently refer to them as "death taxes," attempting to paint them as immoral given that we all eventually die. On the other, those who support this form of taxation attempt to appeal to our innate sense of fairness by referring to the undeserved wealth received by supposedly spoiled rotten rich kids if inheritances are not taxed (McCloskey 2007). Added to these conflicting views is the perspective offered by John Tomasi that "ordinary people may oppose the death tax because they value living in a society of the sort that allows anyone, including *people like them*, to rise to great wealth" (Tomasi 2012, p. 63).

There continues to be uncertainty with regard to which of these non-logical perspectives will prevail into the future or, perhaps to be more precise, if any particular view will be commonly accepted for long. In any case, it seems the debate over whether estate and inheritance taxes, or other forms of wealth taxation, should be introduced, or increased, to repeal inequality is unlikely to dissipate in the foreseeable future (Cowen 2013).

Redistributive Properties of Taxation: Entangled Political Economy Perspectives

The participatory nature of tax policy design, implementation, and enforcement in an entangled political economy suggests that "[t]he [income] tax code is assembled through interaction among many people extending over a good number of years, and will continue to be assembled in this manner" (Hebert and Wagner 2013, p. 166). In the U.S. alone, the tax code of the federal government consists of some 50 volumes covering over 70,000 pages and including nearly four million words. The provisions in the code include deductions, exemptions, and other forms of relief affecting an individual's liability to pay personal income tax. Similar forms of tax complexity have been observed in other developed countries, suggesting the developments described, or the processes determining them, are not accidental.

The setting of tax policy is, to put it simply, a contestable process. The friction between economic, social, and political actors in the determination of who pays what taxes contributes to a discriminatory scenario in which "tax rates can be varied over a wide set of economic characteristics: income and wealth classes, occupations, professions, and industrial categories. Race horse breeders, real estate developers, and resort operators can secure special treatment without constitutional challenge" (Buchanan and Congleton [1998] 2003, p. 130). Furthermore, the development of taxation structures riddled with exemptions, and other forms of relief from actually paying tax, may well frustrate the plans of those policymakers wanting to ameliorate income inequality.

Population segments initially identified as bearing the responsibility to shoulder much of the tax liability will politically counteract in an attempt to relieve their responsibilities. According to Boettke and Martin, "tax burdens apportioned 'progressively' fall asymmetrically across the population, thus laying the groundwork for both rent-seeking and countervailing distributional forces to work from the bottom up … A tax burden concentrated on the rich creates a strong incentives for a small group to lobby to introduce various loopholes and provisions to offset the burden" (Boettke and Martin 2011, p. 10). Of course, there is every chance that rent-seeking will beget rent-seeking in tax policy: "[t]he moment the door is opened to one deduction, we have a flood, and resources will be wasted on lobbying for deductions, as well as on lawyers and tax accounts who exploit them" (Zingales 2012, p. 209).

To the extent that government maintains some semblance of a revenue-collection target, formal exclusions from tax payment contribute to a fiscal culture of "recognition that the best tax is nearly always one that someone else pays" (Hebert and Wagner 2013, p. 170). Milton Friedman ([1962] 2002) explains that even people in similar financial positions could end up paying different income tax amounts, violating "horizontal equity" norms in which those in similar circumstances are treated alike.

The upshot of this discussion is that entanglement likely creates a situation in which a progressive tax rate structure on the statute books may not actually reduce inequality in effect. At any given period of time, the taxation arrangement "entails the use of distributed knowledge that is in no person's possession" (Hebert and Wagner 2013, p. 166), but, when we consider the process of fiscal evolution more deeply, it is by no means assured that policymakers would even know, with any great precision, if their tax policies are helping to reduce economic inequality. It is not implausible that the fiscal process in an entangled political economy is biased towards rent-seeking activity. This bias may give rise to a less effective tax system with respect to inequality abatement: "a progressive tax on income might be thought of as constituting a programme to redistribute income in a downward direction. Yet the tax code is also replete with provisions that work in the reverse direction" (Wagner 2007, pp. 73–74).

A progressive rate structure for income taxation implies that revenue collected will vary from person to person in accordance with the income they earn. Table 4.1 provides a summary of U.S. federal income tax collections according to selected income categories for 2014, essentially indicating that participation by players in America's entangled political

Table 4.1 United States federal income taxation collections by selected income categories, 2014

Income group	Returns (number)	Share of adjusted gross income (per cent)	Share of total income taxes paid (per cent)	Average tax rate (per cent)
Top 1 per cent	1,395,620	20.6	39.5	27.2
Top 5 per cent	6,978,102	36.0	60.0	23.6
Top 10 per cent	13,956,203	47.2	70.9	21.3
Top 25 per cent	34,890,509	68.9	86.8	17.8
Top 50 per cent	69,781,017	88.7	97.3	15.5
Bottom 50 per cent	69,781,017	11.3	2.8	3.5
All taxpayers	139,562,034	100.0	100.0	14.2

Source: Greenberg (2017)

economy has resulted in the bulk of income tax being borne by those towards the top of the income distribution.

There is a view amongst some classical liberals that the relatively smaller share of personal income tax collections borne by those in the bottom half of the income distribution implies that a considerable number of people are insensitive to changes in the cost of providing public sector services:

> To the extent a revenue system operates to present significant shares of taxpayers with zero marginal prices for expansions in government spending, those taxpayers can be expected to support expansions in governmental activity up to satiation point, provided that the governmental activity in question is regarded as good and not bad, meaning that it conforms to the presumption that more of it is better than less of it. (Wagner 2012a, p. 132)

The matter raised by Wagner is of importance from the perspective of a functional democratic polity and sustainable fiscal structure. By the same token it should be recognised not all persons statistically assigned to an income cohort, as is the case in Table 4.1, are necessarily treated in the same measure by fiscal actions. The actual contributions people make to the public fisc are, ultimately, an empirical question which needs to consider not only income tax but all taxes, as well as the incidence of public sector expenditure programmes. The annual versus lifetime balance of taxes paid and benefits received also need to be factored in any estimates.

Undeterred by such complications, a number of protagonists within the contemporary inequality debate, such as Piketty and Stiglitz, have argued for a steepening of the progressive income -tax rate scale on redistributive grounds. From this perspective, it is anticipated that government would faithfully implement a policy imposing higher marginal tax rates upon those well-off, exempting those with lesser means from an increase in their relative income tax burden. Thomas Piketty (2014) advocated a very high top income tax rate of 80 per cent for the American economy. It is supposed that tax hikes would ameliorate inequality in two ways: repressing the appetite for seemingly excessive corporate remuneration packages benefiting a small cohort of income earners; and quelling international tax competition for skilled labour who could potentially earn substantive after-tax premia on their earnings.

Several economists have questioned the efficacy of personal income tax increases as a means to suppress income inequality. In the economics literature, it is clearly held that progressive marginal tax rates diminish, at least on the margins, the incentive for workers to look for new, higher-paying jobs or to offer to work extra hours in their existing workplaces. Any deterrence of upward mobility, as a consequence of more steeply progressive taxation, serves to effectively protect the economic positions of those workers already situated within the higher income-earning echelons. Some economists, such as Stephen Gordon (2016), have hypothesised that high-income earners, with relatively extensive human capital and having the greatest potential to relocate, would seek to bargain with employers for *greater pay* in the face of tax increases. This is but one possibility that could transpire within the interactionist and complex framework of entangled political economy.

A number of participants in the contemporary inequality debate have raised criticisms that certain large companies pay corporate tax rates which are effectively lower than the statutory tax rate. With regard to American corporate taxation, it is contended that "the effective tax rate—the fraction of their income that corporations actually pay in taxes—is much less than 35 percent, with some of the country's premier corporations, like GE, paying no taxes" (Stiglitz 2012, p. 278). An important underlying reason for this discrepancy rests with the availability of deductions, exemptions, and other waivers written into the corporate tax code, enabling firms to effectively have their tax liabilities reduced.

Among the more important corporate tax reliefs offered by governments, in terms of revenue foregone, in developed countries include depreciation allowances to assist companies in defraying the cost of investments they make, credits or other forms of relief for those firms undertaking eligible research and development expenses, deductions for certain sub-national government taxes already paid, and allowances to carry over previous financial losses into subsequent years (OECD 2010). Industry-specific tax incentives may also be available, such as for manufacturing firms or companies in the fossil fuels sector, and incentives for companies to develop certain technologies, such as biotechnology and renewable energy.

There are other grounds for companies potentially being able to assume an effectively lesser liability for corporate income tax. A company operating across national borders, say, may implicitly "shift" profits from high-taxing countries to low-taxing countries via a host of financial and operational adjustments. This "transfer pricing" phenomenon relates to practices that effectively transfer revenues to foreign subsidiaries in countries with lower tax rates—for example, the domestic company (in a high-taxing country) sells goods and services to subsidiaries in low-tax countries at cheaper rates resulting in low revenues in the high-tax country and high revenues and profits in the low-tax country (Barker et al. 2017). Another technique, referred to as "corporate inversion," is the reincorporation of a company overseas to reduce the tax liability it domestically owes in the high-taxing country (Neely and Sherrer 2017).

The fact of corporate tax relief represents little more than a reflection of the entangled political economy perspective of taxation as an emergent process of considerable complexity. Hebert (2014) describes the situation as akin to a game of "cat-and-mouse," in which businesses continuously seek new tax loopholes, whereas tax officials are constantly looking to close loopholes as they arise. The "chase," so to speak, is in no small part influenced by tax accountants and lawyers who not only assist their respective clients (business or government) through the ambiguity and incoherence presented by tax legislation, and associated by-laws and guidelines, but work to inject additional complexities reputedly on behalf of the clients they represent (Hillman 2013).

It is a better reflection of reality to suggest that taxation is not imposed by a separable, organismic political entity solely dedicated to redistributive policy. Recognition should also be given to the proposition that, for many, taxes still resemble "forced exchange" given the fundamentally triadic nature of any given taxation arrangement. As noted by Richard Wagner, "[w]ithout doubt, taxation … generally involves a good number of people in paying for output they do not value, or value less than the sacrificed market output the tax makes necessary" (Wagner 2006, p. 243). The complexities inherent within the tax system reflect a deeper struggle between the taxers, wishing to extend the reach of triadic, questionably valued exchanges, and the taxed, seeking to avoid being on the perceived losing end of such forced exchanges.

Key Features of Government Expenditure in Entangled Political Economy

As is the case for taxation, economists have advanced numerous rationales in support of governmental expenditures. The first we shall consider, which traces an intellectual lineage to the writings of Adam Smith, suggests that some outputs referred to as "public goods" may not be provided efficiently by for-profit economic enterprises, as a consequence of certain technical features attached to the public goods. The feature of "non-excludability" means that the (public) good is available to everybody and, thus, a for-profit producer cannot feasibly set a price to exclude non-payers. Unless the good is produced by government, and compulsorily financed by taxation or some other revenue-raising instrument, people would shirk the responsibility of voluntarily contributing towards the cost of production (this is referred to as "free-riding"). A related characteristic of public goods is "non-rivalry," indicating that the act of consumption of the good by a given individual does not subtract from anyone else's potential to likewise consume the good.

The dichotomy between public goods and private goods, the latter being excludable by price and rivalrous in consumption, serves as a foundation for public finance centred upon an additive political economy perspective. The reality is, however, most goods and services do not match the "pure public good" ideal of complete non-excludability and non-rivalry. "The dichotomy between public and private goods seems to map naturally into a distinction between domains, with government providing public goods and market-based organizations providing private goods," said Richard Wagner, "[t]his distinction, however, does not conform at all well to reality" (Wagner 2007, p. 16).

Other theories have been developed in support of spending by political enterprises. The English economists Henry Sidgwick and Arthur Cecil Pigou have been largely credited with developing the theory of "externality," highlighting the presence of uncompensated benefits or costs associated with certain activities taking place within the economic order. In the case of positive external benefits, it is suggested that economic enterprises are, in fact, under-producing the relevant output which is providing benefit not only to payers but to non-payers. To ensure a greater, more efficient level of production, the policy prescription is for government to provide a subsidy to the relevant activity generating the positive externality.

Most economists agree that the significant involvement in school education by public sector entities is justifiable on externality grounds. This is because the provision of educational instruction to the citizenry produces spillover benefits—productive workplaces, a cohesive society in which individuals can converse with each other, and a functional polity in which people can capably vote and govern themselves—which are at risk of being under-provided if left solely to economic enterprises or to parents (Friedman 1955). It is important to note, however, that education spending authorised by legislators is usually also tied to regulation dictating the compulsory attendance of children in schools.

Redistribution also looms large as a rationalisation for governmental spending. A large component of recurrent governmental expenditure consists of "welfare state" cash payments and in-kind social services for individuals and families identified to be in need. The desire to effect redistribution from less-deserving to more-deserving individuals and groups is arguably the most obvious rationalisation for the welfare state, but fighting inequality is not the only reason why political agents maintain welfare expenditure programmes. In many instances, the actors comprising the state also wish to redistribute in a "horizontal" fashion:

> Social insurance is primarily designed for horizontal redistribution, seeking to allocate income across the life course. Like commercial insurance plans, there is no attempt to redistribute between "rich" and "poor." Instead, the aim is to smooth lifetime income and guarantee well-being in the face of bad luck (like illness) or foreseeable need (like old age). (Esping-Andersen and Myles 2011, p. 640)

In these cases, the government provides income, and other kinds of support where necessary, to support people in the event of unemployment, illness, or other unfortunate events. Boiled down to its essentials, "[t]his is a vision of the welfare state as offering people a helping hand if needed to support their own responsible conduct" (Wagner 2005,

p. 385). It is envisaged that once the personal crisis passes, individuals will suitably return to active economic and social engagements.

The operation of forces outside individual control (e.g. birth, luck) demonstrates it is obvious, even in flourishing civil societies, that people will occasionally require assistance. This issue was discussed at length by Friedrich Hayek in his support for a form of non-discriminatory welfare state: "a certain minimum income for everyone, or a floor below which nobody need fall even when he is unable to provide for himself, appears not only to be a wholly legitimate protection against a risk common to all, but a necessary part of the Great Society in which the individual no longer has specific claims on the members of the particular small group into which he was born" (Hayek [1979] 2013, pp. 394–395). Hayek clarified that the purpose of this "insurance" function is "not that people should be coerced to do what is in their individual interest but that, by neglecting to make provision, they would become a charge to the public" (Hayek [1960] 2006, p. 249).

Some economists have depicted the welfare state as assuming public good characteristics. Harold Hochman and James Rodgers (1969) indicated that charity is not a purely private good, given that the utility the donors receive from lending assistance to beneficiaries depends upon the aggregate amount of donations made out or, equivalently, on the aggregate extent to which poverty is reduced. Under this scenario it is rational for potential donors to withhold assistance, in the hope that others will do so instead. To avoid the threat of charity under-provision due to free-riding, government should intervene by taxing people (richer individuals presumably paying a relatively greater amount) to contribute to the pool of charitable donations. A similar view was outlined by Lester Thurow (1971).

The final justification for the welfare state outlined here could be summed up as "keeping the peace." Buchanan (1976) reinterpreted the Rawlsian difference principle, which indicates that inequalities are justified to the extent the circumstances of those least well off in society are improved, to suggest that the difference principle is necessary to avoid a Hobbesian state of nature in which nobody prospers. Under an accommodation of the difference principle, in this manner a justification can be found for some redistributive function by the state.

The welfare state often evokes a mental image, or impression, of a monolithic and coherent enterprise conducted by political agents. It is from this standpoint that any perceived lack of coherence is seen as anomalous in some way. However, we consider that a realistic use of the shorthand term "welfare state" is to depict a regime characterised by "multiple programs that address narrower and overlapping constituencies of supporters" (Wagner 2010, p. 101). The actually existing constellation of spending programmes and initiatives should be expected in an entangled political economy, as this would reflect the ceaseless, entrepreneurial pursuit of fiscal gains by actors intertwining across the economic, communal, and political orders.

Maintaining a welfare state represents a complex and extensive undertaking. Numerous agencies and bureaus are involved in designing and enforcing welfare policies, providing any combination of payments and services to beneficiaries (unconditionally or conditionally). As part of these administrative efforts, the government often outsources the delivery of services to charities and other non-profit organisations, and, as a result, modern welfare state management will also entail extensive contractual responsibilities. A comprehensive identification of all the welfare programmes in existence is fraught with great difficulty, given definitional issues, regular administrative changes, and variations in reporting across multiple levels of government. An American study by the Cato Institute's Michael Tanner found 126 separate and often overlapping programmes at the federal level alone:

> there are 33 housing programs, run by four different cabinet departments, including, strangely, the Department of Energy. There are currently 21 different programs providing food or food-purchasing assistance. These programs are administered by three different federal departments and one independent agency. There are 8 different health care programs, administered by five separate agents within the Department of Health and Human Services. And six cabinet departments and five independent agencies oversee 27 cash or general assistance programs. All together, seven different cabinet agencies and six independent agencies, administer at least one anti-poverty program. (Tanner 2012, pp. 2–3)

At a 2015 hearing of the U.S. Congressional Ways and Means Committee, 83 federal programmes (of largely an overlapping nature) were identified, costing in excess of U.S. $1 trillion per annum (U.S. House of Representatives 2015). The programmes were intended to help low-income individuals and families by providing food, housing, healthcare, jobs training, education, and energy assistance, as well as cash to underpin effective household budgeting.

The extent and direction of redistribution effected by welfare state activities can only be comprehended with respect to the underlying, bottom-up processes giving rise to such outcomes. The policy actually enacted by government is forged by a hard-fought process of negotiation between individuals across the different domains of society looking to discover favourable subsidy arrangements, but with all other parties in society obliged to wear the accompanying taxes imposed upon them. The outcomes of the welfare state are contingent, and not certain. In other words, "[t]o wish that government would redistribute income to soften the distributional results of market processes is not to ensure that government will actually do so. A government may not have the ability, even if it has a single-minded interest in doing so" (Wagner 1989, p. 12).

In the early 1970s, the University of Chicago economist George Stigler coined a "law," named in honour of his esteemed colleague Aaron Director. This so-called Director's Law indicates that interest-group dynamics create a situation whereby welfare spending (and taxation) implicitly redistributes funds not in favour of the lower class but, rather, to the middle class. The conceptual basis for this proposition is that "[g] overnment has coercive power, which allows it to engage in acts (above all, the taking of resources) which could not be performed by voluntary agreement of the members of a society. Any portion of the society which can secure control of the state's machinery will employ the machinery to improve its own position. Under a set of conditions … this dominant group will be the middle income classes" (Stigler 1970, p. 1).

Several figures have engaged in arithmetical exercises to suggest that Director's Law may be operative in certain developed countries, with a complementary, yet small, body of econometric literature tending to lend some support to the existence of such a phenomenon (Acemoglu et al. 2015; Feld and Schnellenbach 2007; Mohl and Pamp 2008). Milton and Rose Friedman ([1980] 1990) made a rough estimate that expenditures on selected welfare programmes in the U.S. effectively amounted to double the amount of income a non-farming family of four received on the "poverty line." Deirdre McCloskey (2006) later performed her own calculations, showing if one-quarter of the U.S. government tax-take went to the poor, each man, woman, and child in poverty would receive $U.S. 30,000 each per annum (a family of four would receive an annual income of $U.S. 120,000).

It would be inappropriate to treat cohorts of individuals or households, sorted on an income basis, as homogenous with respect to income, or to treat those within each income bracket as identically affected by fiscal action (Wagner 2008). With those caveats in mind, the point of Director's Law is to emphasise the *potential* of non-poor redistribution taking place.

With age-pension payments dominating the welfare landscape, there is a degree of redistribution taking place over the life cycle, as mentioned previously. These payments may (or may not) favour middle-income earners and may (or may not) reduce income and wealth inequalities. Watkins and Brook suggest "the money paid out of Social Security could not have created or even expanded the middle class since Social Security payments were mainly financed by taxes on the middle class. It was a redistribution not from the rich to everyone else but mostly from middle-class workers to middle-class retirees" (Watkins and Brook 2016, p. 31). One might further add that certain welfare payments induce a transfer from asset-poor, cash-rich workers to cash-poor, asset-rich retirees (especially elderly homeowners). It is important, however, to recognise those contributory pensions and other schemes—more prevalent in continental Europe than in the Anglosphere—in which there is some linkage between the mandated contributions individuals (and their employers) make and what individuals receive in payments, and the latter may appear to be upwardly redistributive in the year in which they occur.

Although mainstream economic treatments have a government fashioning welfare state payments to effectively repress economic inequality, or curtail poverty, it may not actually possess the requisite knowledge to be able to perfectly design and implement such expenditure policies. The "knowledge problem," as famously explicated by Friedrich Hayek, represents a foundation for modern classical liberal critiques of governmental policy, and has been frequently applied to the welfare state. The economist Mark Pennington casts doubts on the ability of participants within the welfare state to agree upon, let alone implement, that immaculate programme, or set of programmes, inducing unambiguously pro-poor redistribution. As he put it, "however well motivated people may be to achieve a particular distributive pattern, in a complex society where their decisions must dovetail with those of millions of others they simply cannot know what the appropriate action should be" (Pennington 2011, pp. 134–135).

In a recent study concerning poverty alleviation, Adam Martin and Matias Petersen raise the obvious point that poverty "is a socially embedded phenomenon associated with difficulties related to physical and mental health, social networks, cultural norms, access to legal services, political influence, and public services" (Martin and Petersen 2017, p. 8). For Martin and Petersen, efforts to reduce poverty take on a catallactic character in economic, social, and political environments distilling fragmented, and highly contextual, knowledge. Boettke and Martin (2011) also raise the importance of knowledge when referring to the divergence between "elegant" policies on paper and "messy" policies in practice.

It may be argued the panoply of programmes and initiatives comprising the welfare state actually reflect attempts by political actors to overcome their epistemic limitations. After all, political actors are as capable of learning as others within civil society (Yu 2011), even if the capacity for error-correction (i.e. abolishing programmes discovered not to work, or deemed irrelevant as circumstances change) is hampered by the likes of constituency resistance, legislative intransigence, or internal policy inertia. Social entrepreneurs may also work around existing governmental programmes, experimenting with different models which build the capabilities of the needy and vulnerable (Ziegler 2010). Notwithstanding the veracity of these insights, the ability of political actors to surmount knowledge problems appears deeply constrained by their very omnipresence within the domains of concern (in this case, welfare). As shall be discussed later in this chapter, greater institutional leeway for active involvement by non-political agents will be critical to develop interactive systems in which participants learn, and act on their learning.

The welfare state has long been accompanied by affective rhetoric and appealing sentiment to rationalise the imposition of such policy. In particular, the use of ideological construct looms large in welfare state politics. The cultivation of public acquiescence with triadic exchanges rests upon political entrepreneurship which formulates "a supporting coalition by crafting a transactional structure that entails gainers and losers, while at the same time generating a supporting ideological cover that softens and conceals the redistributive character of the transaction" (Wagner 2016, pp. 125–126).

The "insurance" justification for social security and certain other payments is an iconic example in which political rhetoric and economic and fiscal realities diverge. The insurance narrative suggests that individuals make contributions (i.e. pay insurance premiums) to a pool of finances that may be accessible upon the production of compensation claims, in light of the occurrence of certain unfortunate circumstances. The contributions that individuals make are assessed on the basis of risk profiling, taking into account factors such as age, gender, occupation, habits, and previous behaviours.

In a competitive and open insurance market, people have the ability to select that insurer providing the most appropriate balance between insurance coverage and suggested premium. In many circumstances, reflecting the ceaseless competition within the insurance market to maintain customers (and, through them, deep contribution pools), insurers provide premium discounts and other rewards for members with a longstanding record of *not* accessing the insurance pool.

Although many of the welfare state payments, especially in the Anglosphere, are purported to be insurance mechanisms, the reality is that they are not. The responsibility for financing most payments is allotted to the current cohort of general taxpayers on a "pay-as-you-go" basis, using existing tax systems to finance spending. This is opposed to a "contributory model" in which funds are gathered from taxpayers on the basis of their individual risk-profiles, and then deposited into a financial pool, for a specific purpose, to be subsequently invested in an effort to yield reasonable financial returns. The inculcation of the mass belief that welfare is an insurance system, or at least embodies one, perhaps explains the massive public resistance against even modest proposals for reform, because members of the public believe they have "paid into" welfare all of their lives.

The "stroke of promotional genius," as Hayek labelled the invocation of the language of insurance in welfare policy, provided a degree of political cover for the redistributive function of cash subsidies and in-kind provisions:

> Such a redistribution of income has today become the chief purpose of what is still called social "insurance"—a misnomer even in the early days of these schemes. … From the beginning it had little to do with insurance and has since lost whatever resemblance to insurance it may ever have had. … Though a redistribution of incomes was never the avowed initial purpose of the apparatus of social security, it has now become the actual and admitted aim everywhere. No system of monopolistic compulsory insurance has resisted this transformation into something quite different, an instrument for the compulsory redistribution of income. (Hayek [1960] 2006, p. 251)

Another common way to generate public agreeability with triadic exchanges associated with the welfare state is to proclaim that the recipients of such support are worthy and deserving of their receipt. Any reference to the efforts that non-beneficiaries—whether they are rich or poor—have to make, or burdens they have to endure, is largely underplayed by political sponsors of these programmes, if not ignored altogether. Taking this matter further, Richard Wagner submits that "[w]idespread references to social contracts and similar images exemplify the creation of images that give a veneer of rationality, as if the programme were a product of logical choice. … They all apply a veneer of rationality to what is in no way a logical action" (Wagner 2016, p. 100).

The welfare state is lauded as a pivotal mechanism for government to dampen inequality through spending which reputedly acts to redistribute from the rich to the poor. However, "[a]n aggregate measure that finds some net redistribution in favour of the lower income classes … will contain many net losers among members of the lower income categories, as well as containing many net gainers among the upper income categories" (Wagner 2005, p. 403). Taking these insights one step further, entangled political economy theory suggests that these will tend to be rhetorically papered over by those special interests—including people positioned within the middle to upper echelons of income and wealth distributions—who deem such arrangements to be in their favour.

The "Samaritan's Dilemma" and Monocentric Public Governance

James Buchanan ([1975] 1999b) presents a game-theoretic thought experiment based on the biblical parable of the Good Samaritan, a wealthy passer-by who renders assistance to a beaten traveller left by a roadside. Giving assistance to the stricken traveller would obviously benefit the victim, and possibly provides psychic income for the Samaritan. By the same token, there is the prospect that the act of assistance will encourage the traveller to want to rely upon the charity (instead of entrepreneurship or labouring) of the Good Samaritan for their future upkeep. In the extreme case, the proliferation of needy travellers can overwhelm those Samaritans who would otherwise voluntarily elect to provide aid, with bad behaviour driving out the good.

Tuszynski and Wagner (2016) and Wagner (2017) have contemplated Buchanan's dilemma in depth. The crux of the dilemma seems to be "[g]iving aid to those who make impoverishing choices will encourage others to do the same, thereby worsening the problem. Yet there is no unmistakable way of separating choice from chance" (Wagner 2017, p. 393). In the context of managing government spending programmes, bureaucrats tend to have limited epistemic opportunities to deeply appreciate the circumstances under which a person applying for assistance arrived at their position. The lack of knowledge on the part of governmental providers, not to mention "one-size-fits-all" programme eligibility criteria, limits the capacity of bureaucrats to respond most appropriately—say, through tailored supports encouraging commitments by beneficiaries to develop their own self-supporting strategies in the longer term.

The difficulty for governments in providing personalised supports to lift people out of poverty, and to tackle inequality through expenditure programmes more generally, is expressed in the following terms: "[a] program of raising requires the use of knowledge that is not fully in the possession of any particular person, and involves instead institutionally structured coordination among multiple participants. … Among other things, a program of raising requires programmatic distinctions to be made between good and bad choices, and also requires a resolve to act upon that distinction" (Wagner 2016, p. 133). Andreas Bergh similarly suggests that "[p]rograms that require a lot of knowledge are vulnerable to the Hayekian knowledge problem" (Bergh 2015, p. 23).

Motivational issues are also likely to arise should the provision of assistance to potential beneficiaries be predominated by governmental involvement. Public sector employees, themselves usually represented within the middle to upper reaches of income and wealth distributions by virtue of their relatively generous remuneration, may have an interest in perpetuating the expenditure programmes they administer. Therefore, any reforms overcoming the Samaritan's dilemma would tend to be fiercely resisted.

The problems we have just described tend to be greatly magnified under a monocentric system of public governance. Under monocentricity, decisions are filtered through a very limited number of policymakers generally lacking competitive alternatives (within the economic, communal, or political orders) that would ordinarily provide a check upon the conduct of the provider. Monocentrically positioned as the "helper of last resort," the Samaritan (i.e. the government with the tax-financed capability to provide assistance) cannot refuse requests for aid. The accommodation of "all-comers" under this scenario arises because of a lack of knowledge pertaining to the source of the potential beneficiary's hardship, and nor is the political actor *qua* Samaritan likely to refuse aid requests due to a motive to perpetuate public spending.

It is true that the operators of political enterprises, such as welfare bureaucracies, have a capacity to acquire information. Modern governments maintain large data sets containing information about the demographic, economic, and social characteristics of individuals and households receiving welfare payments. Assuming that the information obtained is contextually appropriate, the ability of policymakers to act upon such information in socially beneficial ways is vital. However, such a state of affairs cannot be guaranteed in ordered regimes in which monocentricity is in the foreground. In the modern welfare state, governments generally cannot refuse to offer aid *ex ante*, but they increasingly promote draconian policies in efforts to, *ex post*, demarcate welfare recipients into either "deserving" and "undeserving" categories. Many of the kinds of policies considered here are rhetorically framed by political actors as techniques for the raising of individual recipients to an improved state of well-being, although the veracity of such claims is questionable given the refusal by the same-said actors to maintain fiscal and regulatory environments conducive to mass-participatory economic development.

Inspired in no small part by applied behavioural economic theory, stating that seemingly "irrational" behaviour is the appropriate subject of fiscal and regulatory policy interventions, governments have increasingly imposed conditions upon welfare programme recipients. These conditions have even tended to infiltrate previously unconditional payment regimes. In Australia, for example, a "compulsory income management" scheme has been devised to ensure that individuals receiving certain welfare payments spend those monies on "priority goods and services" such as good, housing, clothing, education, and healthcare (Thomas and Buckmaster 2010). Spending on "moral bads" such as alcohol, gambling, illicit drugs, and tobacco is actively discouraged. This scheme has been applied to people residing in remote (mainly indigenous) areas within Australia, and those in certain urban areas characterised as having low socio-economic status.

Efforts to overcome the legitimate concern that is the Samaritan's dilemma, but through the highly arbitrary and prescriptive ways described here, appear to run afoul of John Stuart Mill's ([1859] 1985) famous critique of state paternalism. Reducing the ability of welfare recipients to expend monies, in ways they individually see fit, undermines their ability to make economic choices and to learn from those choices. Therefore, strategies such as income management deprive welfare recipients of their liberties by a not-inconsiderable degree. Chris Berg suggests that the deleterious effects of welfare conditionality extend even further: "[i]ncome management undermines the dignity that the welfare state is apparently supposed to advance. And it subjects recipients to intensive scrutiny and surveillance, as even the simplest purchases are monitored by the government" (Berg 2016, p. 19). Gilles Saint-Paul (2011) also notes there is a connection between the intensity of redistributive desire on the part of political agents and the degree of paternalism applied to welfare recipients.

School education has been identified as a policy area affected by similar issues. The trend towards monocentricity in education, for example, has enabled teacher unions to emerge as a very influential collective group. This is illustrated by the capacity of labour unionists to influence political actors so as to enable the former to appropriate some of the returns to politically organised schools through supra-competitive wages (Wagner 2016). Remuneration arrangements within government schools are biased towards seniority, and with performance arrangements given less, or no, prominence in determining salaries or salary movements. These are coupled with observations of an aversion by government schools to retrench underperforming, yet highly paid, teaching staff (Cochrane et al. 2015). It is for these key reasons that human resource management models tend to stand apart from those maintained by non-government schools, and indeed by enterprises within other service industries.

A tendency towards monocentric public schooling is also reflected in the gradual movement towards centralised modes of funding. Steven Teles refers to the panoply of untied and tied grant programmes in American school education, attracting and motivating rent-seeking interests to intertwine themselves with federal political interests. As he describes it, "[t]he complicated structure of federal education policy has thus created an army of Lilliputians who lock in the multitude of grants even though the work of keeping those grants coming often makes it harder to actually run school districts. … the 'blob' of education interests wins, while the capacity of the federal government to actually improve educational opportunity diminishes" (Teles 2013, p. 101; also Glenn and Teles 2009).

It is true that each of the school-education expenditure programmes is individually small in financial magnitude, but collectively accounts for a sizeable share of aggregate school spending. The point is that the gradual tendency towards monocentricity in education provision and finance in the U.S. and elsewhere is not necessarily to the advantage of poor families, whose prerogatives and concerns regarding the entire issue of high-quality schooling often appear demoted in education discourse and policy determination. For classical liberals attuned to the desirability of polycentric orders, the movement towards monocentricity in school sector organisation is seen to have not coincidentally paralleled growing evidence of American educational underperformance (Beaulier et al. 2016).

Classical liberals during the twentieth century, if not earlier, raised the idea that the state need not simultaneously be involved in school education financing *and* provision (Friedman 1955, [1962] 2002; Hayek [1979] 2013; Pennington 2011). There seems widespread liberal support for a more flexible and portable regime of public spending for schools, tied with non-discriminatory and open enrolment regulatory provisions, enabling students from poorer families to enrol in better quality schools. It is for this reason that liberals have long expressed support for "voucher" subsidy programmes for schools and other social services (e.g. healthcare, disability services), to the extent that political enterprises remain engaged with financing roles. The basic idea is that providing vouchers would enable service-users to escape modes of provision traditionally dominated by monocentrically-inclined political enterprises.

The task before us is not to create an unrealistic impression that there is one correct path of services provision and expenditure, that only needs implementing by a truly benevolent and omniscient actor in the political realm. It is certainly not preordained that the interests of the poor will be sufficiently acknowledged and respected in the determination of welfare spending policy, especially if the policy is primarily filtered through monocentric systems of public governance. Perspectives of need and desire are multifaceted and often localised, even contestable, in certain situations. In this context, institutional rules must be discovered, and be allowed to emerge throughout the meso level of action without needless obstacles, allowing multiple interpretations of betterment to take shape.

Acknowledging the reality of government spending as a disparate and fragmented "ecology" of arrangements orchestrated by multiple political enterprises—rather than as a unitary, simplified plan by a point-mass polity—for inequality analysis and policy is profound. Scholars suggest that polycentric principles may provide a useful way for policymakers to sidestep knowledge problems, keep them accountable in a contestable environment, and to contain the influence of concentrated, well-connected interests who, *inter alia*, seek fiscal advantages primarily for themselves and their group members. To be sure, polycentricity is not a recipe for fewer services but for better, if not more, services insofar as consumers desire it. Polycentric forms of provision and financing can potentially be carried out by a vast ecology of enterprising participants in entangled political economy—be they lower levels of government, charitable organisations within the communal order, and other bodies and individuals. Issues concerning the merits of polycentricity will be discussed in further detail in Chap. 7.

Conclusion

Many of those critical of existing distributions of income and wealth call for relatively simple principles for taxation and expenditure policy settings: take from the rich (through tax) and give to the poor (through spending). However, the work of fiscal policy is not undertaken by a benevolent and omniscient political agent who is detached from the rest of civil society. In fact, budgetary policies are enacted by a multiplicity of competitive and collaborative political actors who preside over their own enterprises and ventures, sometimes in cooperation with non-political actors, but more often in acquiescence and under duress on the part of the latter.

Contrasting the impressions of mainstream economic theory that redistribution can be undertaken with precision, entangled political economy opens the possibility that redistributive policies are uncertain in their effects. Taxing and spending arrangements could implicitly create either sideway or upward redistribution. The fact of shifting alliances between economic, communal, and political actors implies that downward redistribution, if it happens to materialise at all, must be interpreted as one possibility among many.

Richard Wagner has drawn upon economic and sociological insights to illustrate how varying tax and expenditure forms alters patterns of economic inequalities. Other figures in the classical liberal tradition have expressed similar perspectives: "[t]he impact upon incomes of this enormous diversion and redistribution is a very complicated subject … It is far from being a simple redistribution from the richer to the poorer. And yet it is to a large degree sustained by a belief in the rightness of redistribution from the richer to the poorer and by the belief that this is what the whole process comes to" (de Jouvenel 1951, p. 20). These kinds of assessments would surely provide pause for even the most ambitious of redistributive projects filtered through governmental action.

James Buchanan famously insisted throughout much of his career that if one deems fiscal outcomes to be unsatisfactory, then one should contemplate amendments to the overarching institutional-rule environment within which the fiscal outcomes are negotiated and assented. This suggests the need to reinvigorate the constitutionalising strain of thought deeply embedded in the classical liberal tradition. There is practically fertile ground for enshrining a fiscal constitution in many developed countries with seemingly runaway budgetary settings, but even so the need for better rules should not be restricted to taxation and expenditure. To enable us to consider a more comprehensive perspective about the impact of governmental policy upon inequality, we need turn to the next chapter, which focuses upon regulation.

Notes

1. Borrowing by political enterprises represents another major element of modern public sector financial management. Under this approach (current and capital), projects are financed today by issuing securities to domestic and international capital markets, but with the expectation that future governmental revenue streams will be of a sufficient magnitude to relieve the debt burden. The implications of the level and distribution of public debt for a functioning political economy have been canvassed at length by researchers in the public choice tradition, and much more recently by scholars versed in entangled political economy. For our purposes, we largely restrict our focus onto fiscal policies affecting presently existing persons.

References

Acemoglu, Daron, Suresh Naidu, Pascual Restrepo, and James A. Robinson. 2015. Democracy, Redistribution, and Inequality. In *Handbook of Income Distribution*, ed. A.B. Atkinson and F. Bourguignon, vol. 2B, 1885–1966. Amsterdam, Netherlands: Elsevier.

Barker, Joel, Kwadwo Asare, and Sharon Brickman. 2017. Transfer Pricing as a Vehicle in Corporate Tax *Avoidance. Journal of Applied Business Research* 33 (1): 9–16.

Beaulier, Scott A., Daniel J. Smith, and Benjamin G. Tegethoff. 2016. Education in a Robust Political Economy. *School System Reform Journal* 1: 1–34.

Beckert, Jens. 2008. Why is the Estate Tax So Controversial? *Society* 45: 521–528.

Berg, Chris. 2016. *The Libertarian Alternative*. Melbourne, Australia: Melbourne University Press.

Bergh, Andreas. 2015. Yes, There are Hayekian Welfare States (At Least in Theory). *Econ Journal Watch* 12 (1): 22–27.

Blount, Simon. 2001. The Art of Taxation. *Australian Tax Forum* 16: 345–360.

Boettke, Peter J., and Adam Martin. 2011. Taking the "G" Out of BIG: A Comparative Political Economy Perspective on Basic Income. *Basic Income Studies* 6 (2): 1–18.

Buchanan, James M. 1976. A Hobbesian Interpretation of the Rawlsian Difference Principle. *Kyklos* 29 (1): 5–25.

———. 1983. Rent Seeking, Noncompensated Transfers, and Laws of Succession. *The Journal of Law & Economics* 26 (1): 71–85.

———. (1967) 1999a. *Public Finance in Democratic Process: Fiscal Institutions and Individual Choice*. The Collected Works of James M. Buchanan, vol. 4. Indianapolis, IN: Liberty Fund.

———. (1975) 1999b. The Samaritan's Dilemma. In *The Logical Foundations of Constitutional Liberty*. The Collected Works of James M. Buchanan, vol. 1, 329–345. Indianapolis, IN: Liberty Fund.

Buchanan, James M., and Roger D. Congleton. (1998) 2003. *Politics by Principle, Not Interest: Toward Nondiscriminatory Democracy*. The Collected Works of James M. Buchanan, vol. 11. Indianapolis, IN: Liberty Fund.

Cochrane, John H., Lee E. Ohanian, and George P. Shultz. 2015. Conclusions and Solutions. In *Inequality and Economic Policy: Essays in Honor of Gary Becker*, ed. Tom Church, Chris Miller, and John B. Taylor, 147–180. Stanford, CA: Hoover Institution Press.

Cowen, Tyler. 2013. Wealth Taxes: A Future Battleground. *The New York Times*, July 20. Accessed October 11, 2017. http://www.nytimes.com/2013/07/21/business/wealth-taxes-a-future-battleground.html

Diamond, Peter A. 1998. Optimal Income Taxation: An Example with a U-Shaped Pattern of Optimal Marginal Tax Rates. *American Economic Review* 88 (1): 83–95.

Diamond, Peter A., and James A. Mirrlees. 1971. Optimal Taxation and Public Production I: Production Efficiency. *American Economic Review* 61 (1): 8–27.

Esping-Andersen, Gøsta, and John Myles. 2011. Economic Inequality and the Welfare State. In *The Oxford Handbook of Economic Inequality*, ed. Brian Nolan, Wiemer Salverda, and Timothy M. Smeeding, 639–664. Oxford, UK: Oxford University Press.

Feld, Lars P., and Jan Schnellenbach. 2007. Still A Director's Law? On the Political Economy of Income Redistribution. Institute for Research in Economic and Fiscal Issues, June. Accessed October 14, 2017. https://fr.irefeurope.org/Still-a-Director-s-Law-On-the-Political-Economy-of-Income-Redistribution,a0378

Friedman, Milton. 1955. The Role of Government in Education. In *Economics and the Public Interest*, ed. Robert A. Solo, 123–144. New Brunswick, NJ: Rutgers University Press.

———. (1962) 2002. *Capitalism and Freedom*. 40th Anniversary ed. Chicago, IL: University of Chicago Press.

Friedman, Milton, and Rose Friedman. (1980) 1990. *Free to Choose: A Personal Statement*. New York, NY: Harcourt

Glenn, Brian J., and Steven M. Teles. 2009. *Conservatism and American Political Development*. Oxford, UK: Oxford University Press.

Gordon, Stephen. 2016. Bargaining Power and the Incidence of Income Taxes on High Earners in Canada. Université Laval, Centre de Recherche sur les Risques les enjeux Économiques et les Politiques Publiques, *Working Paper*, August. Accessed February 27, 2018. https://www.crrep.ca/sites/crrep.ca/files/fichier_publications/crrep_2016_02_0.pdf

Greenberg, Scott. 2017. Summary of the Latest Federal Income Tax Data, 2016 Update. *Tax Foundation*, February 1. Accessed October 9, 2017. https://taxfoundation.org/summary-latest-federal-income-tax-data-2016-update/

Hayek, Friedrich A. (1960) 2006. *The Constitution of Liberty*. Routledge Classics ed. London, UK: Routledge.

———. (1979) 2013. *Law, Legislation and Liberty: A New Statement of the Liberal Principles of Justice and Political Economy, Volume 3: The Political Order of a Free People*. Routledge Classics ed. London, UK: Routledge.

Hebert, David J. 2014. Towards a Catallactic Approach to Taxing and Spending. Doctoral thesis, George Mason University.

Hebert, David, and Richard E. Wagner. 2013. Taxation as a Quasi-Market Process: Explanation, Exhortation, and the Choice of Analytical Windows. *Journal of Public Finance and Public Choice* 31 (1–3): 163–177.

Hill, Claire A. 2010. What Cognitive Psychologists Should Find Interesting About Tax. *Psychonomic Bulletin & Review* 17 (2): 180–185.

Hillman, Arye L. 2013. Rent Seeking. In *The Elgar Companion to Public Choice*, ed. William F. Shughart II, Laura Razzolini, and Michael Reksulak, 2nd ed., 307–330. Cheltenham, UK: Edward Elgar.

Hochman, Harold M., and James D. Rodgers. 1969. Pareto Optimal Redistribution. *American Economic Review* 59 (4): 542–557.

de Jouvenel, Bertrand. 1951. *The Ethics of Redistribution*. Cambridge, UK: Cambridge University Press.

Landsburg, Steven E. 2011. How the Death Tax Hurts the Poor. *The Wall Street Journal*, October 29. Accessed October 11, 2017. https://www.wsj.com/articles/SB10001424052970203554104577001652652545814

Mankiw, N. Gregory, Matthew Weinzierl, and Danny Yagan. 2009. Optimal Taxation in Theory and Practice. *Journal of Economic Perspectives* 23 (4): 147–174.

Martin, Adam G., and Matias Petersen. 2017. Poverty Alleviation as an Economic Problem, February 26. Accessed October 14, 2017. https://papers.ssrn.com/sol3/papers.cfm?abstract_id=2924048

McCloskey, Deirdre N. 2006. *The Bourgeois Virtues: Ethics for an Age of Commerce*. Chicago, IL: University of Chicago Press.

———. 2007. Chap. 1 of *Bourgeois Revaluation*: Ideology is Rhetoric. Vol. 2 of Bourgeois Virtues, October. Accessed October 9, 2017. http://www.deirdremccloskey.org/articles/bt/ch1.php

Meltzer, Allan, and Scott F. Richard. 1981. A Rational Theory of the Size of Government. *Journal of Political Economy* 89 (5): 914–927.

Mill, John Stuart. (1859) 1985. *On Liberty*. Penguin Classics ed. London, UK: Penguin Books.

Mirrlees, James A. 1971. An Exploration in the Theory of Optimum Income Taxation. *The Review of Economic Studies* 38 (2): 175–208.

Mohl, Phillipp, and Oliver Pamp. 2008. Income Inequality, Redistributional Spending & Director's Law—An Empirical Investigation. Paper presented at International Political Economy Society Meeting, November. Accessed October 14, 2017. http://citeseerx.ist.psu.edu/viewdoc/download?doi=10.1.1.535.4521&rep=rep1&type=pdf

Neely, Michelle Clark, and Larry D. Sherrer. 2017. A Look at Corporate Inversions, Inside and Out, Federal Reserve Bank of St. Louis. *The Regional Economist*, 1–3.

Norton, Michael I., and Dan Ariely. 2011. Building a Better America—One Wealth Quintile at a Time. *Perspectives on Psychological Science* 6 (1): 9–12.

Novak, Mikayla. 2015. Death Taxes Punish the Living. *The Canberra Times*, December 11.

Organisation of Economic Co-Operation and Development (OECD). 2010. *Tax Expenditures in OECD Countries*. Paris, France: OECD Publishing.

Pennington, Mark. 2011. *Robust Political Economy: Classical Liberalism and the Future of Public Policy*. Cheltenham, UK: Edward Elgar.

Piketty, Thomas. 2014. *Capital in the Twenty-First Century: The Dynamics of Inequality, Wealth, and Growth*. Translated by Arthur Goldhammer. Cambridge, MA: The Belknap Press of Harvard University Press.

Saint-Paul, Gilles. 2011. The Welfare State and the Rise of Paternalism. *The Montréal Review*, September. Accessed February 15, 2018. http://www.the-montrealreview.com/2009/The-welfare-state-and-the-rise-of-paternalism.php

Schmalbeck, Richard. 2001. Avoiding Federal Wealth Transfer Taxes. In *Rethinking Estate and Gift Taxation*, ed. William G. Gale, James R. Hines Jr., and Joel Slemrod. Washington, DC: Brookings Institution Press.

Scholes, Myron S., Mark A. Wolfson, Merle M. Erickson, Edward L. Maydew, and Terrence J. Shevlin. 2002. *Taxes and Business Strategy: A Planning Approach*. 2nd ed. Upper Saddle River, NJ: Prentice Hall.

Stigler, George J. 1970. Director's Law of Public Income Redistribution. *The Journal of Law & Economics* 13 (1): 1–10.

Stiglitz, Joseph E. 2012. *The Price of Inequality*. New York, NY: W. W. Norton & Co.

Tanner, Michael. 2012. The American Welfare State: How We Spend Nearly $1 Trillion a Year Fighting Poverty-and Fail. Cato Institute, *Policy Analysis No. 694*, April. Accessed September 21, 2017. https://object.cato.org/pubs/pas/PA694.pdf

Teles, Steven M. 2013. Kludgeocracy in America. *National Affairs* 17: 97–114.

Thomas, Matthew, and Luke Buckmaster. 2010. Paternalism in Social Policy—When is it Justifiable? *Parliamentary Library Research Paper No. 8*, December. Canberra, Australia: Parliament of Australia.

Thurow, Lester C. 1971. The Income Distribution as a Pure Public Good. *The Quarterly Journal of Economics* 85 (2): 327–336.

Tomasi, John. 2012. *Free Market Fairness*. Princeton, NJ: Princeton University Press.

Tuszynski, Meg P., and Richard E. Wagner. 2016. Samaritan's Dilemmas, Wealth Redistribution, and Polycentricity. George Mason University, Department of Economics, *Working Paper No. 16-36*, February 19. Accessed October 12, 2017. https://papers.ssrn.com/sol3/papers.cfm?abstract_id=2734725

United States House of Representative. 2015. Chairman Boustany: Better Coordinating Welfare Programs to Serve Families in Need. *Committee on Ways and Means Press Release*, November 3. Accessed October 12, 2017. https://waysandmeans.house.gov/chairman-boustany-better-coordinating-welfare-programs-to-serve-families-in-need/

Wagner, Richard E. 1989. *To Promote the General Welfare: Market Processes Vs. Political Transfers*. San Francisco, CA: Pacific Research Institute for Public Policy.

———. 2005. Redistribution, Poor Relief, and the Welfare State. In *Handbook of Public Finance*, ed. Jürgen G. Backhaus and Richard E. Wagner, 385–405. Boston, MA: Springer.
———. 2006. Choice, Catallaxy, and Just Taxation: Contrasting Architectonics for Fiscal Theorizing. *Social Philosophy and Policy* 23 (2): 235–254.
———. 2007. *Fiscal Sociology and the Theory of Public Finance*. Cheltenham, UK: Edward Elgar.
———. 2008. Polycentricity, Political Economy, and the Welfare State. *Public Finance and Management* 8 (2): 141–167.
———. 2010. Spontaneous Order and Positive Legislation: Ruminating on Daniel Shapiro's Justification of the Welfare State. *Review of Austrian Economics* 23: 97–102.
———. 2012a. *Deficits, Debt, and Democracy: Wrestling with Tragedy on the Fiscal Commons*. Cheltenham, UK: Edward Elgar.
———. 2012b. Rationality, Political Economy, and Fiscal Responsibility: Wrestling with Tragedy on the Fiscal Commons. *Constitutional Political Economy* 23: 261–277.
———. 2014. Entangled Political Economy: A Keynote Address. *Advances in Austrian Economics* 18: 15–36.
———. 2015. The Tax State as a Source of Perpetual Crisis. In *The Oxford Handbook of Austrian Economics*, ed. Peter J. Boettke and Christopher J. Coyne, 445–463. New York, NY: Oxford University Press.
———. 2016. *Politics as a Peculiar Business: Insights from a Theory of Entangled Political Economy*. Cheltenham, UK: Edward Elgar.
———. 2017. *James M. Buchanan and Liberal Political Economy: A Rational Reconstruction*. Lanham, MD: Lexington Books.
———. 2018. The Language of Taxation: Ideology Masquerading as Science. In *For Your Own Good: Taxes, Paternalism, and Fiscal Discrimination in the Twenty-First Century*, ed. Adam J. Hoffer and Todd Nesbit, 77–96. Arlington, VA: Mercatus Center.
Watkins, Don, and Yaron Brook. 2016. *Equal is Unfair: America's Misguided Fight against Income Inequality*. New York, NY: St. Martin's Press.
Yu, Fu-Lai Tony. 2011. *New Perspectives on Economic Development: A Human Agency Approach*. Dordrecht, Netherlands: Springer.
Ziegler, Rafael. 2010. Innovations in Doing and Being: Capability Innovations at the Intersection of Schumpeterian Political Economy and Human Development. *Journal of Social Entrepreneurship* 1 (2): 255–272.
Zingales, Luigi. 2012. *A Capitalism for The People: Recapturing the Lost Genius of American Prosperity*. New York, NY: Basic Books.

5

Regulatory Policies

Introduction

Contemporary governments have at their disposal an array of instruments which they employ in efforts to achieve their policy objectives. In addition to taxation and expenditure, whose aggregates are presented in budget papers on a regular basis, political agents may also attempt to achieve policy aims through the use of government regulation. Regulation entails the specification of formal commands, edicts, and rules pertaining to the behaviour and conduct of individuals and their enterprises. The definition provided here, albeit broad-ranging in its nature, is distinguished from the array of formal and informal mechanisms for control and influence perpetuated by non-political actors.

Whatever the form that regulation comes in, there is little doubt that regulatory instruments represent a pivotal instrument adopted by political actors to change economic performance, to alter social activity, and to condition political action. Mainstream political economy conceptualises regulation as an imposition upon the economy, designed to ensure a better outcome from the perspective of the underlying policy objective to be met. The entangled political economy framework, alternatively, suggests

M. Novak, *Inequality*, Palgrave Studies in Classical Liberalism,
https://doi.org/10.1007/978-3-319-89417-1_5

that regulatory output reflects an emergent "push-and-pull" of both collaborative and competitive activities between networked political and non-political interests. In this setting, complexity is to be assumed as a feature, and not an aberration, of the regulation-making process.

In response to traditional, but now contested, presumptions that regulation is strictly conducted in the public interest, economists have drawn upon several heterodox strands of political economy to highlight the redistributive properties of regulation which shape the distribution of income and wealth. Generally speaking, regulation may have the effect of redistributing resources either from producers to consumers, from consumers to producers, or from one group of consumers or producers to another. This regulatory redistributive effect, in turn, has implications for the overall distribution of income and wealth. The contemporary inequality debate has instigated academic and policy interest in the potential role of regulation in redistributing income and wealth in unexpected, and perhaps perverse, ways.

Interpreting regulatory policy through an entangled political economy lens is, therefore, the primary objective of this chapter. The next section provides a description of key regulatory aspects from the vantage point of entangled political economy. This is followed by a discussion about the effect of regulation upon economic inequality. The predominance of regulatory policy also raises important questions regarding the quality of regulatory settings and the institutional environment within which regulatory agencies operate, which is also discussed in this chapter. In conclusion, this chapter briefly provides some observations relating to the effectiveness of regulatory policy to redress inequalities of income and wealth.

Regulation and Entangled Political Economy: General Reflections

Governments enact and maintain regulations to influence activities undertaken, and decisions made, within society. There is an abundance of narratives which impress upon the given reader a sense that government regulation is an all-encompassing feature of modern life, with one such example as follows:

> Imagine a typical day: We wake up in the morning to the sounds of a commercially regulated radio station or National Public Radio coming over a patented and Federal Communications Commission-registered clock radio operating on power supplied by either a government-regulated power company or a public utility. We brush our teeth with toothpaste produced under a government patent and trust that it has been judged safe (if not effective) by a federal agency. We use municipally operated water and sewer systems without thinking of the complexity of their operation. We dress in clothes produced under governmental restrictions and eat food prepared in accordance with government regulations and inspected by the government. We drive on a public highway, following government-enforced traffic laws, to a university substantially funded by federal, state, and sometimes local dollars to study from books copyrighted and catalogued by the Library of Congress. Though the day has hardly begun, our lives already have been touched by public organizations in a multitude of ways. (Denhardt et al. 2014, p. 19)

Regulation stands alongside taxation and expenditure as an instrument at the disposal of political actors to impose changes within the economic and communal orders, and this fact has given rise to debate concerning the substitutability or complementarity of regulation with respect to its fiscal policy counterparts.

Economists such as Posner (1971), Brennan (2004), and Brennan and Kliemt (2008) indicate that, in their view, regulation serves as a substitute for taxation. "Those who are at the helm of the ship of state," Brennan and Kliemt write, "can pursue their aims, ends or values by means of rule fixing or by revenue raising and allocation. For them, the regulatory and fiscal options become substitutes in the pursuit of their own gubernatorial ends" (Brennan and Kliemt 2008, p. 252). A government, for example, can seek to reduce carbon dioxide and other greenhouse gasses emitted by producers by directing taxing the emissions, providing subsidies to encourage producers to reduce emissions or to offset the emissions in other ways (e.g. subsidising tree planting activities), or regulating the producers in order to direct them to abate their emissions. Any of these strands of intervention may be implemented to achieve the same general policy objective.

In some circumstances, regulation may serve as a complementary activity to budgetary operations. Governments regulate to compel parents to send their children to school, *and* they spend taxpayers' funds to provide schooling facilities and teaching staff. To take up another case example, in respect to health policy, in Australia, the government both "spends" to prop up private health insurance coverage—by providing a tax rebate for members to purportedly help cover the cost of their premiums—and simultaneously regulates to promote enduring insurance memberships, by threatening to raise premiums for those who refuse to take up cover over the age of 30.

Although there is little doubting the prevalence of government regulation, there is considerable ambiguity surrounding a concrete definitional basis, let alone a rigorous classification schema, for such activity, which incidentally might explain some of regulation's political appeal. Demarcating "economic" and "social" regulations in accordance with its intention to impact economic and social conduct, respectively, is one way to classify regulation. From an entangled political economy perspective, it is clear that the soundness of such a classification is susceptible to the fuzziness of policy boundaries, and of economic and social developments more generally (Prosser 2010).

A regulatory taxonomy can also be derived with respect to the kind of legal, or other, instrument by which it is made. Regulation given effect by primary and secondary (subordinate) legislation that is passed through, and assented by, the legislative assembly is sometimes referred to as a "black-letter" law. In keeping with the spirit of mapping kinds of regulation with colour scheme, there also exists a range of "grey-letter" laws of varying shades. These include accreditation schemes, agreements, codes, declarations, determinations, guidelines, policies, and standards that entail "government involvement in the development or monitoring of the regulatory arrangement, or through the provision of funding associated with a regulatory regime" (Commonwealth Interdepartmental Committee on Quasi-Regulation 1997, p. 7). Adding to this complex tapestry are forms of co-regulation, such as legislative support for rules developed and administered by representatives of economic enterprises (e.g. industry associations), and other instruments such as international treaties (Productivity Commission 2007).

In addition to the matter of regulatory definition, there have been numerous attempts to quantify the extent of regulation in force at any given period of time. One of the more popular methods in this regard is to count the number of pages of primary or subordinate legislation (Dawson and Seater 2013; Crews 2017), or the number of words which appear within legislation. Despite the high frequency of use of these proxy measures for regulatory extent, page and word formatting is subject to publishing variation. The number of words appearing in regulatory instruments also does not necessarily denote a command or an order for non-political actors to undertake certain actions. Mulligan and Shleifer (2005) offer an arguably superior substitute for raw-word count in the form of their accounting of the number of bytes contained in legislation (with each byte represented by a character), but even that method is not immune to criticism that the count is conducted indiscriminately.

Perhaps the best available measure of regulatory extent to date has been provided by staffers at George Mason University's Mercatus Center, who have developed a methodology known as "RegData" (Al-Ubaydli and McLaughlin 2015). The distinctive contribution of RegData is that it proxies the extent of regulation by the number of restrictive clauses—for example, encapsulated in words such as "must," "prohibited," "required," and "shall"—contained in legislation. The number of restrictive clauses imposed through U.S. federal legislation has grown from over 405,000 words in 1970 to in excess of one million words in 2015 (McLaughlin and Sherhouse 2017). This pattern of growth is mostly replicated in other developed countries.

Regulations have long received endorsement by many economists as a potential solution to market failure, ensuring fairer and more efficient market operations in the public interest. Regulatory imposition is seen to rectify asymmetric information between seller and buyer in relation to the attribute or performance of goods and services, potentially leading to exploitation and the erosion of confidence and trust in market transactions. To avoid the prospect of monopolistic economic enterprises overpricing and under-providing outputs, to the detriment of consumer welfare, it is considered that government should regulate to control the economic conduct of the monopoly. Externality effects upon third parties not directly involved in a market transaction are also seen, under certain circumstances, to rationalise regulation.

The anti-market failure, "public interest" model of regulation is, at its core, a model of additive political economy. Government injects its regulatory prerogatives into the economic or communal spheres, as if a surgeon operating upon a patient, with the intention of rectifying market failure. There may be costs associated with such intervention, of course, but the presumption is that the benefits of regulation imposed by the distant and aloof political agent will far outweigh any downsides attributed to such activity.

The development of an alternative theory of regulation by public choice theorists, and economists based at the University of Chicago such as George Stigler, Richard Posner, and Sam Peltzman, presented a keen challenge to the orthodox market-failure/public-interest regulatory conceptions. Regulators were modelled to be influenced by the demands of economic enterprises, and other interests, to craft regulations so as to ensure the latter's interests are protected, indeed promoted, by the regulatory environment. Protection in this context may be interpreted as regulations effectively maintaining prohibitive entry barriers against new entrepreneurs that seek to undermine the economic positions of incumbent players.

In addition to rent-seeking pressures, Fred McChesney (1997) shed light upon the phenomenon of "rent extraction." Recognising that the interaction between economic and political agents is not unilateral (in the direction of requests by non-political representatives for particularised favours feeding into the political process), McChesney conceived that political actors propagate a self-interested agenda. As Anderson notes, "[t]he legislature will sometimes pass a vaguely defined statute to be enforced in an unpredictable manner, in order to identify and pressure interest groups to make payment, and to increase the demand from those groups for relief from cost-increasing government regulation" (Anderson 1994, p. 297). Rent extraction occurs when political actors identify and target interest groups to provide rewards to politicians, perhaps serving as another avenue through which monstrous moral hybrids form and populate the meso-population structure.

Insofar as these theories have deepened our understanding of the regulatory environment, and how political action contributes to it, they nonetheless implicitly persist with the additive political economy framework. For many policy experts, since regulations alter the substantive content of property rights and contractual liberties, they "appear as interventions into economy" (Wagner 2016, p. 38). As pointed out by Bruce Benson, "[m]arkets are still modeled as fields, … and the autonomous agents still rationally maximize utility, subject to known benefits and constraints" (Benson 2011, p. 193). Regulation in an entangled political economy frame is, instead, seen as the by-product of emergent and complex actions between and across networks of actors situated within the economic, communal, and political orders of society.

If there is to be any sense of commonality to be found in the interactionist pursuits of human beings, it is their broadly shared interest to strike deals characterised by mutual advantage. This sentiment seems to ring as true in the field of regulatory development as it does in any other domain of human action, though it should not be presumed that the interests and motivations of every party involved in regulation-setting are necessarily harmonised:

> Various individuals or groups can benefit from regulation: bureaucrats who seek more power or influence, legislators who can extort rents from regulated firms by threatening even more stringent regulations, regulated firms that want to deter the entry of potential rivals, labor unions that want to require all firms to provide the same working conditions to their members, employees who want to increase demand for the skills required by regulations, or owners of capital who want to increase demand for the types of capital used intensively in complying with regulatory requirements. With such a richness of possible beneficiaries, one might explain any given regulation, perhaps incorrectly, by identifying *ex post* some group that benefits from it. (Glazer 2013, p. 284)

For some scholars, the regulatory forms which emerge from entanglements between political and non-political agents appear to bear some vague similarities with a "spontaneous order," given that the observed regulations seem largely a by-product of decentralised, complex human actions. The intersubjective, and often conflicting, division of knowledge impacting the regulatory policy sphere suggests that "[a]s agreements are reached, statutes modified, and regulations written, a package of outcomes emerges that no one has chosen, not even senior members of the legislative and executive branches of government. Each participant pursues opportunities for gain within a networked system of complex interaction where the overall outcome is not a product of intentional choice" (Smith et al. 2011, p. 48).

Irrespective of the relationship between regulatory and fiscal policies, there is little practical doubt that regulation remains a primary method through which political actors engage in triadic exchange relations. On a speculative note, perhaps a reason for political partiality towards regulation is that "[r]egulations are like many small excise taxes, and are an excellent application of Puviani's approach to fiscal illusion. The bill for regulation is not presented directly in one lump sum. It is presented indirectly and in hidden fashion, and is presented in many small pieces" (Wagner 2012, p. 139). Given Mancur Olson's (1965) observation that beneficiaries of regulatory settings tend to be smaller, insider groups receiving concentrated advantages, it is likely to be difficult for the losers to organise themselves to petition government to reverse the ill-effects of regulation.

The ability of certain individuals and groups to secure gains through the shiftable regulatory environment depends upon multiple factors. Whilst there is the great potential for individuals, enterprises, and others to generate novel regulatory ideas, and to rally support behind those initiatives, the scope for entrepreneurialism of this kind is in itself determined by the historical development of regulations which potentially constrain what regulatory possibilities appear politically feasible.

The degree of regulatory complexity is another important factor. Complexity not only provides rent-seekers with potential avenues to secure important political concessions, but it also serves as an arena in which such advantages become vigorously contested by rivalrous individuals and groups. "Part of the commercial strategy of many enterprises," wrote Wagner, "will involve the use of regulatory proceedings to increase the durability of entrepreneurial rents and to redistribute such rents" (Wagner 2010, p. 115). In other words, an important motivation for soliciting entanglements with certain political actors is to secure rents flowing from regulatory imposition.

The Wagnerian conception of regulation as an inherently dynamic process, rather than the propulsion of coercive force onto passive societal entities, is similar to other process-laden theoretical approaches that have emerged over the last two decades. An interesting example is provided by legal scholar Julia Black's "decentred" view of regulation, which emphasises "[r]egulation is a two-way or three or four-way process, between all those involved in the regulatory process, and particularly between regulator and regulatee in the implementation of regulation. … regulation is 'co-produced'" (Black 2002, p. 7). The idea of regulatory co-production will be revisited later in this book, in the context of a discussion about styles of polycentric regulatory governance.

Proposed regulation may not only attract lobbying by some to secure advantages. Novel ideas on the regulatory front may elicit "defensive" lobbying by others to repel the possibility of win-win-lose triadic exchanges. "The granting of permissions," suggests Richard Wagner, "emerges through a process where many competitors participate in trying to influence the terms on which permission is granted, and in some cases even trying to prevent" (Wagner 2010, p. 116). The contingency of outcomes under entangled political economy implies that "[r]egulations will tend not to benefit *all* producers or *all* consumers, but rather *subgroups* which can organize with the appropriate characteristics for effectively obtaining a regulatory benefit" (Anderson 1994, p. 296; emphasis added). Of course, it is worthwhile to contemplate the possibility that political actors themselves engage in rent extractions from remainder sub-groups of society.

Paretian non-logical motivation infuses the regulatory scene at least as much as it does the realms of taxation and expenditure policy deliberation. The famous "Bootleggers and Baptists" conception of alliance formation in regulatory policy is particularly noteworthy in this context. Bruce Yandle (1983, 1999; also Smith and Yandle 2014) contends the pecuniary interests of the "bootleggers"—whose sales of illicit alcohol would increase by virtue of a regulated ban on alcohol sales—would align with the moralistic interests of the Baptists—who, for their part, wished to see the banning of alcohol on days of worship. If rhetorical appeals can, indeed, serve as a persuasive, and thereby useful, means to defuse enmity towards rent-seeking conduct, then it is entirely possible for seemingly strange coalitions of interest to emerge in order to share the spoils.

More generally, regulation can in itself serve as a signal that the political class cares about certain problems, even if regulation is not a particularly effective solution. To be more specific, "regulation has come to perform something of a sacramental function. It is taken as an outward sign that a society cares about something, even if the efficacy of a regulation cannot be demonstrated. Indeed, for many … , to 'regulate' something are interchangeable with a desire to make it better" (English 2014, p. 263). Robin Hanson (2008) refers to similar, non-logical mechanisms at play with regard to spending on medical services.

Consequences of Regulation for Income and Wealth Redistribution

A core insight of entangled political economy is that competitive impulses are prevalent throughout society, and can be conducted in ways traversing the boundaries of economic, social, and political actions. As has been stressed throughout much of the contemporary economic literature, even by theorists who implicitly presume the existence of additive political economy, regulations have the potential to quell market-based competition. It is against this background that "regulations that restrict competition replace genuine accomplishment with faux accomplishment for the beneficiaries of such regulation" (Wagner 2016, p. 25).

It is useful to consider the effects of regulation upon competition amongst economic enterprises through the application of network theory. Differential advantages are gained as a consequence of regulation effectively blocking off possibilities for economic agents to create certain connections within entangled political economy: "regulation is mainly about the creation of alliances within a network of relationships, wherein some nodal positions gain advantage relative to other positions" (Wagner 2010, p. 130). Martin (2015) indicates that sufficient degeneracy underpins the resiliency of a network structure, allowing feasible alternative options to be discovered and implemented should existing connections fail to endure. However, there is the risk that regulation "can eliminate degeneracy by requiring entrepreneurial plans to pass through particular nodes … Such regulatory nodes are almost the exclusive source of monopoly in society, because there is no way that a commercial plan can contract around that node" (Wagner 2010, pp. 116, 130).

James Broughel illustrates how regulations have the potential to stifle certain (inhibited or banned) forms of economically valuable knowledge propagation and diffusion whilst advancing (allowable) others: "[u]nfortunately, if society restricts discovery pathways, it can never be sure if access is being blocked to only harmful innovations or also beneficial discoveries" (Broughel 2017, p. 55). Wagner (2010) similarly shows that an entrepreneurial plan can be represented as a kind of directed graph, extending into the future from some originating point. In the interim, nodes of focused action can be altered and revised by substitutable or complementary plans in the spirit of "utopia competition" (Almudi et al. 2017).

Figure 5.1 presents a modest refinement of Wagner's portrayal of entrepreneurial amendment to bring it more in line with Broughel's insights,

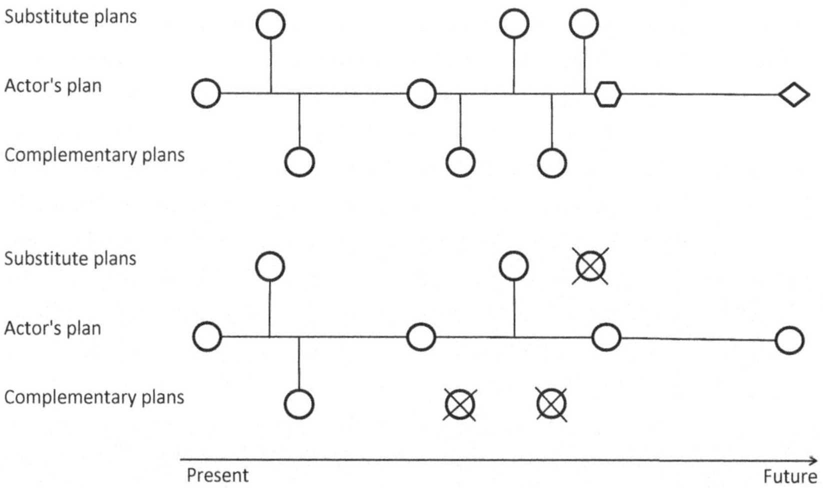

Fig. 5.1 Entrepreneurial plans as directed graphs affected by regulation. Source: Wagner (2010); Author's illustrations

with the addition of proscriptive regulatory measures which redirect the shape of entrepreneurial planning. The top panel of the figure depicts the path of entrepreneurial planning in an environment whereby no regulation is imposed by government. Different stages of the given actor's plan are represented by the four nodes on the horizontal line running from the present to some future point in time. Substitute plans are injected at various intervals of the entrepreneurial planning stages, reducing the value of the actor's plan, whereas complementary plans increase value. The impact of substitutes and complements has the effect of feeding revisions to the actor's original plan, as shown by the morphing of the original circle initially into a truncated hexagon and, eventually, into a diamond.

The bottom panel of the figure incorporates not only the influence of other economic agents upon the given actor's entrepreneurial plan, but shows regulatory impacts as illustrated by the nullification of substitute or complementary economic plans suggested by others. The imposition of regulation erases some of the substitute and complementary plans, and as such enables the original entrepreneurial plan to go unchanged, and unchallenged, in the absence of the toing-and-froing of novel alternative plans impressed upon the actor's consideration.

The regulatory realignment of competitive forces in society has significant implications from an inequality perspective. The erection of regulatory barriers against aspiring new entrants implicitly provides a significant source of rent for incumbent economic enterprises, whose sizes would be larger, and ages would be older, than would otherwise be the case. As stated by Wagner: "[s]ize is important because the amount of wealth involved can be used by market-based enterprises to secure more favorable treatment from political enterprises. … Age is also important because many connections take time to craft. Those who belong to the nouveau riche lack the density of connections that the long-time rich possess" (Wagner 2007, p. 95). These tendencies also help to explain the observation of path-persistence on the part of privileged access-networks within the political realm (Clark 2014; Clark et al. 2017).

Financial sector regulation is seen by many to be a reasonable case in point, with much scrutiny of the sector and the terms of its regulatory control in the years leading up to, and following, the GFC. Financial institutions receive both direct and indirect support from government.

Critics of such arrangements have suggested that the kinds of favouritism extended to the financial sector by political actors enable banks and other financial institutions to play an outsized role in the economy (Baker 2016; Creighton 2015; for an alternative perspective see Kirchner 2016).

Some researchers contend that financial enterprises tend to extract significant rents at the expense of the rest of the community (Anderson 1994; Kroszner 1999; Zingales 2012; Lindsey and Teles 2017). The implicit value of support for the financial sector, which tends to advantage larger banks with greater asset portfolios conceived systemically too important to fail, has been estimated by the International Monetary Fund to be up to U.S. $70 billion for the U.S., U.S. $110 billion for Japan and the United Kingdom, and U.S. $300 billion for the Euro area (IMF 2014).

There is also the risk that support for the financial sector by government perversely fuels incentives for financial institutions to engage in the very kinds of risky behaviour that regulation supposedly is meant to discourage:

> the too-big-to-fail status gives large banks a competitive edge and incentives to take on additional risk. If investors believe the largest banks are too big to fail, they will be willing to offer them funding at a discount. Together with expectations of rescues, this discount gives the too-big-to-fail banks incentives to engage in riskier activities. This, in turn, could drive the smaller banks that compete with them to take on further risks, exacerbating the negative effects of having too-big-to-fail banks in the financial system. (Afonso et al. 2015, p. 2)

Roger Koppl has explicated a "Big Player" network effect in several writings (Koppl 2002; also Butos and Koppl 1993; Koppl and Yeager 1996). What distinguishes a Big Player from one that is not-so-big is the former's combination of "the power to influence some market, a degree from immunity from competition, and use of discretion in the exercise of his power" (Koppl 2002, p. 17). The Big Player effect appears to be prominent within the financial sector. A central bank, financial-sector regulatory agencies, or state-protected financial institutions can potentially disrupt the harmony of sectoral-wide expectations by virtue of their discretionary influence. This disruptive potential perhaps adds to the importance, not to mention the intrigue, surrounding entanglement. As Richard Wagner astutely notes, a Big Player may have a disproportionate influence over the systemic qualities emerging through a complex system of human interrelationships (Wagner 2016), and could be held partly responsible for entrenching networked zones of concentration and inequality.

Regulation of the financial sector, to the extent that it catalysed the concentrated growth of especially large financial institutions, may have worsened economic inequalities. This is attributed to the suggestion that "[i]n an industry that is protected from competition and receives rent money—such as finance—the labor force captures part of the rent" (Zingales 2012, p. 65). Several empirical studies lend support to the fact that workers in the finance sector are amongst some of the well-off in society. Kaplan and Rauh (2010) show that employees of hedge fund, private equity, and venture capital businesses account for a substantial share of the very wealthy cohort in the United States. Bell and Van Rennen (2013) undertook an analysis of financial sector remuneration and occupational structure in the United Kingdom, observing that a significant share of wages for those in the top one per cent of the income distribution was attributed to bankers, and this had barely changed since the GFC. Denk (2015) and Cournède et al. (2015) found evidence pointing to similar trends occurring in continental Europe. Of course, one should be mindful of the counteracting view that remuneration paid out to finance sector workers represents an appropriate return on the intensive education and skills they have acquired.

Inasmuch as regulation may foster upward redistribution through the enhancement of the economic role of the financial sector, it may also provide numerous opportunities for political actors to impress and impose their aspirations and priorities across the economic order. Smith et al. (2011) provide a vivid, entangled political economy account of the ways in which American financial sector bailouts and support provided something of a "back door" for politicians and bureaucrats to alter the operational environment of banks and insurance companies. The U.S. $700 billion Troubled Asset Relief Program (TARP) originally intended to give the government authority to purchase "toxic assets" held by banks.

In practice, it extended support to a range of entities (some of which did not require assistance) deemed to be systemically important to the financial system. As Smith and his colleagues noted:

> TARP represented a shift in the underlying constitutional order of how political enterprises relate to market enterprises with respect to financial intermediation, property rights, and the ability of boards and directors and corporate officers to manage their enterprises. This new enterprise was not grounded in the same bedrock as the political enterprises it replaced. The defining of new entanglement territory was soon evident as the means to induce financial stability began to change rapidly in terms of the rhetoric and actions of the key political actors involves in its administration. (Smith et al. 2011, p. 54)

Richard Wagner (2010, 2012, 2016, 2017) identified similar issues with respect to economic and political interdependence in the field of credit provision. Nowadays regulatory authorities are intimately involved in the operation of credit markets, standing in between otherwise dyadic exchanges which would occur between borrower and lender on terms which they mutually agree with, and in observance with the general principles of private property and freedom of contract.

It is eminently possible that other regulatory settings established by government implicitly facilitate a redistribution of income and wealth effectively from the lower to the middle echelons of the distribution, and from the middle to the top. Take housing as an example. The house-pricing surge, observed in numerous developed countries (Demographia 2018), has bolstered the value of wealth possessed by those already established in the housing market. At the same time, these trends increasingly deprive those on lower incomes (including young individuals and couples) of an opportunity to own a home in their preferred location. In a perceptive appraisal of Thomas Piketty's (2014) claim that worsening wealth inequality is attributable to the observed growth in the rate of return on capital as a share of national income, Matthew Rognlie (2014) found that the trend Piketty identified appears almost entirely attributable to appreciating house prices.

From a basic economic perspective, relative prices of services such as housing are influenced by both demand- and supply-side considerations. Population growth contributes to rising house prices from a demand perspective, although the efforts of populist commentators to rhetorically sheet home a significant portion of blame for housing price trends upon migrants have been challenged by the authors of several empirical analyses (Akbari and Aydede 2012; Sá 2015; Cochrane and Poot 2016). Another determinant of housing demand is the availability of economic, social, and climactic features and opportunities, collectively known as "quality-of-life" factors.

Supply considerations also matter in the determination of housing price trends, wherein a lack of adequate growth in the supply of homes contributes to the escalation of house prices more generally. Contending that existing homeowners in expensive markets "have become increasingly successful at stopping the creation of new housing," Brink Lindsey and Steven Teles write that, "they have artificially boosted housing prices in those markets, creating a windfall for existing homeowners. In the process, they have also made it harder for newcomers to move into cities with surging incomes, pushing them to parts of the country with less opportunity" (Lindsey and Teles 2017, p. 110).

Our view is that restrictions upon expanding the supply of housing have contributed to the observed concentration of wealth in certain developed countries. The question to be answered is as follows: If housing supply limitations are contributing to the uptick in house prices, thereby feeding into inequality, what affects the supply limitations? From a classical liberal perspective, regulation plays a non-insignificant role in perpetuating the supply constraint. In general terms, regulatory settings prevent the ample provision of new houses—and limit the dissipation of wealth embodied in housing—which would be expected to naturally take place in the long run as workers and their families shift from locales with fewer opportunities to those with greater opportunities.

In reality there are numerous forms of land-use regulation taking effect mainly at a local or regional level, though with some national political influence in the background. One generic kind of regulation which impacts housing prices is zoning provisions, dividing up parcels of property within a given geographic space in accordance with how such properties are to be used. Zoning regulations not only specify that property is to be put to use either as residential housing or commercial premises, but they impose other conditions on property development including the approved size of lots, the density and height of structures to be built on the land, preferred architectural features, and so on. The policy purpose for imposing zoning regulation is to ensure that economic and social developments are undertaken in an orderly, coordinated fashion, with due consideration given to the impact of property use upon environmental amenity and the aesthetic character of neighbourhoods. The market-failure rationale for zoning and other land-use regulations suggests that the lack of intervention by political actors with respect to how land is used would, somehow, lead to haphazard property developments imposing significant negative externalities upon members of the community (Pennington 2002).

The notion that individuals and enterprises, if left to their own devices, would build impracticably and in ways divorced from quality-of-life considerations remains a popular view amongst members of the planning profession and regulators. Zoning regulatory arrangements, however, are not designed and enforced without consequence. The especially prescriptive forms of zoning apparent in many major metropolitan housing markets have been associated with the phenomenon of upward redistribution:

> The regressive nature of zoning begins with its animating purpose: to protect homeowners' property values at the expense of access to housing for everybody else. In other words, it transfers wealth from the less affluent to the more affluent (given that homeowners generally have both higher incomes and higher net worth than renters). Zoning's exclusionary means then add insult to the injury of its regressive end: zoning accomplishes its objectives by keeping poor people away from rich people. (Lindsey 2015, p. 24)

Aside from zoning, local and regional governments in several countries have introduced so-called urban growth boundaries to contain urban residential and commercial property developments within a certain area. Urban growth boundaries are said to be necessary to prevent agricultural land, parks, and open spaces from being encroached upon by urban sprawl (Staley 2002; Ikeda and Washington 2015). The circumscription of development along the urban fringe, and into areas outside the perimeter of the urban growth boundary, is also likely to aggravate wealth inequality to the extent that the stock of cheaper housing is limited—in turn, benefiting existing homeowners within the boundary who enjoy the wealth effects associated with house-price increases.

There is a burgeoning empirical literature alluding to the impact of various land-use regulations upon housing markets. Glaeser et al. (2005a) established that the flow-on impact on American house prices resulting from regulatory permission to build on land is significant. The costs exuded by land-use regulation implicitly adds 20 per cent to the price of houses in Baltimore, Boston, and Washington DC, 30 per cent in Los Angeles and Oakland, and 50 per cent in Manhattan, San Francisco, and San Jose. An investigation by the same authors of the Manhattan housing market found that apartment prices in the district are roughly twice the costs associated with their construction, pointing to the effect of regulatory constraints embedded in higher prices (Glaeser et al. 2005b). Quigley and Raphael (2005) examine the factors behind rapidly rising house prices in California, finding a positive correlation between regulatory stringency and house prices. Green et al. (2016) identified a similar relationship with respect to Canadian cities. Keith Ihlanfeldt (2004) surveys the literature and finds evidence to the effect that zoning and other land-use regulations inflate housing prices.

Proponents of entangled political economy emphasise that regulation is ultimately a participatory exercise. By no means, however, does this imply that regulations will be designed and enforced in a manner consistent with the generalised interest of all members of the public. Fischel (2003) advances the hypothesis that American zoning regulations became a popularly used exclusionary device against potentially low-income homeowners in wealthier neighbourhoods from the 1970s onwards. Using the frequency of the words “land use” in U.S. state appeals court records as a proxy of regulatory stringency, Ganong and Shoag (2017) appear to confirm our suggestion that interest-group effects have become influential in the determination of land-use regulation.

The presence of exploitable gains attributable to the regulatory environment may lead to numerous situations in which the interests of people who do not own their own home are also sidelined. This is especially the case if land-use controls come to be used "as a kind of surrogate for home value insurance" (Lindsey 2015, p. 23). One example whereby regulation of land foments clashing interests concerns the development of affordable dwellings dedicated for low-income earners: "developers of low-income housing are prevented from buying land in suburban communities that have strict minimum acreage requirements. The parties thereby excluded are an alliance of the rich and the poor, of the business establishment and of minority racial or ethnic groups" (Epstein 1985, p. 263).

Another assortment of regulatory arrangements—collectively (and rather euphemistically, for reasons to be explained later) known as "intellectual property"—has also been identified as another major cause of upward redistribution. We consider patents (an exclusive authority, license, or right preventing others from imitating and selling and invention) and copyright (an exclusive authority, license, or right preventing others from publishing or otherwise reproducing artistic, literary, or music material) as being key elements of intellectual property for our purposes (WIPO 2017).

The modern justification for intellectual property is deeply infused in the language of market failure theory. The concern is that an absence of regulation in this area would lead to an underprovision of innovative activities and, through that, an undermining of economic growth. The fruits of innovative activity, as embodied in novel goods and services propagated throughout the economic order, are costly for the entrepreneurial innovator to produce. By the same token, innovations are claimed to be easily replicable by potential imitators during the meso-trajectory phase of adoption. The concern is that originating entrepreneurs would receive insufficient returns for their innovative activity, resulting in insufficient profitability and a diminished incentive to invest in potentially innovative ventures into the future.

An evolutionary perspective of economic theory challenges the mainstream view that replicability would necessarily undermine innovation-led economic growth, given that replication itself is an indispensable feature of evolution. Imitation serves as a signal of endorsement by others in relation to the usefulness of the originating, novel innovation. In addition, copying the good ideas and inventions of others assists individuals to overcome knowledge problems regarding how to subsist, and indeed flourish, in society (Potts 2013, 2014).

In recent decades, patent and copyright provisions have tended to become more prescriptive. During the late 1990s, federal legislators in America extended the term of copyright provisions to 70 years after the death of an author, and for works of corporate authorship to 120 years after creation or 95 years after publication (whichever applies sooner). This move restricted the use of the likes of Disney's "Mickey Mouse" images for public domain use farther into the future. The domain of enforcement against copyright breaches has extended into the criminal realm, with more punitive fines, prison terms, and asset forfeitures applying to those found in breach of the relevant legislation (Baker 2016; Lindsey and Teles 2017; Zingales 2012).

From the standpoint of entangled political economy, intellectual property poses as yet another participatory exercise in regulatory design and enforcement. Competing and collaborating interests from all strands of civil society are drawn into an exercise in which they attempt to negotiate the terms of triadic exchanges. In this context, the advantageous bargain, attempted to be secured through patenting and copyrighting, would reflect a sense of political assent to a monopolistic use of ideas and inventions deemed to be "innovative." The costs are to be absorbed by entrepreneurs wishing to replicate the innovation, and consumers wear the relatively higher prices resulting from the political grant of monopoly.

The many critics of intellectual property regulation have readily pointed out that these regulatory frameworks represent little more than a politically instituted contrivance empowering holders of patents and copyrights to enjoy greater income and wealth through the capture of monopoly rents. The prospect of intellectual property regulation closing off opportunities for Schumpeterian creative destruction is highlighted by Boldrin and Levine (2013), who suggest that political demands for more stringent regulation come from the representatives of mature, established enterprises who seek economic immunity from existing and future innovators.

It has also been suggested that copyright and patent provisions also play their part in propping up "winner-takes-all" superstar effects, observed in industries such as entertainment and software development (Baker 2016; Zingales 2012). Stringent intellectual property regulations may also undermine equality of opportunity, insofar as careers are insufficiently open to all those aspiring and innovative talents wanting to promulgate novelty throughout the economy and society.

The inequalities magnified by intellectual property are apparent in several industries. Take medicine as an example. Although we recognise that research and development undertaken to develop new and improved medicines is risky and routinely expensive, intellectual property regulation is likely to raise the price of prescription drugs. This accordingly provides a profit windfall for the companies possessing the relevant patent that cannot be dissipated by competitors. Drug patents also reduce the affordability of product for consumers, especially for those on low incomes. The inequality-inducing effects of intellectual property regulation were forcefully drawn to public attention as a result of Martin Shkreli (nicknamed "Pharma Bro") purchasing the then-expired patent for anti-malarial drug Daraprim, and rapidly increasing the U.S. dosage price from U.S. $13.50 per pill to U.S. $750 per pill (Pollack 2015).

Whilst we interpret intellectual property as enacted and maintained by government to promote meso-level economic concentration and inequality, it is recognised that intellectual property has numerous supporters, and not merely the direct participants engaging within this regulatory edifice. It seems that such support rests, to some extent, upon the linguistic reference to patents and copyrights as "property," according these regulatory arrangements a modicum of respectability which would be ordinarily and aptly given to private property.

The technique to conflate intellectual property with private property is, of course, another example of a non-logical stratagem to quell the resentments of those who lose out as a result of regulation. Putting some nuanced complexities aside, the pivotal difference between intellectual and private properties rests upon the fact that, in the case of the former, regulatory edicts circumscribe to some extent the uses to which goods and services are to be put by the user, whereas for the latter no such restriction occurs because property is freely used and disposed of by the individual possessing it (Boldrin and Levine 2013).

Regulatory Governance in an Entangled Political Economy

Contradicting rhetorical political statements to the effect that developed countries have retrenched their governmental activities, liberalised their economies, and slashed regulatory "red tape," what has actually been observed is a partial, *ad hoc* switching between modes of intervention. Governmental activity has switched away from public sector ownership of enterprises, and the heavy taxing of corporate profits, towards the widespread regulation of all enterprises. Other notable features of this emergent "regulatory state" is the growing influence of international agreements and treaties in domestic regulation policymaking, the centralisation of regulation policy determination within countries, and the diffusion of regulatory governance which, among other things, invokes a semblance of organisational and political independence for regulators (Jordana et al. 2011).

The modern predominance of regulation as a political strategy to effect change places a great emphasis upon the importance of effective modes of "regulatory governance." This term refers to the nature, integrity, and effectiveness of regulatory organisational forms and administrative procedures in ensuring that regulatory objectives are being achieved. Questions of regulator accountability and transparency, and the performance of regulatory operations at reasonable cost, are some of the major issues for researchers investigating the regulatory governance field.

A number of significant regulatory governance developments have emerged amongst developed countries these past few decades. They raise legitimate questions over the extent to which regulatory activity remains genuinely accountable and responsive to the interests of those being regulated. In the cases of monetary policy, competition policy, financial regulation, industrial relations, intellectual property management, and more, legislators have devolved more of the responsibility for regulation policy design and enforcement to regulatory agencies. Many of those agencies, in turn, have been given the status of statutory independence, with much of their (discretionary) authority to undertake action delegated to them by legislatures.

There are some good reasons for politicians to delegate regulatory roles and responsibilities to regulators. Politicians do not necessarily possess the knowledge and skills required to conduct regulatory policies—such as the setting of interest rates and minimum wages, or to establish rulings on certain competition policy and other cases. As was illustrated by "political business cycle" research during the 1970s and 1980s—revealing how political actors would manipulate (regulatory and other) policies to try to retain office—it has also been presumed, from a public choice perspective, that politicians lack sufficient incentives to align their interests with the principals (citizen-voters) to which they are ultimately accountable.

Some classical liberals, such as Chris Berg (2008, 2015), suggest the pendulum of regulatory governance swung too far in favour of the regulators *vis-à-vis* the politicians. From this perspective, regulatory agencies have been given an inordinate set of powers to design and enforce regulations. Previously understood forms of democratic accountability were unwound as legislators assigned regulatory agencies additional powers to exercise discretion regarding how it shall act. "The consequences of such institutions are not yet well understood," warns Berg, "non-majoritarian institutions vested with considerable legal power are susceptible to becoming 'governments in miniature'" (Berg 2008, p. 59). The tendency to consolidate agencies within the regulatory policy network via the introduction of "mega-regulators," with responsibilities to regulate vast swathes of an economy, also tests traditional chains of democratic accountability between rulers and the ruled.

Other economists have noted that delegating regulatory staff a wide scope of discretion entails risks, not only due to the classic knowledge problem explicated by Hayek. Drawing from the behavioural economics literature, it is suggested that even highly educated bureaucrats share, with the rest of us, the generic human tendency to act in a cognitively biased manner (Berggren 2012; Rizzo and Wittman 2009; Tasic 2009, 2011). Referring to the implications of expertise from a political economy perspective, Koppl suggests that "[t]he risk of expert failure is greater when experts enjoy an epistemic monopoly and when they choose for others rather than merely advising them" (Koppl 2015, p. 343). These concerns cast doubts over the merits of perpetuating monocentric tendencies within entangled political economy, via the delegation of concentrated authority to a relatively small number of political enterprises.

The ecology of human interaction we denote as entangled political economy features not only large-scale regulatory authorities but many smaller entities which, themselves, wield significant and discretionary influence. Richard Epstein stresses the potential for arbitrariness in the enforcement of zoning and other land-use regulations by smaller-scale, local regulatory bodies:

> most systems of land use control are not normally self-executing. Instead, they set out in very general terms the desired ends—preservation of aesthetic qualities, prevention of urban sprawl, maintenance of individual neighborhoods, or whatever. Thereafter the operation of the system depends upon discrete applications, usually culminating in decisions by a local planning board, often in response to some highly particularized request of local groups. An enormous slippage thus occurs between the articulation of a general principle and its concrete application. (Epstein 1985, p. 264)

The challenge of reconciling application approvals with regulatory objectives opens up the opportunity for much intrigue in the approval process. In the land-use regulatory context, this includes the potential for individuals to form alliances and coalitions with a view to petition against any proposed development application. Regulation-induced conflict may either lead to the nullification of given approvals by the regulator, or lend itself to the regulator seeking bargains with would-be developers to exact concessions in exchange for approval (Calder 2017). In some of the worse cases of corruption, concessions to smooth over potentially contentious development applications could come in the form of political contributions and donations (Teles 2015; Murray and Frijters 2016, 2017).

International considerations have crept into domestic regulatory governance concerns, in what could be regarded as a case of *global* entangled political economy. The "Uruguay Round" of international trade negotiations led to, amongst other things, the Agreement of Trade-Related Aspects of Intellectual Property Rights (TRIPS) specifying intellectual property regulatory standards that are to be adhered to by all signatory nations. The TRIPS outlined lengthy copyright terms and an expansive definition of patents to be granted to "any inventions, whether products or processes, in all fields of technology, provided that they are new, involve an inventive step and are capable of industrial application" (Devereaux et al. 2006; WTO 2017). Other trade agreements, such as the North American Free Trade Agreement, have incorporated additional, intellectual property-related matters such as data protections and marketing exclusivity with respect to pharmaceutical products (Baker 2016).

The proliferation of patent and copyright procedures on a global scale appears to have contributed to the "globalisation" of arbitraged effort by economic and political enterprises to secure privileges (Dourado and Tabarrok 2015). Davidson and Potts (2017) observe that the global coverage of intellectual property regulation adds another dimension to domestic lobbying activity, animated by the desire of domestic innovators to have their domestic government protect their interests against potential predation by overseas governments and their attached crony interests.

Entangled political economy is characterised by the participation of numerous individuals and their agencies and organisations in policy development processes, with clear implications for operational capabilities across the economic, communal, and political orders. Alongside the legislators and regulators, members of the judiciary and the legal profession pose as Big Players, deciding what form intellectual property regulation will take. In 1982, a Court of Appeals for the Federal Circuit was established with exclusive jurisdiction over patent cases in America. The judiciary has played a key role in broadening the scope of patent regulation by allowing DNA sequences and life forms and, later, software and business methods to be patented (Baker 2016; Lindsey and Teles 2017).

It isn't only judicial developments that have contributed to an explosion in U.S. patent applications. The broader legal system itself appears to have morphed into a focal point, through which the distributive conflicts at the heart of intellectual property disputes have taken place. The incentive to secure gains in ambiguous legal environments have played their part in facilitating the emergence of a most peculiar form of enterprise—the so-called "patent troll" which aggregates patent portfolios for the purpose of initiating patent lawsuits against other enterprises (Boldrin and Levine 2013; Lindsey 2015; Tabarrok 2013). It has been estimated that the legal costs arising from encounters with patent trolls in America runs into the billions of dollars annually (Bessen et al. 2011)

Conclusion

A recurring theme in this book, one which is emphasised repeatedly by Richard Wagner, is that there is a gulf between rationalisations for action and explanations that attempt understanding of the action which has been rationalised. The divorce between rationalisation and explanation is as apparent with respect to regulation as it is in every other conceivable field of policy conduct.

Normative theories of regulation, economically grounded in the "market failure" narrative of mainstream economics, represent a rationalisation for what regulatory making should be if economic and social perfection were to be established. Economically and socially fallen participants cannot secure better arrangements, and so benighted government comes to the rescue with regulatory commands and edicts to prod individuals, and the enterprises they operate, towards a superior state of affairs.

The explanatory arm of regulatory theory and analysis came to the fore with the development of Virginian and Chicagoan political economy frameworks, of Buchanan and Stigler, respectively. These theories sought to explain regulation as the manifestation of interest-group engagement with government. We argue entangled political economy presents a new branch in the positive, explanation-laden approach to regulation—retaining a role for interest groups but accentuating the inherent dynamism that is part and parcel of the regulatory process.

The entangled political economy approach to regulation encapsulates evolving and complex networks of competing, and collaborating, participants, jostling and interacting to secure rents as embodied in favourable regulatory arrangements. The distinct possibility raised by this explanatory theory is that political actors, together with a small band of interests, will perceive they have forged gains through the regulatory process, ignoring or overlooking the equally distinct possibility that there is a much larger band of societal members whose economic and social interests have been compromised.

Economists have traditionally deflected theoretical attention away from the distributional effects of regulation, properly recognising that regulations create disincentives which do not conform to basic liberty principles but contending that distributional matters are better reserved for taxation and expenditure policies (Veljanovski 2010). The contemporary inequality debate has doubtlessly forced the economists' hand in relation to the matter, at least in terms of a growing awareness of the impacts of regulation upon income and wealth inequality.

The ceaselessly shifting patterns of policy, entangling with action performed within the economic and communal orders, do not necessarily lend themselves to definitive conclusions concerning the distributional impacts of all regulations. What is not ruled out by the analysis presented here is that regulations may be manipulated, in some circumstances and at the margins, to assist in ensuring an upward redistribution of income and wealth. Regulation provides abundant opportunities for rents to be seized with the consequence that income flows to the rich, and that the wealthy can accumulate even more wealth. Regulations often work as entry barriers, shutting down economic competition that can help break down concentrated network effects, a matter to be set aside for a later chapter.

References

Afonso, Gara, João A.C. Santos, and James Traina. 2015. Do "Too-Big-to-Fail" Banks Take on More Risk? *The Journal of Financial Perspectives* 3 (2): 1–29.

Akbari, Ather H., and Yigit Aydede. 2012. Effect of Immigration on House Prices in Canada. *Applied Economics* 44 (13): 1645–1658.

Almudi, Isabel, Francisco Fatas-Villafranca, Luis R. Izquierdo, and Jason Potts. 2017. The Economics of Utopia: A Co-Evolutionary Model of Ideas, Citizenship and Socio-Political Change. *Journal of Evolutionary Economics* 27 (4): 629–662.

Al-Ubaydli, Omar, and Patrick A. McLaughlin. 2015. RegData: A Numerical Database on Industry-Specific Regulations for All United States Industries and Federal Regulations, 1997–2012. *Regulation & Governance* 11 (1): 109–123.

Anderson, Gary M. 1994. The Economic Theory of Regulation. In *The Elgar Companion to Austrian Economics*, ed. Peter J. Boettke, 294–299. Cheltenham, UK: Edward Elgar.

Baker, Dean. 2016. *Rigged: How Globalization and the Rules of the Modern Economy Were Structured to Make the Rich Richer*. Washington, DC: Center for Economic and Policy Research.

Bell, Brian, and John Van Reenen. 2013. Bankers and Their Bonuses. *The Economic Journal* 124: F1–F21.

Benson, Bruce L. 2011. A Neo-Mengerian Examination of the Regulatory Process. *Studies in Emergent Order* 4: 193–208.

Berg, Chris. 2008. *The Growth of Australia's Regulatory State: Ideology, Accountability and Mega-Regulators*. Melbourne, Australia: Institute of Public Affairs.

———. 2015. *Liberty, Equality & Democracy*. Ballarat, Australia: Connor Court.

Berggren, Niclas. 2012. Time for Behavioral Political Economy? An Analysis of Articles in Behavioral Economics. *The Review of Austrian Economics* 25 (3): 199–221.

Bessen, James E., Michael J. Meurer, and Jennifer Ford. 2011. The Private and Social Costs of Patent Trolls. *Regulation* 34 (4): 26–35.

Black, Julia. 2002. Critical Reflections on Regulation. *Australian Journal of Legal Philosophy* 27: 1–35.

Boldrin, Michele, and David K. Levine. 2013. The Case Against Patents. *Journal of Economic Perspectives* 27 (1): 3–22.

Brennan, Geoffrey. 2004. The Political Economy of Regulation: A Prolegomenon. In *Changing Institutions in the European Union: A Public Choice Perspective*, ed. Giuseppe Eusepi and Friedrich Schneider, 72–94. Cheltenham, UK: Edward Elgar.

Brennan, Geoffrey, and Hartmut Kliemt. 2008. Regulation and Revenue. *Constitutional Political Economy* 19 (3): 249–260.

Broughel, James. 2017. *Regulation and Economic Growth: Applying Economic Theory to Public Policy*. Arlington, VA: Mercatus Center of George Mason University.

Butos, William N., and Roger G. Koppl. 1993. Hayekian Expectations: Theory and Empirical Applications. *Constitutional Political Economy* 4 (3): 303–329.

Calder, Vanessa Brown. 2017. Zoning, Land-Use Planning, and Housing Affordability. Cato Institute, *Policy Analysis No. 823*, October. Accessed October 28, 2017. https://object.cato.org/sites/cato.org/files/pubs/pdf/pa-823.pdf

Clark, Gregory. 2014. *The Son Also Rises: Surnames and the History of Social Mobility*. Princeton, NJ: Princeton University Press.

Clark, Gregory, Andrew Leigh, and Mike Pottenger. 2017. Immobile Australia: Surnames Show Strong Status Persistence, 1870–2017. CESifo Group, *Working Paper Series No. 6650*, September 13. Accessed October 24, 2017. https://papers.ssrn.com/sol3/papers.cfm?abstract_id=3043103

Cochrane, Bill, and Jacques Poot. 2016. Past Research on the Impact of International Migration on House Prices: Implications for Auckland. *New Zealand Ministry of Business, Innovation and Employment*, April 13. Accessed October 27, 2017. http://www.mbie.govt.nz/publications-research/publications/housing-and-property/nidea-report-immigration-housing-literature-review.pdf

Commonwealth Interdepartmental Committee on Quasi-Regulation. 1997. *Grey-Letter Law*. Belconnen, Australia: Productivity Commission.

Cournède, Boris, Oliver Denk, and Peter Hoeller. 2015. Finance and Inclusive Growth. OECD, *Economic Policy Paper No. 14*, June. Accessed October 25, 2017. http://www.oecd.org/eco/monetary/finance-growth-inequality.htm

Creighton, Adam. 2015. Bank Sector Too Big and Too Greedy in Australia and US. *The Australian*, May 22.

Crews, Clyde Wayne, Jr. 2017. *Ten Thousand Commandments: An Annual Snapshot of the Federal Regulatory State—2017 Edition*. Washington, DC: Competitive Enterprise Institute.

Davidson, Sinclair, and Jason Potts. 2017. The Stationary Bandit Model of Intellectual Property. *Cato Journal* 37 (1): 69–88.

Dawson, John W., and John J. Seater. 2013. Federal Regulation and Aggregate Economic Growth. *Journal of Economic Growth* 18 (2): 137–177.

Demographia. 2018. *14th Annual Demographia International Housing Affordability Survey: 2018*. Accessed January 28, 2018. http://www.demographia.com/dhi.pdf

Denhardt, Robert B., Janet V. Denhardt, and Tara A. Blanc. 2014. *Public Administration: An Action Orientation*. 7th ed. Boston, MA: Wadsworth.

Denk, Oliver. 2015. Financial Sector Pay and Labour Income Inequality: Evidence from Europe. OECD, Economics Department, *Working Paper No. 1225*, June. Accessed October 25, 2017. http://www.oecd-ilibrary.org/economics/financial-sector-pay-and-labour-income-inequality_5js04v5wjw9p-en

Devereaux, Charan, Robert Z. Lawrence, and Michael D. Watkins. 2006. *Case Studies in US Trade Negotiation. Volume 1: Making the Rule*. Washington, DC: Peterson Institute for International Economics.

Dourado, Eli, and Alex Tabarrok. 2015. Public Choice Perspectives on Intellectual Property. *Public Choice* 163 (1–2): 129–151.

English, William. 2014. Economic and Ideological Corruptions of the Regulatory State. *Society* 51 (3): 262–267.

Epstein, Richard A. 1985. *Takings: Private Property and the Power of Eminent Domain*. Cambridge, MA: Harvard University Press.

Fischel, William A. 2003. Public Goods and Property Rights: Of Coase, Tiebout, and Just Compensation. In *Property Rights: Cooperation, Conflict, and Law*, ed. Terry L. Anderson and Fred S. McChesney, 343–364. Princeton, NJ: Princeton University Press.

Ganong, Peter, and Daniel Shoag. 2017. Why Has Regional Income Convergence in the U.S. Declined? National Bureau of Economic Research, *Working Paper No. 23609*, July. Accessed October 28, 2017. http://www.nber.org/papers/w23609

Glaeser, Edward L., Joseph Gyourko, and Raven E. Saks. 2005a. Why Have Housing Prices Gone Up? National Bureau of Economic Research, *Working Paper No. 11129*, February. Accessed October 28, 2017. http://www.nber.org/papers/w11129

———. 2005b. Why Is Manhattan So Expensive? Regulation and the Rise in Housing Prices. *The Journal of Law and Economics* 48: 331–369.

Glazer, Amihai. 2013. Regulatory Policy. In *The Elgar Companion to Public Choice*, ed. William F. Shughart II, Laura Razzolini, and Michael Reksulak, 2nd ed., 284–290. Cheltenham, UK: Edward Elgar.

Green, Kenneth P., Josef Filipowicz, Steve Lafleur, and Ian Herzog. 2016. *The Impact of Land-Use Regulation on Housing Supply in Canada*. Vancouver, Canada: Fraser Institute.

Hanson, Robin. 2008. Showing That You Care: The Evolution of Health Altruism. *Medical Hypotheses* 70 (4): 724–742.

Ihlanfeldt, Keith. 2004. Exclusionary Land-Use Regulations within Suburban Communities: A Review of the Evidence and Policy Prescriptions. *Urban Studies* 41 (2): 261–283.

Ikeda, Sanford, and Emily Washington. 2015. *How Land-Use Regulation Undermines Affordable Housing*. Arlington, VA: Mercatus Center.

International Monetary Fund (IMF). 2014. *Global Financial Stability Report: Moving from Liquidity- to Growth-Driven Markets*. Washington, DC: IMF.

Jordana, Jacint, David Levi-Faur, and Xavier Fernández i Marin. 2011. The Global Diffusion of Regulatory Agencies: Channels of Transfer and Stages of Diffusion. *Comparative Political Studies* 44 (10): 1343–1369.

Kaplan, Steven N., and Joshua Rauh. 2010. Wall Street and Main Street: What Contributes to the Rise in the Highest Incomes? *The Review of Financial Studies* 23 (3): 1004–1050.

Kirchner, Stephen. 2016. Economy's Engine Room Right Size for Job. *The Australian Financial Review*, January 10.

Koppl, Roger. 2002. *Big Players and the Economic Theory of Expectations*. New York, NY: Palgrave Macmillan.

———. 2015. The Rule of Experts. In *The Oxford Handbook of Austrian Economics*, ed. Peter J. Boettke and Christopher J. Coyne, 343–363. New York, NY: Oxford University Press.

Koppl, Roger, and Leland B. Yeager. 1996. Big Players and Herding in Asset Markets: The Case of the Russian Ruble. *Explorations in Economic History* 33: 367–383.

Kroszner, Randall S. 1999. Is the Financial System Politically Independent? Perspectives on the Political Economy of Banking and Financial Relation. University of Chicago, George J. Stigler Center for the Study of the Economy and the State, *Working Paper No. 151*, June. Accessed October 25, 2017. https://www.chicagobooth.edu/assests/stigler/151.pdf

Lindsey, Brink. 2015. *Low-Hanging Fruit Guarded by Dragons: Reforming Regressive Regulation to Boost U.S. Economic Growth*. Washington, DC: Cato Institute.

Lindsey, Brink, and Steven M. Teles. 2017. *The Captured Economy: How the Powerful Enrich Themselves, Slow Down Growth, and Increase Inequality*. Oxford, UK: Oxford University Press.

Martin, Adam. 2015. Degenerate Cosmopolitanism. *Social Philosophy and Policy* 32 (1): 74–100.

McChesney, Fred S. 1997. *Money for Nothing: Politicians, Rent Extraction, and Political Extortion*. Cambridge, MA: Harvard University Press.

McLaughlin, Patrick A., and Oliver Sherhouse. 2017. RegData 3.0. Accessed October 23, 2017. http://quantgov.org

Mulligan, Casey B., and Andrei Shleifer. 2005. The Extent of the Market and the Supply of Regulation. *The Quarterly Journal of Economics* 120 (4): 1445–1473.

Murray, Cameron K., and Paul Frijters. 2016. Clean Money, Dirty System: Connected Landowners Capture Beneficial Land Rezoning. *Journal of Urban Economics* 93: 99–114.

———. 2017. *Game of Mates: How Favours Bleed the Nation*. Brisbane: Publicious Pty. Ltd.

Olson, Mancur. 1965. *The Logic of Collective Action: Public Goods and the Theory of Groups*. Cambridge, MA: Harvard University Press.

Pennington, Mark. 2002. *Liberating the Land: The Case for Private Land-Use Planning*. London, UK: Institute of Economic Affairs.

Piketty, Thomas. 2014. *Capital in the Twenty-First Century: The Dynamics of Inequality, Wealth, and Growth*. Translated by Arthur Goldhammer. Cambridge, MA: The Belknap Press of Harvard University Press.

Pollack, Andrew. 2015. Drug Goes from $13.50 a Tablet to $750, Overnight. *The New York Times*, September 20. Accessed October 29, 2017. https://www.nytimes.com/2015/09/21/business/a-huge-overnight-increase-in-a-drugs-price-raises-protests.html

Posner, Richard A. 1971. Taxation by Regulation. *Bell Journal of Economic and Management Science* 2 (1): 22–50.

Potts, Jason. 2013. Rules of Spontaneous Order. *Cosmos + Taxis* 1 (1): 30–41.

———. 2014. Innovation is a Spontaneous Order. *Cosmos + Taxis* 2 (1): 1–10.

Productivity Commission. 2007. *Performance Benchmarking of Australian Business Regulation*. Melbourne, Australia: Productivity Commission.

Prosser, Tony. 2010. Models of Economic and Social Regulation. In *The Regulatory State: Constitutional Implications*, ed. Dawn Olier, Tony Prosser, and Richard Rawlings, 34–49. Oxford, UK: Oxford University Press.

Quigley, John M., and Steven Raphael. 2005. Regulation and the High Cost of Housing in California. *American Economic Review* 95 (2): 323–328.

Rizzo, Mario J., and Douglas Glen Wittman. 2009. Little Brother is Watching You: New Paternalism on the Slippery Slopes. *Arizona Law Review* 51: 685–739.

Rognlie, Matthew. 2014. A Note on Piketty and Diminishing Returns to Capital, June 15. Accessed October 27, 2017. http://gabriel-zucman.eu/files/teaching/Rognlie14.pdf

Sá, Filipa. 2015. Immigration and House Prices in the UK. *The Economic Journal* 125 (587): 1393–1424.

Smith, Adam, Richard E. Wagner, and Bruce Yandle. 2011. A Theory of Entangled Political Economy, with Application to TARP and NRA. *Public Choice* 148: 45–66.

Smith, Adam, and Bruce Yandle. 2014. *Bootleggers and Baptists: How Economic Forces and Moral Persuasion Interact to Shape Regulatory Policies*. Washington, DC: Cato Institute Press.

Staley, Samuel R. 2002. Zoning, Smart Growth, and Regulatory Taxation. In *Politics, Taxation, and the Rule of Law*, ed. Donald P. Racheter and Richard E. Wagner. Boston, MA: Springer.

Tabarrok, Alex. 2013. Innovation Policy and Australia. Grattan Institute. Accessed October 29, 2017. https://grattan.edu.au/wpcontent/uploads/2014/05/908_tabarook_alliance_21.pdf

Tasic, Slavisa. 2009. The Illusion of Regulatory Competence. *Critical Review* 21 (4): 423–436.

———. 2011. Are Regulators Rational? *Journal des Economistes et des Etudes Humaines* 17 (1): 1–16.

Teles, Steven M. 2015. The Scourge of Upward Redistribution. *National Affairs* 25: 78–95.

Veljanovski, Cento. 2010. Economic Approaches to Regulation. In *The Oxford Handbook of Regulation*, ed. Robert Baldwin, Martin Cave, and Martin Lodge, 17–38. Oxford, UK: Oxford University Press.

Wagner, Richard E. 2007. *Fiscal Sociology and the Theory of Public Finance*. Cheltenham, UK: Edward Elgar.

———. 2010. *Mind, Society, and Human Action: Time and Knowledge in a Theory of Social Economy*. London, UK: Routledge.

———. 2012. *Deficits, Debt, and Democracy: Wrestling with Tragedy on the Fiscal Commons*. Cheltenham, UK: Edward Elgar.

———. 2016. *Politics as a Peculiar Business: Insights from a Theory of Entangled Political Economy*. Cheltenham, UK: Edward Elgar.

———. 2017. *James M. Buchanan and Liberal Political Economy: A Rational Reconstruction*. Lanham, MD: Lexington Books.

World Intellectual Property Organization (WIPO). 2017. What is Intellectual Property? Accessed October 29, 2017. http://www.wipo.int/about-ip/en/

World Trade Organization (WTO). 2017. Annex 1C: Agreement of Trade-Related Aspects of Intellectual Property Rights. Accessed October 29, 2017. https://www.wto.org/English/docs_e/legal_e/27-trips.pdf

Yandle, Bruce. 1983. Bootleggers and Baptists: The Education of a Regulatory Economist. *Regulation* 7 (3): 12–16.

———. 1999. Bootleggers and Baptists in Retrospect. *Regulation* 22 (3): 5–7.

Zingales, Luigi. 2012. *A Capitalism for The People: Recapturing the Lost Genius of American Prosperity*. New York, NY: Basic Books.

6

Social Exclusion

Introduction

Relationships between people in an entangled political economy undoubtedly reflect the affirming values attached by many to an active sense of participation within society itself. This idea of participation is not wholly determined by economic or financial interests—that is, the desire to interact in an effort to generate value or procure profits by exchanging goods, services, and assets. The extent and kinds of involvement in entangled political economy are also patterned by the "habits of heart and mind" (Wagner 2010, p. 8), influencing the terms and conditions with which individuals are prepared to engage each other.

Reflecting the importance of these considerations in entangled political economy, network structures are impacted by a persisting human trait of association or, more precisely, wishing to belong. In practical terms, however, belonging has often taken on status-laden attributes. Certain "in-groups" of people are accorded more favourable status, over and above engagement with cohorts of people deemed to be belonging to the "out-groups." The identification of groups, or classes, of people as "in" and "out" of favourable status and esteem reflects a complex array of

M. Novak, *Inequality*, Palgrave Studies in Classical Liberalism,
https://doi.org/10.1007/978-3-319-89417-1_6

factors. Governments, for example, have over the centuries used legislation, regulation, taxation, and spending in an effect to promote and maintain group distinctions which crystallise status variations.

Our contention is that the treatment of individual persons as imbuing a certain identity, or being affiliated with a certain group, will have some bearing upon economic inequality. Specifically, status perceptions associated with certain people, and the activities they undertake, can play a role in the emergence of incomplete, partial network structures that facilitate inequalities of income and wealth. The implication is that, along some margins, certain individuals will become disadvantaged in their efforts to secure adequate resources and, further still, opportunities, because they are seen to be a member of an out-group. The resultant accumulation of advantages and disadvantages along groupish lines will, thus, have some impact upon the broadly observed meso-level patterns of income and wealth evident within a given society.

This chapter will provide an outline of the implications of group identity for inequality through the prism of the entangled political economy framework. The next section will describe the concept of personal and group identities using developments in evolutionary theory, followed by a discussion of the rationale for individual and group identities. The historical record and contemporary experience illustrates that identity has been used to exercise discrimination against so-called out groups, with government policy playing a key role in entrenching group biases. These matters are also canvassed in this chapter, followed by an explanation of the impacts of racist, sexist, and xenophobic biases upon economic inequality. This chapter concludes with a brief reflection of the implications of group discriminations.

Defining Identity: An Evolutionary Approach

One of the distinguishing characteristics of *Homo sapiens* is their tendency to ascribe a sense of *identity* to themselves, and to others. The concept of identity is a somewhat enigmatic one, with many interpretations apparent; therefore, efforts to provide a unifying definition are fraught with great difficulty. It is suggested in some quarters that identity pertains to expectations, representations, and understandings about just who a person is, what sort of person they are, and how they relate to others (Fearon 1999). This conceptualisation is surely a broad one, and many issues are subsumed within it, such as the construction of identity by individuals and by groups of individuals, the utilisation of identity by individuals as a role-playing activity inducing collaboration or competition within society, and the application of identity for legal and policy purposes.

Identity is the subject of an extensive literature particularly within the disciplines of psychology, anthropology, and sociology, with economists also indicating a formal interest in recent times (Akerlof and Kranton 2000, 2010; Davis 2003, 2011; Hermann-Pillath 2013). The evolutionary economist Carsten Hermann-Pillath has devoted considerable attention to identity issues, relating them to the long-standing economic interest in individual agency: "[a]gency is seen as a property of individuals which results from identity: identity establishes personhood and is embedded into human groups, both synchronically as confluence of population-level processes of social categorizations and diachronically as narratives that distinguish individuals relative to others" (Hermann-Pillath 2013, p. xxvi). The demarcation of identity into individual (personal) and group (social) categories represents a basic attempt at categorisation that is made by most identity researchers, and, for that matter, by many people in most walks of life. Essentially, a given person may have their own sense of self developed ever since childhood in an idiosyncratic way, and this is contrasted by the identities subscribed to by other persons.

Mapping individual identity to one's own sense of agency is one matter to be considered. As numerous scholars have emphasised, individual identity is also influenced by which groups in society they are affiliated with (Tajfel and Turner 1979). Indeed, people often express their own sense of self with reference to their group-memberships (e.g. age, race, gender, kinship, nationality, religion, sexual preference, ideological or political affiliation, and civic association membership). There is a bilateral sense in which individual and group identities relate to each other, because individuals can be also classified by other people, and their agencies, in terms of (by and large, group) identity. As a consequence of these effects, we observe in modern societies a pervasive yet evolving relation between individual and group identities.

In a formal treatment, Hermann-Pillath (2013) invokes a concept of the "sign" (a physical attribute or object) serving to connect individuals into (meso level) groups within the networked structure of society. This idea draws upon Bruno Latour's (2005) actor-network theory, which conceives complex relations between physical and non-physical attributes or objects. Connectivity by groups with a given sign influences action within, and the overall performance of, networks: "if a group manifests high degrees of solidarity, this is based on certain signs that connect the individuals in the group, which activate certain emotional mechanisms in a recurrent fashion, such that the group-level pattern of solidarity emerges" (Hermann-Pillath 2013, p. 278).

Putting these concepts through their paces, we observe that one of those signs through which interactions have been mediated is skin colour. It is well known that people have curiously tended to be grouped into racial categories, even to this day, on the basis of the colour of one's skin. However, the limitations associated with *objectively* enunciating group identities on the basis of signs, those "observer independent objects in the sense of being physical entities" (Ibid., p. 281), are illustrated by the overwhelming modern social-scientific insight that race is a social construct. This view, to be sure, clashes with "folk" notions to the effect that race is somehow a biological phenomenon. Nonetheless, the "race-as-biology" perception is misplaced—studies indicate the observed degree of genetic variation between people *within* racial categories is greater than the interpersonal variation *across* race (for a summary, see Clair and Denis 2015).

Perhaps a more plausible way in which signs are attached to group identity is through the association of different kinds of commodities, and patterns of conduct, to groups. Clothing, food, music, venues, and even vocabulary and manner of speech may be stereotypically identified as predominantly being in use by certain groups of people, and not others. Even so, changing tastes and other factors mean that people will idiosyncratically alter their senses of attachment to shiftable signs. As members of the various groups interact and mingle with each other, it would be expected that cross-group adoption and modification of signs would take place, in a phenomenon labelled in recent years as "cultural appropriation" (for defences of such practices, see, for example, Brown 2016; Malik 2017; Veer 2017).

Jason Potts (2008, 2011) has extended the body of economic research into identity to reinforce an inherently evolutionary approach to identity formation. Eschewing the mainstream economic approach that identity is exogenously given to the individual, Potts conceives of identity as "a 'generic asset' subject to investment, adaptation and maintenance" (Potts 2011, p. 85). Although identity can be seen as a micro-level phenomenon inherent in an individual agent, meso-level groups emerge when multiple individuals happen to have internalised similar (internally and externally signalled) rules—which ultimately revolve about identity as a way of being, doing, and knowing—and there is common recognition amongst a population of people that similar rule-internalisations have, indeed, taken place.

A particularly interesting facet of Potts's account of identity dynamics is the connection between individual identity and group identity through the prism of entrepreneurship: "it is conceivable to talk of 'identity entrepreneurs' who extract value from novel identity constructions that might be adopted by other agents. The social milieu in this view is not given, but continuously emerges from the interactions of differently endowed and specialized agents, each proposing, configuring and projecting identity constructs creatively assembled from connections and refractions from other agents" (Ibid., p. 90). Nick Cowen (2013) affirms—in specific reference to gender and sexual identities—that identity is a contingent phenomenon, entrepreneurially subjected to modification as individuals (and especially members of minority groups who share similar group affiliations) navigate their social environments in often novel ways. It is also possible to appreciate ethnic and racial identities as socially constructed entrepreneurial processes (Byng 2012). Therefore, identity is subject to contestation and cooperation between, and amongst, individuals participating in an entangled political economy.

The preceding discussion suggests identity need not necessarily be an essential or physicalist notion, borne of qualities more readily the subject of observance by others. In addition, identity should not necessarily be viewed as a fixed quality inherent within people. The meso-level structure of group identities within society is affected by the relative size of group-membership categories which already exist, and the rate at which individuals "self-categorise" by way of expressing an affiliation with certain groups (reflecting that individuals can assume multiple identities at once, and reject others). Group identity is dynamic, grounded in the ever-shifting combination and recombination of affiliation with the attributes of others (Davis 2014). This contrasts identity as an equilibrating notion wherein people persistently conform to the functions, norms, and ideals associated with given identities (Akerlof and Kranton 2000, 2010).

Why Do We Identify Ourselves and Others?

Complications arising from the evolutionary account of identity aside, Paul Rubin (2002) points out that human beings appear to share a widespread tendency to quickly and resolutely assign others as members, or non-members, of certain groups. Furthermore, individuals themselves enunciate and express their affiliation with commonly understood group identities, including those which have persisted through the meso-retention phase of cultural and social evolution.

Group identities are often seen as an important way in which people can signal their affiliation with, and support for, certain alliances and coalitions, whose underlying purpose is to secure gains over and above those secured through individual exertions. Although it is possible to conceptualise a group cohort of an astonishingly large size—for instance, the cosmopolitan, humanist, and indelibly liberal "brotherhood and sisterhood of all humankind"—studies suggest that most individuals seem to cognitively accommodate a relatively small number of nested relationships among those trusted and well-known to them for the purposes of furthering material cooperation and social support. This tendency poses as a rather obvious tension which must be addressed in the interest of managing tectonic clashing within society.

Robin Dunbar (1992) famously suggested that the average person can maintain a close relationship with 150 other people. A group size beyond this threshold figure is believed to be susceptible to fragmentation. Large groups tend to be plagued by coordination failures to detect free-riders and cheaters, who insufficiently contribute towards joint efforts to perpetuate group survival. In addition, groups which consist of large numbers may be less cohesive in avoiding defection, and resisting those seeking to challenge entrenched group norms (Tomasello et al. 2012). As mentioned previously, Mancur Olson (1965) suggests that concentrated interests consisting of small-number groups may be organisationally and strategically more cohesive in capturing inequality-inducing rents from the political process.

Cooperative outcomes are difficult to attain, even in small-sized group settings, unless underlined by a modicum of trustful relations amongst entangled agents. The recognition of an existing, shared identity amongst individuals generates "bonding" social capital, in the form of better trust and stronger connections within a given meso-level group. Given the assumption of multiple identities by individuals, it is also possible for a "bridging" social capital to develop between members of disparate groups (Putnam 2000; Chamlee-Wright 2008; Meadowcroft and Pennington 2008). It is worth noting in this context the theoretical contribution of Ronald Burt (1992). His conception of "structural holes" stresses the role of certain network players—situated between multiple, relatively dense networks—which disseminate valuable information between the networks. These "link entrepreneurs" can become trusted players by members presently embedded within strongly connected network structures, irrespective of varying identities, helping to further cultivate social capital more broadly.

Group identities also aid in overcoming cultural and social knowledge problems by promoting consistent expectations concerning the ways and means by which diverse people conduct themselves. The maintenance of certain norms, traditions, and values by group members "develop sound expectations about one another's behaviour, even if cases where we are not in direct contact. If two people share a culture, it is likely that they will be able to anticipate one another's day-to-day activities—including their economic activities—so that they can adjust their own to them" (Tebble 2017). To put this in another way, the emergence of a form of identity which is reasonably accepted by most people can help make individuals legible to others.

It is possible that the presence of multiple group identities can lead to inter-group variations in expectations, complicating any desire to navigate interpersonal engagements across groups. However, those costs are likely to be more manageable should members of various groups welcome the involvement of outsiders, at least to a meaningful extent, and with expectations openly communicated to members and non-members alike. Commingling in an entangled political economy can help promote social learning. Individuals with an ability to better relate to people subscribing to different identities are more likely to be adaptable in the face of shifting conditions, possessing greater potential to become prosperous compared to those actors with more "clannish" appetites (Rubin 2002).

Although classical liberalism in its modern guise is most commonly associated with individualism, groups practically play a vital role in promoting civil society that all liberals cherish. The genius of the liberal ideal of an "open society" is that an ability to attain an identity, and to derive benefits from affiliation with identity, is the result of voluntary choice, instead of the consequence of some preordained, collective assignment to meso-retained group categories. The philosopher Loren Lomasky has noted that, "[b]y minimizing the scope of the mandatory, liberalism maximizes the domain of the voluntary. That, of course, includes voluntary association. … Groups will wax and wane in response to the desires of the individuals who enter into them or defect" (Lomasky 2002, pp. 64, 65).

As mentioned, the open society, perhaps best represented as a complex adaptive process (Buckley 1968; Novak 2018), represents an integral part of a broader system of liberty. It provides the greatest possibility for each and all to fulfil some of their more important desires—including the enjoyment of liberty itself. Group identity, to the extent it is the by-product of voluntaristic forms of cooperative efforts to secure and share joint gains, plays an integral role enabling individuals to fulfil their aspirations and to write their own life stories.

The "Groupishness" of Human Behaviour as a Source of Discrimination and Exclusion

Although identity is an instrumental feature of our sense of self, the reality is that identity is not wholly individually determined. Social and bio-political considerations may condition the extent to which an individual fully self-determines at least their group identity. At the time of our birth, or close enough to it, many aspects of identity are chosen for us by parents and relatives, and are duly registered by government agencies. These identity attributes cannot be amended easily, or in a costless manner, later in life. Childhood socialisation also plays a major influence upon an individual's lifelong senses of individual and group identity, as explained in great detail by Norbert Elias ([1939] 2000). Immense peer, cultural, and social pressures are also imposed upon adults to conform to norms and practices associated with certain group affiliations.

Even if we counter with the strong assumption that identity is, instead, wholly the product of individual influence, there may still be adverse consequences attached to the kinds of selections that a person makes. This is attributable, in no small part, to the propensity of human beings to act "groupishly" towards one another—treating members of out-groups (whomever and however defined) less favourably than would otherwise be the case. Haidt (2012) refers to the human tendency towards groupishness as being situated in mechanisms which promote adeptness by way of promoting the interests of one's favoured groups in competition against others. A large number of studies appear to confirm the existence of favourable in-group biases in social interaction (Sherif et al. 1961; Tajfel 1970; Greenwald et al. 1998; Hewstone et al. 2002).

In an important account of the moralistic basis of inter-group conflict, Joshua Greene identified several ways in which social biasedness can exacerbate frictions between those affiliated with different group identities:

> First, human tribes are tribalistic, favoring Us over Them. Second, tribes have genuine disagreements about how society should be organized, emphasizing, to different extents, the rights of individuals versus the greater good of the group. Tribal values also differ along other dimensions, such as the role of honor in prescribing responses to threats. Third, tribes have distinctive moral commitments, typically religious ones, whereby moral authority is vested in local individuals, texts, traditions, and deities that other groups don't recognize as authoritative. Fourth, tribes, like the individuals within them, are prone to biased fairness, allowing group-level self-interest to distort their sense of justice. Fifth, tribal beliefs are easily biased. Biased beliefs arise from simple self-interest, but also from more complex social dynamics. Once a belief becomes a cultural identity badge, it can perpetuate itself, even as it undermines the tribe's interests. Finally, the way

> we process information about social events can cause us to underestimate the harm we cause others, leading to the escalation of conflict. (Greene 2013, p. 99)

The purpose of these points is not to dismiss the importance of group identity as such, but to underline a suggestion that individuals can be prone to *thinking* in groupish terms. As noted by Greene, "[s]ocial space is complex and multidimensional, but at least one thing is clear from both common sense and boatloads of social scientific research: We humans pay exquisitely close attention to where people reside in our egocentric social universes, and we tend to favor people who are closer to us. Call this tendency *tribalism*, which is sometimes known as *parochial altruism*" (Ibid., pp. 49–50). Recalling a brief discussion in Chap. 3, John Hartley and Jason Potts similarly refer to a "universal adversarialism" wherein "our groupishness is also groupish: we make in-groups and out-groups" (Hartley and Potts 2014, p. 274).

A fraught issue, consequent to the adoption of universally adversarial attitudes, has been the development of status hierarchies. To put it simply, the members of in-groups are valorised, whereas, by contrast, out-group members are denigrated (Fourie 2012; Spinner-Halev 1995). The lack of due consideration to identifiable members of out-groups often manifests itself in prejudice—the harbouring of negative attitudes, opinions, and viewpoints towards individual members of out-groups, and to out-groups more generally—and discrimination, referring to negative actions and behaviours conducted against out-group members, and the out-group in its entirety. Research conducted by Sarah Fiske (2009; also Harris and Fiske 2006) points to a disturbing trend that prejudice and discrimination could descend into a promulgation of dehumanising attitudes directed towards members of certain out-groups.

Fractious group relations pose a significant, though not insurmountable, challenge to those counteracting processes which innovatively strive to break down group-categorical barriers. Studies have indicated that discrimination and prejudice can be reduced through frequency of interaction (Allport 1954; Kurzban et al. 2001; Brown and Hewstone 2005). The intersectionality presented by adherence to multiple group identities potentially serves as another hedge against group adversity, as individuals attempt to reconcile the imperatives of the multiple groups they affiliate with or support:

> Individuals can have pro-own-group allegiances to different social groups that on average practice anti-other group behavior toward one another, and individuals can even find themselves being anti-own group in circumstances where their other group loyalties are pre-eminent. Thus the sharp dividing line between pro-own-group and anti-other-group behavior is blurred, and *intra*group conflict interacts with *inter*group conflict. (Davis 2015, p. 1216)

The economic order is one environment in which "social distance" may be reduced, with classical liberals conceiving that market-based interactions foster peaceful relations between people. It is possible to envision broader circumstances wherein intertwining relationships with entangled political economy act as disinfectants against groupism—in the sense that open-ended and criss-crossing economic, social, and political relationships would facilitate networking and social learning amongst people of many backgrounds and perspectives. It is conceivable the exercise of universal adversarialism can be redressed through the accumulation of experiences in dealing with others, necessarily arising from networked human entanglement, as well as the adoption and practice of toleration towards others. Group frictions are more likely to hold sway over a prolonged period, by contrast, if economic, social, and political interactions are limited or misshapen in any substantive manner.

Public Sector Enforcement of Group-Based Discriminatory Norms

The political scientist James C. Scott (1998) contends that a perennial project of statecraft is to make the individual members of society legible for the purpose of facilitating fiscal and regulatory policies. As noted by Scott, through his description of the ratification of surnames as identity markers, we similarly view the long-held governmental practice of codifying individual and group identities as a key component of the broader political quest to render diverse individuals legible. Legibility of the population (subjects) by political agents (rulers) is, of course, closely associated with manipulability of the subjects in fiscal and regulatory terms.

We can take this insight into the "politics of identity" a step further. Amplifying the power to tax and regulate appears well served by "sedentarising," or rendering fixed, official identity classifications. This notion, combined with factors such as conservative cultural attitudes, serves as a potential explanation for why identity so often serves as a flashpoint for social tectonics in entangled political economy—the inherently evolutionary conception of identity, as outlined previously, clashes with the political interest to engender fixity of identity norms.

In truth, the human tendency to undermine the aspirations, interests, and values of those deemed as possessing out-group identities often found historically safe harbour in the form of discriminatory government policies. Formal discrimination is typically associated with political efforts to codify and control identity. In an entangled political economy there would be little doubt that political action bears some responsibility for the consequent inequalities arising from such discriminatory treatments. Moreover, the manipulation of inter-group animosities and tensions for the purposes of concentrating political power and influence seems, on the basis of historical if not contemporary experience, to have been important factors behind the perpetuation of malign social phenomena such as racism, sexism, and xenophobia.

Researchers versed in public choice theory interpret the government-enforced magnification of in-group/out-group animosity as an important application of interest-group theory. Jennifer Roback (1984, 1986, 1989, 1991) notably promulgated a research programme illustrating how selective interests lobbied government to implement and maintain racialist policy settings. Formal discrimination also adjusts the relative costs, and benefits, of identifying oneself as members of the advantaged in-groups and disadvantaged out-groups. All else being equal, the dispensing of fiscal or regulatory advantages for in-groups is likely to encourage more people attempting to identify themselves as in-group members, and label rivals as out-group members, at least on the margins. Roback (1991) also illustrates that government-enforced discrimination often led to legal challenges regarding who is, and is not, eligible to receive benefits on the basis of group identity.

The "Baptist and bootlegger" positioning of competing interests also features in the politics of identity. Art Carden (2012) observed that "[i]dentity channeled through the political process likely creates 'Baptist and bootlegger' coalitions of pure rent-seekers and observers who derive identity utility from keeping others limited to what they think should be their socially prescribed roles." Several researchers have identified labour unions as an influential "bootlegging" interest group pressing for restrictions against the entry of women, immigrants, and racial minorities into the domestic labour market. Union representatives in the U.S. expressed fears that entry by African-Americans and migrants into unionised occupations would undercut the wages of white workers (Bernstein 2000, 2001; Moreno 2010). It has been noted that some of the major American labour unions themselves were resistant to admit African-Americans into their ranks, at least up to and during the mid-twentieth century (Hill 1961).

Interest-group attempts to entrench discrimination were often deeply infused with moralising statements and conduct. The proclamation of non-logical rationalisations for state-sponsored racial discrimination was abundant in the U.S. during the era of slavery, and the *de jure* segregation in the American South from the late nineteenth century to the 1960s. Higgs (1977) and Grynaviski and Munger (2017) noted that racists regarded African-Americans as, allegedly, less than human, somehow necessitating the dispensation of "positive duties of care" for slaves on the part of slaveholders. Some racists maintained pseudo-scientific beliefs to proclaim the inferiority of African-Americans relative to Europeans. Others cast about stereotypes to the effect that blacks were unintelligent, unproductive, and prone to criminality. These stereotypical arguments, unfounded in reality, were used by the propagators of government-enforced racism as rhetorical cover for the economic, social, and political subordination of blacks and other minorities in inter-group relations.

Government controls over immigration during a large part of the twentieth century also bore a close relation to racist attitudes. A notorious example of the intersection of racism and xenophobia came in the form of the "White Australia" policy, heavily restricting the entry of non-European migrants into Australia during the early twentieth century. Following punitive restrictions against Asian and Pacific Islander immigration during the preceding decades, the newly federated Australia in 1901 imposed the *Immigration Restriction Act*. The legislation included a "language dictation test" provision requiring that applicants for entry must write a passage of 50 words in a European language as directed by an immigration officer (Australian Government 2017), essentially designed to discourage immigration from Africa and Asia with few native European-language speakers.

The *Immigration Restriction Act 1901* and subsequent amending legislation heralded decades of discriminatory Australian immigration policy, eventually unwound by the early 1970s. The White Australia policy, whilst in place, was generally supported by the major political parties and drew backing from loose coalitions elsewhere within Australian society. The latter groups included unions and businesses, seeking to protect white labourers from rigorous labour market competition, and others looking to promote more explicitly racist or xenophobic objectives. However, these measures were not uniformly accepted; for example, the classical liberal William Foxall (writing under the *nom-de-plume* "Gizen-no-teki") outlined a penetrating early criticism of the foundations of White Australia policy (Foxall 1903; Kemp 2011).

Governments enacted policies to restrain the influx of specific populations entering their countries and, in some cases expelled minority groups (such as Australia's Pacific Islander population during the late nineteenth and early twentieth centuries). Australia, Canada, New Zealand, and the U.S. imposed legislation to prohibit the immigration of Chinese labourers into their countries. In New Zealand, the *Chinese Immigrants Act 1881* restricted the entry of Chinese people in accordance with the weight of the ship they arrived on, and a poll tax was also imposed upon migrants from China. Subsequent legislation increased naturalisation fees for Chinese arrivals, raised poll taxes, introduced literacy and reading tests, and imposed fingerprint identification for Chinese people temporarily departing New Zealand (O'Connor 1968; Ferguson 2003). These forms of governmental discrimination were complemented by widespread stigmatisation of Asians in political discourse, popular media, and public places.

The entangled character of public policy meant that immigration and citizenship standards often intertwined with other policies, such as defence and national security, to rationalise the exclusion of minorities. During World War I, Australian, British, and Canadian authorities detained German-born residents and others on the presumption that they may advance the cause of wartime enemies, whereas the likes of Australia and U.S. established internment camps for people of Japanese origin during World War II. Of course, Nazi Germany became most notorious for the systemic repression and violence meted out against its Jewish citizens, and Jews in occupied countries, including through its concentration camp system (Stone 2017).

Legislators and bureaucrats also mingled with interest groups, such as labour unions and large businesses, to economically discriminate against women. Leonard (2016) indicates that misogynist, and sometimes racialist, sentiments were used to rationalise regulatory and other measures blocking women's labour market participation. It had been argued in several quarters that biological and other considerations dictated that women were primarily suited to be child-bearers and "homemakers," whereas men were better equipped to be "breadwinning" factory and office-site workers on behalf of their family. Other matters, such as the supposed threat of low-wage-earning women to male employment, were also invoked to restrict female participation in the workforce (Novak 2015).

The kinds of discriminatory restrictions levelled against women in developed countries were quite extensive in their reach. Women were subjected to occupational segregation legislation, banned from some lines of work and with numbers restricted in others, as well as limitations upon the number of hours they can work (Kirkby 1987). The public services of several countries, including Australia, Ireland, and the U.S., and large companies introduced "marriage bar" legislation obliging single working women to relinquish their positions upon marriage (Goldin 1990). It has also been noted that income tax exemptions, and similar privileges embedded within the tax system, were established so as to effectively discourage the uptake of work by potentially secondary wage-earners (mainly women) within a household (McCaffery 1997; Skwire 2018). Part of the explanation for the governmental welfare state during the early twentieth century rested upon fiscal initiatives—for example, maternity and child payments—with the intention of promoting birth rates and keeping women in the home (Tucker 2016).

Malign group-oriented attitudes to the effect that women were subservient to men were also reflected in general economic regulations pertaining to property rights and contracting. Coverture legislation in the U.S., United Kingdom, and elsewhere generally prevented individual women from signing contracts, inheriting property, or owning their own property (at least not without the express consent of their husbands) (Salmon 1986; Combs 2006; Cowie 2009). These restrictive provisions were eventually relaxed, and later abolished. These reforms were the result of factors such as interjurisdictional competition for a larger population base (Lemke 2016b), as well as opinion-shifting arguments for greater group-equality between women and men (Novak 2016).

On several occasions, Richard Wagner (2009, 2010, 2017) invokes Martin Buber's notion that the calibre of human relationships broadly resembles either "I-Thou" or "I-It" categories. In essence, "I-Thou" relationships are typified by mutuality and respect between two individuals, or groups of individuals. In the case of "I-It" relationships, there is a tendency for one person (or group of persons) to treat another as an object to be acted upon and manipulated. "The use of people as objects and not as subjects is surely a cardinal operating principle of state-based enterprises," Wagner (2010, p. 177) states. This contention does not appear misplaced against the record of the politicisation of gender, nationality, race, and many other forms of individual and group identity.

Implications of Group-Discrimination for Income and Wealth Inequalities

One should reasonably wish to redress discriminatory behaviour and conduct to the greatest extent practicable, and not merely for ethical and moral reasons. Discrimination is also better avoided on consequentialist grounds. Scanlon (2018) refers to the potential impacts of caste and class distinctions, and of discrimination, upon inequality, whereby individuals deemed to belong to the out-groups are denied employment and other important avenues for economic interaction. Severely restricting economic and social participation of minorities, government discrimination often attempted to give in-group members something of a privileged "head start," accessing the best of life's opportunities. In more general terms, Bowles et al. (2014) and Rothstein (2017) discuss the legacy effects of past episodes of *de jure* discrimination with regard to minority access to education, housing, and other services.

Many observers suggest the loosening of impediments against previously derided and victimised out-groups has yielded some important results. Average, or median, income and wealth for previously discriminated group-members has grown. Ethnic and racial minorities and women are, on average, enjoying significant improvements in other measures of well-being over a relatively short period of time (Higgs 1977; Smith and Welch 1989; Margo 1993; Welch 2003; Goldin 2006, 2014). Although improvements along these lines have been observed, it is clear that statistically unequal outcomes between groups persist. In the terminology applied by Douglas Rae, there remains a degree of "bloc-regarding inequality." There is also an important distinction between bloc-regarding inequality and so-called "individual-regarding inequality," which assesses outcomes among individuals only:

> [b]lack and white median incomes, for example, might be precisely equal, yet there could be tremendous inequality among blacks, among whites, and within society as a whole. The same point holds … for all other examples of bloc-regarding equality, whether by race, sex, age, native tongue, or sexual preference, and whether aimed at the distribution of income, power, prestige, or leisure. Bloc-regarding equality asks for something very different from individual-regarding … equalities. (Rae 1981, p. 35)

From an entangled political economy perspective, the implications of the commingled relationships between actors within society, including for economic inequality, are necessarily *complex*. Therefore, statistical comparisons providing a representation of bloc outcomes, necessarily "collapsing" people into group categories, conceal much of the variations between individuals. A risk-loving individual, for example, may receive a higher rate of pay because of "compensating differentials," or that amount of additional remuneration needed to compensate for riskier or more dangerous work. Alternatively, a workaholic who decides to work multiple jobs would receive additional wages (Wagner 2017).

One way in which discrimination potentially exudes harm is through the revelation of preferences or "tastes" for discriminatory treatment against out-group members. An iconic theoretical treatment in this context was provided by Gary Becker. As he put it, "[w]hen an employer discriminates against employees, he acts as if he incurs non-pecuniary, psychic costs of production by employing them; when an employee discriminates against fellow employees or employers, he acts as if he incurs non-pecuniary, psychic costs of employment by working with them; when a consumer discriminates against products, he acts as if he incurs non-pecuniary, psychic costs of consumption by consuming them" (Becker 1971, p. 153).

Becker's model of discrimination was primarily applied to the case of racial discrimination of African-Americans by American whites. The model can be applied to conceivably any instance in which discrimination is conceptualised as a manifestation of underlying preferences to withhold economic cooperation from members of perceived out-groups. Whereas non-liberals often raise the worry that discrimination is not obliterated in the classical liberal state-of-the-world, the upshot of the Beckerian analysis is that discriminators are confronted with the relatively greater costs associated with indulging their preferences—with the costs of discrimination becoming more apparent in more competitive market settings.

Another strand of discrimination theory developed by mainstream economists is that of "statistical discrimination," largely associated with the works of Arrow (1972) and Phelps (1972). Statistical discrimination theories indicate that employment discrimination arises in light of a lack of sufficient information about worker characteristics. In the absence of any specific information about the productivity performance of individual workers, an employer may believe that non-white workers are less productive than white workers. It is on this basis that employers discriminate against non-whites when undertaking hiring decisions. Practically, this means that employers are likely to hire fewer non-whites and, when doing so, on lower wage rates.

These neoclassical models, including Becker's, suffer from the inherent limitations of all exercises positing a comparative-static, equilibrating conception of economic action. Economists versed in market-process perspectives submit that the prevalence of statistical discrimination is likely to dissipate, in light of entrepreneurial action by labour market participants to disclose better information about individual worker characteristics (McCabe 2009). Even discrimination under Becker's taste model can be redressed by entrepreneurial action, insofar as the unemployment of minorities—who would ordinarily be hired in greater number absent discrimination—represents an error on the part of discriminatory suppliers potentially subject to correction.

Market interactions can even help resolve discrimination arising from consumer tastes, which was another possibility that Becker raised in his treatise. Under this possibility, suppliers refuse to hire racial and other minorities because of the threat of discriminating consumers boycotting the purchase of goods and services, or, in some other way, wish to have their demand for discrimination embodied in the furnished bundle of outputs for sale onto the market. In other words, discrimination materialises as firms meeting consumer preferences for discrimination are rewarded.

It is anecdotally observed that, for the largest part, entrepreneurs do not necessarily cater to the discriminatory tastes of customers. Indeed, economic entrepreneurs can invoke strategies revealing to consumers the costs associated with their taste for discrimination (Coyne et al. 2007, 2010). By way of an example, it is considered that consumers are likely to change their minds about discrimination if the employment of "unpopular" (discriminated against) labour input coincides with an improvement in final product quality. Coyne and his colleagues refer to an interesting case example of this: the hiring of African-American baseball players by U.S. Major League Baseball teams. In essence, it is suggested discrimination by baseball fans dissipates as the incorporation of African-American players on a given team contributes to an improved winning record.

Economic positions may have been much more closely aligned with status positions in entangled political economies of the past. This is the result of group-discriminatory public policies, creating a more easily identified correspondence between income earnings, wealth holdings, and group identities. "If we are to take the repression of blacks as an exemplar," wrote Fabio Rojas, "then we would think that social inequality often results when one group uses violence, custom, and state policy to exclude another group from important opportunities and resources. In addition to normal variations in ability, personality, and temperament, inequality is also shaped by the relationship between larger groups in society, especially how superior groups relate to lower-status groups via violence and monopolization of resources" (Rojas 2017, pp. 22–23).

In an open, liberal society, characterised by the erasure of formal discrimination, individuals irrespective of their background are more willing and able to exercise personalised choices. Exercising those choices may eventually be reflected in statistical measures of group-based, bloc inequalities of income and wealth. The easing of restrictions concerning how individuals and groups are to engage one another (Lemke 2015, 2016a, b) may have complicated group-based narratives of inequality to an extent, because the more overt forms of discrimination were no longer present to consign certain group members as economic and social outcasts. The most pressing consideration here is that inequality is an emergent outcome, consequent to entanglement, and that such inequality should not necessarily be construed as normatively undesirable. After all, unequal distributions in such cases are not reflective of liberty-inconsistent patterns of interaction yielding "bad" inequality.

However, as the contemporary discussions about gender and racial pay gaps illustrate, there remains significant concern that group economic disparities have not closed. Non-formal manifestations of discrimination and prejudice have also remained the subject of critical scrutiny. An example of this are the studies into "unconscious bias" which indicate that individual job applicants with non-white sounding names are less likely to receive job interviews, even though their skills are similar, if not identical, to white applicants (Bertrand and Mullainathan 2004; Wood et al. 2009). Others have noted that stereotyping—say, in the realm of gender relations, that girls are allegedly not as capable as boys in excelling at mathematics and science—could also fashion individual choices later in life which translate into occupational segregation. The decline of state sanctions, often complemented by violent vigilantism and stifling cultural and social norms, does not suggest, however, that all forms of discrimination have abated. Therefore, a study of the inequality effects of social exclusion remains a valid exercise from the vantage point of entangled political economy.

Conclusion

The effects of identity and status upon income and wealth inequalities have been the subject of extensive research in recent years. Racism, xenophobia, and sexism are viewed by many researchers, in sociology, psychology, and, increasingly, economics, as primary channels through which such status-oriented effects can be discerned. Our interest in the foundations and implications of identity rests upon a core proposition of entangled political economy theory: interpersonal interactions are shaped by rules which shape the incentives actors face when making their decisions, and which mobilise information to facilitate social learning (Boettke 2012). Identity, how we complexly see ourselves and others, is conceived here as an integral part of the overall rule-structure that individuals and their agencies rely upon to navigate their worlds as they seek out exchange opportunities with others.

The enforcement of non-general, discriminatory fiscal and regulatory policies designed on a group basis raises the probability that out-group members will find themselves stuck within the lower reaches of income and wealth distributions. This is the case so long that the policies effectively impede minority out-group members from opportunities to forge their own meaningful network connections. It is understood that government can heavily influence discriminatory attitudes towards groups of people, given the heightened esteem and prestige generally surrounding political action. At the same time, government policy is informed by prevailing attitudes of group-adversarialism held by certain members of society.

Discrimination against unfavoured out-group members risks aggravating economic inequality. Fundamentally, attempts by political actors to sustain group distinctions openly flout evolutionary notions of identity formation and persistence which reflect wholesale, bottom-up engagement with experimentation, interaction, and selection (Potts 2011). Identity evolution is synonymous with economic, social, and political growth and change, patterns defiled by countervailing political efforts to keep group-identity cleavages in place for the purposes of control and influence. In this view, discrimination on the basis of race, gender, nationality, and so on, has much the same kinds of deleterious impacts as trade protections shielding incumbent producers from entrepreneurial challenge beyond the country's borders.

As the effect of the more overt forms of discrimination enshrined in the political process wanes, greater attention is accorded to group-based differences in economic, social, and political achievements. There remains much debate about the predominating causes underpinning the reproduction of group differences, but factors, such as the legacy of past policies, social attitudes, and the discriminatory effects of existing policies, have been frequently cited in research. Given the core ethical principle of classical liberalism that persons are not to be treated as the ends of others, these matters concerning the intersection of economic and social inequalities will be revisited later in this book.

References

Akerlof, George A., and Rachel E. Kranton. 2000. Economics and Identity. *The Quarterly Journal of Economics* 115 (3): 715–753.

———. 2010. *Identity Economics: How Our Identities Shape Our Work, Wages, and Well-Being*. Princeton, NJ: Princeton University Press.

Allport, Gordon W. 1954. *The Nature of Prejudice*. Cambridge, MA: Addison-Wesley.

Arrow, Kenneth J. 1972. Models of Job Discrimination. In *Racial Discrimination in Economic Life*, ed. Anthony H. Pascal. Lexington, MA: Heath.

Australian Government. 2017. *Immigration Restriction Act 1901*. Federal Register of Legislation. Accessed November 12, 2017. https://www.legislation.gov.au/Details/C1901A00017

Becker, Gary S. 1971. *The Economics of Discrimination*. 2nd ed. Chicago, IL: University of Chicago Press.

Bernstein, David E. 2000. Racism, Railroad Unions, and Labor Regulations. *The Independent Review* 5 (2): 237–247.

———. 2001. *Only One Place of Redress: African-Americans, Labor Regulations, and the Courts from Reconstruction to the New Deal*. Durham, NC: Duke University Press.

Bertrand, Marianne, and Sendhil Mullainathan. 2004. Are Emily and Greg More Employable Than Lakisha and Jamal? A Field Experiment on Labor Market Discrimination. *The American Economic Review* 94 (4): 991–1013.

Boettke, Peter. 2012. The Liberalism of Classical Liberalism. *Bleeding Heart Libertarians blog*, January 26. Accessed November 13, 2017. http://bleedingheartlibertarians.com/2012/01/the-liberalism-of-classical-liberalism/

Bowles, Samuel, Glenn C. Loury, and Rajiv Sethi. 2014. Group Inequality. *Journal of the European Economic Association* 12 (1): 129–152.

Brown, Taleed J. 2016. Cultural Appropriation is Love. *Foundation of Economic Education blog*, October 31. Accessed November 11, 2017. https://fee.org/articles/cultural-appropriation-is-love/

Brown, Rupert, and Miles Hewstone. 2005. An Integrative Theory of Intergroup Conflict. *Advances in Experimental Social Psychology* 37: 255–343.

Buckley, William F. 1968. Society as a Complex Adaptive System. In *Modern Systems Research for the Behavioral Scientist: A Sourcebook*, ed. William F. Buckley, 490–513. Chicago, IL: Aldine Publishing Company.

Burt, Ronald S. 1992. *Structural Holes: The Social Structure of Competition*. Cambridge, MA: Harvard University Press.

Byng, Michelle D. 2012. You Can't Get There from Here: A Social Process Theory of Racism and Race. *Critical Sociology* 39 (5): 705–715.

Carden, Art. 2012. Identity Economics: How Our Identities Shape Our Work, Wages, and Well-Being. *Foundation of Economic Education blog*, March 28. Accessed November 9, 2017. https://fee.org/articles/identity-economics-how-our-identities-shape-our-work-wages-and-well-being/

Chamlee-Wright, Emily. 2008. The Structure of Social Capital: An Austrian Perspective on Its Nature and Development. *Review of Political Economy* 20 (1): 41–58.

Clair, Matthew, and Jeffrey S. Denis. 2015. Racism, Sociology Of. In *International Encyclopedia of the Social & Behavioral Sciences*, ed. James D. Wright, vol. 19, 2nd ed., 857–863. Amsterdam, Netherlands: Elsevier.

Combs, Mary Beth. 2006. *Cui Bono?* The 1870 British Married Women's Property Act, Bargaining Power, and the Distribution of Resources Within Marriage. *Feminist Economics* 12 (1–2): 51–83.

Cowen, Nick. 2013. What Would Hayek Say About Gendered Violence? In *What Would Hayek Say Today (Really?)*, ed. Legatum Institute, 27–29. London, UK: Legatum Institute.

Cowie, Andrew James. 2009. A History of Married Women's Real Property Rights. *Australian Journal of Gender and Law* 6: 1–21.

Coyne, Christopher J., Justin P. Isaacs, and Jeremy T. Schwartz. 2010. Entrepreneurship and the Taste for Discrimination. *Journal of Evolutionary Economics* 20: 609–627.

Coyne, Christopher J., Justin P. Isaacs, Jeremy T. Schwartz, and Anthony M. Carilli. 2007. Put Me in, Coach, I'm Ready to Play. *Review of Austrian Economics* 20: 237–246.

Davis, John B. 2003. *The Theory of the Individual in Economics: Identity and Value*. New York, NY: Routledge.

———. 2011. *Individuals and Identity in Economics*. New York, NY: Cambridge University Press.

———. 2014. Social Capital and Social Identity: Trust and Conflict. In *Social Capital and Economics: Social Values, Power, and Identity*, ed. Asimina Christoforou and John Bryan Davis, 98–112. New York: Routledge.

———. 2015. Stratification Economics and Identity Economics. *Cambridge Journal of Economics* 39 (5): 1215–1229.

Dunbar, Robin. 1992. Neocortex Size as a Constraint on Group Size in Primates. *Journal of Human Evolution* 22 (6): 469–493.

Elias, Norbert. (1939) 2000. *The Civilizing Process: Sociogenetic and Psychogenetic Investigations*. Revised ed. Translated by Edmund Jephcott. Oxford, UK: Blackwell Publishing.

Fearon, James D. 1999. What is Identity (As We Now Use the Word)? Stanford University, Department of Economics, November 3. Accessed November 8, 2017. https://web.stanford.edu/group/fearon-research/cgi-bin/wordpress/wp-content/uploads/2013/10/What-is-Identity-as-we-now-use-the-word-.pdf

Ferguson, Philip. 2003. The Making of the White New Zealand Policy: Nationalism, Citizenship and the Exclusion of the Chinese, 1880–1920. Doctoral thesis, University of Canterbury.

Fiske, Sarah. 2009. From Dehumanization and Objectification, to Rehumanization: Neuroimaging Studies on the Building Blocks of Empathy. *Annals of the New York Academy of Sciences* 1167: 31–34.

Fourie, Carina. 2012. What is Social Equality? An Analysis of Status Equality as a Strongly Egalitarian Ideal. *Res Publica* 18 (2): 107–126.

Foxall, Edward William. ("Gizen-no-teki"). 1903. *Colorphobia: An Exposure of the White Australia Fallacy*. Sydney, Australia: R. T. Kelly.

Goldin, Claudia. 1990. *Understanding the Gender Gap: An Economic History of American Women*. New York, NY: Oxford University Press.

———. 2006. The Quiet Revolution That Transformed Women's Employment, Education, and Family. *American Economic Review* 96 (2): 1–21.
———. 2014. A Grand Gender Convergence: Its Last Chapter. *American Economic Review* 104 (4): 1091–1119.
Greene, Joshua. 2013. *Moral Tribes: Emotion, Reason, and the Gap Between Us and Them*. New York, NY: Penguin Press.
Greenwald, Anthony G., Debbie E. McGhee, and Jordan L.K. Schwartz. 1998. Measuring Individual Differences in Implicit Cognition: The Implicit Association Test. *Journal of Personality and Social Psychology* 74 (6): 1464–1480.
Grynaviski, Jeffrey D., and Michael C. Munger. 2017. Reconstructing Racism: Transforming Racial Hierarchy from "Necessary Evil" into "Positive Good". *Social Philosophy and Policy* 34 (1): 144–163.
Haidt, Jonathan. 2012. *The Righteous Mind: Why Good People Are Divided by Politics and Religion*. New York, NY: Pantheon Books.
Harris, Lasana T., and Susan T. Fiske. 2006. Dehumanizing the Lowest of the Low: Neuroimaging Responses to Extreme Out-Groups. *Psychological Science* 17 (10): 847–853.
Hartley, John, and Jason Potts. 2014. *Cultural Science: A Natural History of Stories, Demes, Knowledge and Innovation*. London, UK: Bloomsbury.
Hermann-Pillath, Carsten. 2013. *Foundations of Economic Evolution: A Treatise on the Natural Philosophy of Economics*. Cheltenham, UK: Edward Elgar.
Hewstone, Miles, Mark Rubin, and Hazel Willis. 2002. Intergroup Bias. *Annual Review of Psychology* 53: 575–604.
Higgs, Robert. 1977. *Competition and Coercion: Blacks in the American Economy, 1865–1914*. New York, NY: Cambridge University Press.
Hill, Herbert. 1961. Racism Within Organized Labor: A Report of Five Years of the AFL-CIO, 1955–1960. *The Journal of Negro Education* 30 (2): 109–118.
Kemp, David. 2011. Edward William Foxall: A Classical Liberal in a Racist Age. *Policy* 27 (3): 35–43.
Kirkby, Diane. 1987. "The Wage-Earning Woman and the State": The National Women's Trade Union League and Protective Labor Legislation, 1903–1923. *Labor History* 28 (1): 54–74.
Kurzban, Robert, John Tooby, and Leda Cosmides. 2001. Can Race Be Erased? Coalitional Computation and Social Categorization. *Proceedings of the National Academy of Sciences* 98 (26): 15387–15392.
Latour, Bruno. 2005. *Reassembling the Social: An Introduction to Actor-Network Theory*. Oxford, UK: Oxford University Press.

Lemke, Jayme S. 2015. An Austrian Approach to Class Structure. *Advances in Austrian Economics* 19: 167–192.
Lemke, Jayme. 2016a. Class Structures as Complex Systems. *Liberty Fund, Liberty Matters blog*, November 4. Accessed November 10, 2017. http://oll.libertyfund.org/pages/lm-class
———. 2016b. Interjurisdictional Competition and the Married Women's Property Acts. *Public Choice* 166 (3–4): 291–313.
Leonard, Thomas C. 2016. *Illiberal Reformers: Race, Eugenics & American Economics in the Progressive Era*. Princeton, NJ: Princeton University Press.
Lomasky, Loren. 2002. Classical Liberalism and Civil Society. In *Alternative Conceptions of Civil Society*, ed. Simone Chambers and Will Kymlicka. Princeton, NJ: Princeton University Press.
Malik, Kenan. 2017. In Defense of Cultural Appropriation. *The New York Times*, June 14. Accessed November 11, 2017. https://www.nytimes.com/2017/06/14/opinion/in-defense-of-cultural-appropriation.html
Margo, Robert A. 1993. What Is the Key to Black Progress? In *Second Thoughts: Myths and Morals in U.S. Economic History*, ed. Deirdre N. McCloskey, 65–69. New York, NY: Oxford University Press.
McCabe, Joshua T. 2009. Toward an (Austrian) Economics of Discrimination. Paper presented at Austrian Student Scholars Conference, October 31. Accessed November 9, 2017. http://www2.gcc.edu/dept/econ/ASSC/Papers2009/McCabe_Discrimination.pdf
McCaffery, Edward J. 1997. *Taxing Women: How the Marriage Penalty Affects Your Taxes*. Chicago, IL: University of Chicago Press.
Meadowcroft, John, and Mark Pennington. 2008. Bonding and Bridging: Social Capital and the Communitarian Critique of Liberal Markets. *Review of Austrian Economics* 21: 119–133.
Moreno, Paul. 2010. Unions and Discrimination. *Cato Journal* 30 (1): 67–85.
Novak, Mikayla. 2015. Gender Hierarchy During the Progressive Era: Thoughts and Practices. Cato Institute, *libertarianism.org*, February 11. Accessed November 12, 2017. https://www.libertarianism.org/columns/gender-hierarchy-during-progressive-era-thoughts-practices
———. 2016. Feminism and Liberty's Emancipation Sequence. Cato Institute, *libertarianism.org*, January 15. Accessed November 12, 2017. https://www.libertarianism.org/columns/feminism-libertys-emancipation-sequence
———. 2018. Civil Society as a Complex Adaptive Phenomenon. *Cosmos + Taxis* 5 (3–4): 3–13.
O'Connor, P.S. 1968. Keeping New Zealand White, 1908–1920. *New Zealand Journal of History* 2 (1): 41–65.

Olson, Mancur. 1965. *The Logic of Collective Action: Public Goods and the Theory of Groups*. Cambridge, MA: Harvard University Press.
Phelps, Edmund S. 1972. The Statistical Theory of Racism and Sexism. *American Economic Review* 62 (4): 659–661.
Potts, Jason. 2008. Economic Evolution, Identity Dynamics and Cultural Science. *Cultural Science* 1 (2): 1–7.
———. 2011. *Creative Industries and Economic Evolution*. Cheltenham, UK: Edward Elgar.
Putnam, Robert D. 2000. *Bowling Alone: The Collapse and Revival of American Community*. New York: Simon & Schuster.
Rae, Douglas. 1981. *Equalities*. Cambridge, MA: Harvard University Press.
Roback, Jennifer. 1984. Southern Labor Law in the Jim Crow Era: Exploitative or Competitive? *The University of Chicago Law Review* 51: 1161–1192.
———. 1986. The Political Economy of Segregation: The Case of Segregated Streetcars. *The Journal of Economic History* 46 (4): 893–917.
———. 1989. Racism as Rent Seeking. *Economic Inquiry* 27: 661–681.
———. 1991. The Separation of Race and State. *Harvard Journal of Law and Public Policy* 14 (1): 58–62.
Rojas, Fabio. 2017. *Theory for the Working Sociologist*. New York, NY: Columbia University Press.
Rothstein, Richard. 2017. *The Color of Law: A Forgotten History of How Our Government Segregated America*. New York, NY: Liverlight Publishing.
Rubin, Paul H. 2002. *Darwinian Politics: The Evolutionary Origin of Freedom*. New Brunswick, NJ: Rutgers University Press.
Salmon, Marylynn. 1986. *Women and the Law of Property in Early America*. Chapel Hill, NC: University of North Carolina Press.
Scanlon, T.M. 2018. *Why Does Inequality Matter?* Oxford, UK: Oxford University Press.
Scott, James C. 1998. *Seeing Like a State: How Certain Schemes to Improve the Human Condition Have Failed*. New Haven, CT: Yale University Press.
Skwire, Sarah. 2018. "History Through a Classical Liberal Feminist Lens". In *What is Classical Liberal History?*, ed. Michael J. Douma and Phillip W. Magness, 159–169. Lanham, MD: Lexington Books.
Sherif, Muzafer, O.J. Harvey, B. Jack White, William R. Hood, and Carolyn W. Sherif. 1961. *Intergroup Conflict and Cooperation: The Robbers Cave Experiment*. Norman, OK: University Book Exchange.
Smith, James P., and Finis R. Welch. 1989. Black Economic Progress After Myrdal. *Journal of Economic Literature* 27 (2): 519–564.

Spinner-Halev, Jeff. 1995. Difference and Diversity in an Egalitarian Democracy. *The Journal of Political Philosophy* 3 (3): 259–279.

Stone, Dan. 2017. *Concentration Camps: A Short History*. Oxford, UK: Oxford University Press.

Tajfel, Henri. 1970. Experiments in Intergroup Discrimination. *Scientific American* 223: 96–102.

Tajfel, Henri, and John Turner. 1979. An Integrative Theory of Intergroup Conflict. In *The Social Psychology of Intergroup Relations*, ed. William G. Austin and Stephen Worchel, 33–47. Monterey, CA: Brooks/Cole.

Tebble, Adam. 2017. Liberty and Equality in an Age of Diversity: Adam Tebble's Epistemic Liberalism: A Defence. *Institute for Humane Studies blog*, July 17. Accessed November 8, 2017. https://theihs.org/blog/liberty-and-equality-in-an-age-of-diversity-adam-tebbles-epistemic-liberalism-a-defence/

Tomasello, Michael, Alicia P. Melis, Claudio Tennie, Emily Wyman, and E. Herrmann. 2012. Two Key Steps in the Evolution of Human Cooperation: The Interdependence Hypothesis. *Current Anthropology* 53 (6): 673–692.

Tucker, Jeffrey. 2016. The Misogynist Origins of American Labor Law. *Foundation of Economic Education blog*, February 17. Accessed November 12, 2017. https://fee.org/articles/government-s-war-on-women-1900-1920/

Veer, Pierre-Guy. 2017. Cultural Appropriation Is Intellectual Property on Stilts. *Foundation of Economic Education blog*, June 29. Accessed November 11, 2017. https://fee.org/articles/cultural-appropriation-does-not-exist/

Wagner, Richard E. 2009. Property, State, and Entangled Political Economy. In *Markets and Politics: Insights from a Political Economy Perspective*, ed. Wolf Schäfer, Andrea Schneider, and Tobias Thomas, 37–49. Marburg, Germany: Metropolis.

———. 2010. *Mind, Society, and Human Action: Time and Knowledge in a Theory of Social Economy*. London, UK: Routledge.

———. 2017. *James M. Buchanan and Liberal Political Economy: A Rational Reconstruction*. Lanham, MD: Lexington Books.

Welch, Finis. 2003. Catching Up: Wages of Black Men. *The American Economic Review* 93 (2): 320–325.

Wood, Martin, Jon Hales, Susan Purdon, Tanja Sejersen, and Oliver Hayllar. 2009. *A Test for Racial Discrimination in Recruitment Practice in British Cities*. UK Department for Work and Pensions, *Research Report No. 607*. Accessed November 10, 2017. http://www.natcen.ac.uk/media/20541/test-for-racial-discrimination.pdf

Part III

Reforms

7

Economic Constitutionalism and Inequality

Introduction

In this book we have put forward the claim that inequality can be viewed as the emergent result of choices by individuals and their agencies. Since numerous patterns of entanglement are conceivable, vastly different outcomes potentially abound from a distributional standpoint. The notion of inequality in entangled political economy contravenes deterministic theories, conceiving that economic inequalities will inexorably worsen (Piketty 2014), as well as the idea of an "optimal" degree of inequality (Okun 1975). In addition, it cannot be reasonably considered that inequality represents the objects of deliberate, non-emergent choice (Wagner 1983, 2017).

The processual nature of inequality does not suggest that it cannot be interpreted as desirable or undesirable on the grounds of informed, but nevertheless normative, judgement. As mentioned previously, it is possible to make a distinction between "good" and "bad" inequality (Watson 2015; Geloso and Horwitz 2017). The classical liberal commitment to voluntaristic and mutually beneficial modes of human action implies that inequalities resulting from triadic, "win-win-lose"

M. Novak, *Inequality*, Palgrave Studies in Classical Liberalism,
https://doi.org/10.1007/978-3-319-89417-1_7

exchanges are categorised as forms of "bad" (or, we might suggest, liberty-inconsistent) inequalities.

In previous chapters, it had been conjectured that several facets of governmental policy have a tendency to increase disparities within income and wealth distributions. Certain fiscal and regulatory policy settings were surmised to embody pro-rich redistributive elements, whereas others, still, limit the capacity for those positioned within the lower distributional bands to economically progress. Policy-induced inequality is, for the greatest part, undesired from a classical liberal perspective. However, the realities of entangled political economy suggest that the actions which give rise to such outcomes cannot be eliminated but can, at best, be influenced. This insight lends itself to an emphasis upon the rule-architectures which structure the conduct of policy development. The proposition that rules structure the legitimised kinds of action to be undertaken by the heterogeneous players involved in public policy serves as a venerable component of classical liberalism.

This chapter aims to provide a sketch of the principles underpinning a rules-based economic policy order which may help ameliorate the incidence of politically induced inequality. Subsequent to a brief survey of the relevant literature outlining the need for rules, this chapter outlines the case for fiscal rules restraining the manipulability of taxation and expenditure policies to effect upward redistribution. This discussion is followed by an explanation of the need for a "regulatory constitution," or interlocking systems of high-quality regulatory policies and governance standards. Given the prominence attached to competition policy in the contemporary inequality debate, this issue will be given a separate treatment in this chapter. This chapter concludes by reaffirming the importance of sound rules for a pro-growth *and* pro-equality economic order.

Necessity of Rules-Based Economic Order, and Perpetual Challenge of Maintaining Good Rules

Throughout history, political authorities have long demonstrated an unwelcome tendency to enact illiberal public policies. Policy innovations have often abridged property, and have frustrated the capacity of individuals looking to forge their own economic connections. Policy decisions by governments have corroded certain aspects of associational life and fostered enmities between social groups which would otherwise be non-existent. Many governments of the past have withheld voting rights and limited political access, and some governments continue to do so. In the worst-case situation, governments, even to this day, have enacted policies, threatening and extinguishing precious human life.

The common temptation is to believe that the problem of selfish and opportunistic political conduct can be resolved by a simple replacement of personalities in positions of power. The limitations of this strategy become clear when it is conceded that the discovery and selection of other-regarding, non-opportunistic angels for political offices is an impossible and unrealistic task. Presupposing that every person is potentially a political knave with an interest in advancing their own self-interested causes (Hume [1741] 1985), classical liberal thinkers have advanced the need for abstract, non-discriminatory, and consistently enforced rules aligning the interests of non-political (*principal*) and political (*agent*) actors.

Classical liberals vigorously engage in the task to find better rules because of their aversion towards certain threats posed to the liberal order, which may be aptly described as "patternless projections of authority" (Ratnapala 2003, p. 16). Through a somewhat similar thought process, Buchanan (2008) suggests that should we want better outcomes than, say, the incessantly piecemeal but often counterproductive political interferences undertaken in the name of vanquishing inequality, then we ought to seek better rule-structures to live by.

Other arguments in support of rule-structures—including those replicated and commonly used rules known as (formal and informal) institutions (Dopfer and Potts 2008)—have been advanced over the years. As noted in a recent text focusing on the economic foundations of institutions, "[b]y channelling the structure of pay-offs, incentives and disincentives, institutions effectively rule out certain actions and narrow the range of possible reactions. Thereby they make the actions of others more predictable and give social interaction a certain structure" (Kasper et al. 2012, p. 103). In an economic context, appropriate rules are conducive to the realisation of market-tested betterment, whereby entrepreneurial suppliers and discerning consumers reach consensus over the terms and conditions of exchanges for value-added goods and services.

Rules which suitably protect justly acquired properties from predation both settle disputes and foster a socially cooperative environment. They also foster dyadic exchanges and catalyse advances in productive entrepreneurship. Finally, a sound rule-environment aligns intersubjective expectations among non-intimates, helping reduce the costs associated with broad-scale economic exchange throughout society (Palagashvili et al. 2017). From the classical liberal perspective, there is no coincidence that those societies which have institutionally conferred dignity, with regard to the capability of entrepreneurs and other market participants to discover their own opportunities for enrichment, have fared better in terms of improved living standards over the long term (McCloskey 2010, 2016).

The inherent complexities of entangled political economy may suggest to some a concomitant need for complex rules. In a perceptive analysis, Richard Epstein (1995) contrarily suggests what is most desirous are *simple rules for a complex world*. Epstein argues for simpler rule-structures—presumably more abstract, certain, general, and equal in coverage—on the basis of minimising the administrative burdens and costly errors associated with complex rules. In short, the application of rules should not unduly stretch individuals' cognitive limitations. Hayek once raised a complementary point: "[h]uman intelligence is quite insufficient to comprehend all the details of the complex human society, and it is the inadequacy of our reason to arrangement such an order in detail which forces us to be content with abstract rules" (Hayek [1965] 1967, p. 88).

Simple, but not simplistic, rules allow people to act on their own knowledge, rendering their own connections based on mutuality and respect. These connections, animated by credible, understandable, and enforceable commitments, are the essences of the foundational institutions for an entangled political economy informed by the principle of liberty (Postrel 1998; Wagner 2016). In this light, the suggestion that the most efficacious way to deal with life's complexities is for legislatures to exercise broad-scale planning, providing discretionary potential to introduce complex formal rules, should be ruled out of hand as a fool's errand.

Arguably one of the greatest achievements of classical liberalism as a philosophical system rests upon its emphasis upon *constitutionalism*. This refers to a coherent system of institutional measures, of both a substantive and procedural nature, constraining the ability of political actors to mete discrimination towards, and expound domination over, those who do not wield political offices. An influential group of twentieth-century scholars, including Friedrich Hayek, Bruno Leoni, and Lon Fuller, held that the "rule of law" concept is central to maintaining a constitutionalised rule-structure. Specifically, the law is to be applied to each and all in equal measure, with no exceptions applicable, and legal precepts should be capable of being widely understood to cultivate both legal compliance and acceptance.

Constitutionalism is often depicted as being synonymous with certain political institutions of a more formal nature. These include a written constitution elucidating the nature, extent, and division of political powers[1]; regular and transparent general elections in which citizen-voters select political candidates as members of the legislature; the separation of powers between the legislature (executive and legislative branches) and the judiciary; accountability of government enterprises to the legislative assembly; and the division of governmental functions and roles across different levels of government.[2] These and similar arrangements are supposed to ensure accountability of those wielding political powers to those subjected to legislative, fiscal, and regulatory actions.

The "constitutional thinking" of classical liberalism has been innovatively extended to express the idea that economic and fiscal settings should, in themselves, be conceived as an essential part of the overall constitutional fabric of modern life. Our primary focus in this section is upon the intellectually distinctive ordo-liberal approach towards an effective economic order. This approach was initially developed by an intellectual coalition of German economists and lawyers against the background of an economically dysfunctional Weimar Republic and a murderous Nazi regime. Ordo-liberalism remains a viable research agenda, as adjudged by the works filtered through its headline journal, *Ordo*, and those appearing in other publication outlets.

According to the ordo-liberals, the liberal purposes of the state to protect life, limb, and property risk subversion by certain entanglement styles between economic and political agents, which gives rise to rent-seeking privileges. These practices induce calculational chaos into the profit-seeking, market-based economic order, and violate the spirit of consistency and steadiness characterising a constitutionally ordered economic policy (Eucken 1948a, b). In the theoretical frame of ordo-liberalism, especially as presented by its first generation of intellectuals such as Walter Eucken and Franz Böhm, a distinction was made between a "theory of orders" (*Ordnungstheorie*) and "order policy" (*Ordnungspolitik*). The former compares the generic working properties of alternative institutional-constitutional ordering arrangements pertaining to human relationships, whereas the latter explicates desired policy principles to be pursued by political agents consistent with the tenets of a given set of institutional-constitutional settings (Vanberg 2014; Kolev 2015).

As Richard Wagner has noted, the ordo-liberals determined that an *Ordnungstheorie* centred upon interactions governed by equality and mutuality was much preferred to interactions based upon hierarchy, status, and domination (Wagner 2017). Economic, communal, and political orders operating in accordance with liberal values are also much more conducive to human flourishing than collectivist alternatives. The extreme concentration of political power within a socialist entangled economy is also very likely to generate highly skewed income and wealth distributions, due to the institutionalisation of rent-seeking conduct and the establishment of status positions flowing from such a development (Henderson et al. 2005).

Having established the quintessential desirability of the liberal system for informing (rule-ordered) economic connections, ordo-liberal scholars set out policies intended to create "a broad consistency between the operating principles of enterprises established on the public square and those established on the market square" (Wagner 2007, p. 141). The so-called "constitutive principles" (*konstituierende Prinzipien*) for a functional liberal economic order is as follows:

- *Private property*: Property rights need to be well-defined and secure from expropriation by private or public sector parties, and owners of justly acquired property should be free to dispose, transfer, and use their property;

- *Freedom of contract*: Individuals and organisations are free to enter into contractual arrangements with others regarding the production, distribution, and exchange of goods and services, and contracts should not preclude the participation of certain agents in the market;
- *Liability*: Individuals, firms, and other economic participants should face complete liabilities as it pertains to their errors and mismanagement, particularly as they adversely impact other parties;
- *Open markets*: Individual producers and consumers should be free to enter and exit domestic and international markets;
- *Monetary stability*: The provision of inflation-free money is necessary to ensure that the value of currency remains stable, thus facilitating robust expectations about relative prices and their movements; and
- *Consistency of economic policy*: Policies enacted by the government should mutually reinforce each other to avoid unnecessary structural adjustment and other costs borne by economic agents (Eucken [1952] 1982; Kasper and Streit 1993; Kolev 2015).

The implementation of these constitutive principles ensures that policy rules are consistently *and* persistently applied, giving entrepreneurs every confidence to freely coordinate with others. Policy adherence to the underlying constitutive principles of an economic order ensures that the qualities of productive entrepreneurship and profit-seeking competition pervade economic action, minimising the prospect of "monstrous moral hybrid" enterprises dominating the economic scene.

An indication of a living and viable research programme is the ability of scholars of varied intellectual persuasions to apply and reinterpret themes from an originating body of research—established, in the case of ordo-liberalism, several decades ago—to address new issues and questions. Noting the complementarities between ordo-liberal and evolutionary economic theories, Kurt Dopfer and Jason Potts (2008) established that ordo-liberal constitutive principles represent a key element of "generic policy" shaping the structure and performance of meso-level networks.

The definition of generic policy is necessarily a broad one; it refers to "coordination and change in the underlying generic order itself, as composed of technologies, industries, institutions, mechanisms, legal, cultural and political systems, etc." (Ibid., p. 94). Generic policy is, by the same token, a nested intellectual construction with three layers of understanding. The "zero-order" level of generic policy aims to effect coordination and change to constitutional rules. The next level concerns "first-order" policies, which seek coordination and change within so-called "operational rules." The operational rules merely reconfigure the *outcomes*, not the rules, of the generic order. Finally, Dopfer and Potts specify the existence of "second-order" policies which shape the underlying capabilities to produce commodities, generate and adopt novelty, and to adapt to change.

The ordo-liberal constitutive principles are firmly consistent with the zero-order level of policy rules specified by Dopfer and Potts. The zero-order policy class attempts "to change the underlying structure of property rights, competition law, legal trade agreements, environmental regulation, labor laws, monetary and financial institutions, public infrastructure, and generally all social, political and cultural institutions that affect the economic order" (Ibid., p. 95). Congruent with James Buchanan's intuition that better outcomes are a function of better rule sets, Dopfer and Potts likewise disallow first-order policies as a basis for effecting distributional change:

> The goal of economic policy is always to seek improvements in the generic conditions of a market economy. It seeks to rectify coordination failure in rules and rule populations and to facilitate the evolutionary self-organizing process of change in rules and rule populations. This is to be plainly distinguished from policy that seeks operational effect by intervening in exchange or production and the consequent patterns of price and income. … economic policy should be focused on intervention in the rules that generate operational outcomes, not the operational outcomes themselves. (Ibid., p. 96)

Richard Wagner (1996, 2007, 2012a) notes that proponents of the ordo-liberal school did not actually rule out first-order, outcome-oriented policy interventions. Indeed, the ordo-liberals referred to their economic-outcome policies as "regulative principles." Policy can attempt to alter outcomes within entangled political economy, but they must be in conformity with the underlying constitutive (zero-order) principles. The concept of "market conformity" (*marktkonform*) performs as a compass guiding the formulation of many policy propositions: "[w]ithout market conformability, there would be commingling between commercial and guardian syndromes, which would inject such feudal nodes of operation as status and privilege into social life" (Wagner 2017, p. 163).

The underlying motivation of market conformity is to avoid, as best as one can, tectonic clashes that arise as economic and political enterprises become deeply entangled with each other. Raising the idea that regulative principles also legitimately exist, however, some of the key figures of ordo-liberal thought unwittingly left the policy door ajar for quite expansive modes of fiscal and regulatory policies. Many ordo-liberals expressed deep concerns about inequality, but the key players such as Eucken and Röpke disagreed over the appropriateness of progressive income taxes, inheritance taxes, subsidies to individuals and businesses, prescriptive competition policy, and other initiatives purported to reduce inequalities of income and wealth.

In theory, constitutionalising the economic order is intended to align expectations and promote trust. Achieving such objectives, as previously mentioned, gives confidence to agents to undertake entrepreneurial action in the service of others. We also argue that limiting the possibility of a politics that redistributes income and wealth for the few, but at the expense of the many, is another sound reason for an economic constitution. Even so, entanglement cannot be assumed away. The place for rule-making within entangled political economy, therefore, should be that entanglements are appropriately managed, without exhausting any person's freedom to act and create novel ideas (and also subject to conjecture and refutation by those surrounding them).

The "perpetual challenge," as Suri Ratnapala (2003) would refer to it, is to maintain this constitutionally ordered political economy. Achieving this task is no small order given that, amongst other things, a constitution itself is subject to change. Constitutional change may proceed in formalistic, *de jure*, fashion, or in a non-formal, *de facto*, sense, as economic, social, and political actors seek gains. Rajagopalan and Wagner (2013) and Salter and Wagner (2017) make it abundantly clear that, within open-ended social systems, there are constant "investments" made by actors with the intention of redrawing the boundary lines of what is constitutionally accepted domains of political action. One cannot rule out efforts by actors to have special, unequalising privileges constitutionally entrenched. The conception of a "living constitution" implies that, even at the level of fundamental ordering rules, questions regarding the appropriate balance of cooperation and conflict within society remain hotly contested.

Finally, it should be recognised that constitutionalism represents far more than the retention of certain kinds of policy as formal institutions. Informal norms are essential in facilitating communication amongst diverse persons, creating trust and helping to reduce the costs attributable to exchange. A critical basis for the genius of classical-liberal economic constitutionalism is that an emphasis upon constitutive principles neatly maps to a set of long-standing, but nevertheless emergent, moral attitudes, dispositions, and mores:

> The refraction of an economic order through a legal order reveals a moral order of human conduct. The legal principle of private property entails a moral belief that it is wrong to take what is not yours. It also entails a morel belief that private property provides a just basis for ordering human relationships. The legal principle of freedom of contract maps into the moral belief that people should keep their promises or otherwise make good on the damages that result if they do not. It also entails the moral belief that whatever associations and organizations people create are appropriate. The legal principle of liability or tort entails the moral claim of an obligation to redress the wrongs done to others. (Wagner 2010, p. 47)

These considerations underline the importance of rules and policies for the vibrancy and resilience of that interdependent tapestry of orders—economic, communal, and political—comprising entangled political economy. A distinctive contribution of classical liberal thought is that economic production and trade, civic associational care and giving, and democratic deliberation and voting are not activities that intrinsically clash but rather, when constitutionally ordered, reinforce each other to promote growth and change (Madison 1997; Nell 2017).

Taxation and Expenditure Policies: Imagining a Fiscal Constitution

Richard Wagner (2017) is correct in his assessment that the articulation of principles in support of dyadic economic interactions is a relatively straightforward matter, yet translating those principles into a concrete agenda for implementation is an immensely difficult proposition. This is certainly true with respect to taxation and expenditure that shape a fiscal commons which, as clearly illustrated by the budgetary positions of most developed countries, is being overused (Jakee and Turner 2002; Raudla 2010; Wagner 2012a, b).[3] The challenge before us is to sketch out some key elements of fiscal constitutionalism that could realistically tackle some of the worst vestiges of liberty-inconsistent inequality.

Direct taxes featuring progressive tax rates have long been advocated as a chief fiscal means by which governments attempt to alleviate inequality of income. Arguments for progressive income tax have extended to suggest that the income of rich incumbents sourced through rent-seeking effort can, and should, be eliminated through "corrective" tax action. However, the income tax system in its existing form does not distinguish between incomes generated via rent-seeking or by satisfying the needs of employers and customers. An effort to "tax rents," therefore, would indiscriminately reduce incomes generated through value-added connections between people. This would likely harm the economic interests of those people engaging in productive efforts (Hillman 2009), dampening the incentive effects arising from the materialisation of liberty-consistent, "good" inequalities attributable to effort and choice.

Classical liberal economists have pointed to other potentially adverse unintended consequences due to the implementation of progressive income taxation. Wilhelm Röpke (1960), a prominent figure of ordoliberalism, castigated steeply progressive taxes for depriving wealthy individuals of the capacity to use their private spending to assist others. A strong opponent of monopolisation, Röpke observed that the progressive income tax revenues collected by political agents will be used to effectively crowd out non-governmental endeavours. These include activities in the arts, culture, philanthropy, and the sciences, which are largely funded by the wealthy.

In recent decades, economists have recommended "broad-base, low-rate" (BBLR) as a preferable design framework for taxation. In the case of personal income taxation, a BBLR-consistent structure is best exemplified by a purely "flat tax" with one low, proportional tax rate and no exemptions (Hall and Rabushka 2007). Similarly, Buchanan and Congleton ([1998] 2003) indicate that a flat rate income tax on all sources of income with no exceptions would be consistent with the "generality norm" of non-discriminatory fiscal treatment. With regard to sales or consumption taxes, BBLR principles would dictate a low, single rate of tax applicable to most, if not all, goods and services produced in the economy.

For many economists, BBLR represents the "polar star" of tax reform. However, the suggestion that political actors would faithfully implement and defend a perfect BBLR tax arrangement stretches credulity from an entangled political economy standpoint. This is because fiscal politics may be more realistically construed as a two-stage framework. The ideal tax structure is initially contemplated but is later amended by the forces of "realpolitik," as economic and political interests get themselves entangled in negotiations over the distribution of effective tax liabilities (Hebert and Wagner 2013). The essence of fiscal interaction in entangled political economy is that individuals, and the representatives of enterprises, ultimately prefer that someone else pays tax. These attitudes towards taxation relate to continuous political controversies surrounding the base of taxation ("Should fringe benefits or capital gains be included or excluded from the income tax base?," "Should fresh food be in or out of the sales tax base?") and/or their rate ("Shouldn't the well-off pay more in personal income tax?").

To be sure, generality in tax treatment still remains a desirable aim, upholding a semblance of the rule of law in fiscal policy that also appears congruent with constitutive principles. Its application would, at the very least, send a signal that rent-seeking efforts in support of differentially advantageous tax liabilities are discouraged in a liberal-democratic society. In practical terms, though, tax design will tend to move towards, or away from, non-discriminatory attributes, depending upon the precise forms and substances of those entanglements arising within society. Ideological dispositions towards tax policy would be another factor which affects the direction of policy movement with respect to the tax-generality ideal.

Public choice scholarship has placed great analytical import upon the fact that taxation (and revenue raising more generally) is inextricably linked with the spending side of the budgetary account. Therefore, tax policy considerations should not be considered independently of the uses to which taxation revenues are put. Consistent with this, Wagner suggests that a sole focus on BBLR to ensure fiscal non-discrimination is inadequate given that "[a]ny pattern of distortionary or discriminatory taxation can be accomplished alternatively through the expenditure side of the budget in the presence of nondiscriminatory taxation" (Wagner 1989, p. 249).

It is conceived that, broadly speaking, the distributional pattern of expenditures undertaken by governments is practically more discriminate than taxes. This was raised by Buchanan and Congleton ([1998] 2003) in their assessment of American government during the late twentieth century. This observation is, in no small part, a reflection of the expansive provision of goods and services authorised by legislatures and carried out by bureaucracies. In the parlance of mainstream economic theory, governments realistically provide only very few, if any, "pure" public goods whose technological aspects connote non-excludability of use and non-rivalry in consumption. Political actors do provide a wide array of outputs embodying varying degrees of publicness, giving rise to the potential for non-uniform provision to the public.

Classical liberals have suggested that the late nineteenth century marked the passing of substantive and autonomous non-political provision (also financing) of education, healthcare, and social and welfare services (Green and Cromwell 1984; Beito 2000; Bartholomew 2004; Pennington 2011). To the extent that non-political actors continue to provide the kinds of services mentioned, these seem increasingly subject to subsidisation and regulatory activities by political agents. The resultant indeterminacy of the boundaries between the orders of civil society in this context is unsurprising, given that the provision of outputs not only caters to economic and social values but to political prerogative as well. Even so, many liberals would regard an extensive entanglement between non-government organisations and governments as being deeply problematic, with strong political influence creating "monstrous moral hybrids" that inhabit the communal order.

There is little doubt that reforming the expenditure side of government budgets remains challenging, but not all hope is lost from a liberal perspective. Indeed, mutually reinforcing evolutionary developments affecting consumer preferences and capabilities, production costs, and technology potentially enhance the capacity of non-political agents to provide goods and services presently construed to be the preserve of political activity (Foldvary and Klein 2003; Kuznicki 2017). The range of goods and services classed as "impure" public goods could certainly be provided in a polycentric fashion. Under such a scenario, a multitude of actors (governmental and non-governmental) are simultaneously involved in services provision, meaning that no single player dominates the ecological arena of provision. As the works of Elinor and Vincent Ostrom remind us, the emergence of polycentric, and highly deconcentrated styles of provision can also reinforce the benefits associated with diversity, experimentation, and learning.

As mentioned previously the welfare state is not a monolithic construct, and is influenced by a large number of participants whose activities stretch across the economic, communal, and political orders. The welfare state is a complex "kludge" with many moving parts (Teles 2013), but with those moving parts gradually subject to monocentric puppeteering (by way of subsidies and regulations) by a central government. However, scholars engaging in the entangled political economy research programme would generally agree that welfare, and other social services, delivered polycentricaly would be much more effective in helping people realise their life projects. By "effective," we mean the likelihood that aid, advice, care, and support will equip individuals, families, and communities with improved capabilities to help themselves to improve their situations—a form of "raising up," in a manner of speech.

There are two related considerations concerning the normative preference accorded to polycentricity. Firstly, as indicated by Richard Wagner, "[m]onocentric governments have difficulty making credible commitments about offering or withholding aid because this form of government possesses a grantor of last resort. In contrast, a polycentric system has no position of a grantor of last resort" (Wagner 2016, p. 134). From an ordo-liberal perspective, the moral hazard of diminished personal responsibility which potentially accompanies the monocentric provision of welfare flouts the constitutive principle of liability (Siems and Schnyder 2014).

Secondly, there are knowledge problems to bear in mind. In a polycentric system, potential providers have a better capacity to acquire detailed and intimate knowledge about the beneficiary aspirations, desires, and needs through on-the-spot collaboration. Under a monocentric regime—exhibiting a universal, standardised mode of provision, and often accompanied by paternalistic compliance arrangements—such individualised attention is highly likely to be an extremely costly and epistemically challenging exercise.

Most classical liberals explicitly endorse a much greater role for non-political agents to design and maintain welfare-state-*cum*-mutual-assistance projects within a broader, polycentric regime of diverse experimentation. In a broad sense, this kind of reform suggests a significantly lesser role for legislators and bureaucrats in providing forms of (pecuniary and non-pecuniary) care and support for needy and vulnerable individuals, families, and communities. Although we have previously described the problems associated with the panoply of public sector expenditure arrangements collectively known as the welfare state (e.g. fiscal cost, complexity, paternalistic treatment of beneficiaries), it is equally conceded that unwinding governmental intervention in this area presents a keen reform challenge. In simple terms, the process of "getting from here to there" is likely to prove a formidable one at best.

For some classical liberals, the "end-game" for welfare reform is not the abolition of governmental involvement altogether, but a radically simpler scheme of tax-financed cash provision. Classical liberals (and libertarians) such as Milton Friedman, Charles Murray, and Matt Zwolinski endorse a "universal basic income" (UBI) regime, or variations thereof. It is suggested that implementation of the UBI would eliminate the web of cash (and, under most UBI models, in-kind) assistance, remove the costs of maintaining large welfare bureaucracies, and put an end to "poverty traps" resulting from welfare-tax interactions. Another argument is for extending a UBI "safety net" to all adults, regardless of their present income and wealth positions. The UBI encourages people to take economic risks and engage in productive entrepreneurial conduct—in so doing, extending the scale of network interactions fundamentally governed by liberal ordering principles.

One could make the argument that, if people do see it as either necessary or advantageous to provide tax-financed welfare, it should be provided through a UBI. Acknowledging that the existing welfare state lacks congruency with the generality principle, Buchanan and Congleton ([1998] 2003) put forward an equal-per-head transfer payment (financed by proportional-rate taxation) as an ideal scheme consistent with equality under the law and fiscal non-discrimination. A publicly provided UBI would preferably be set at a reasonably low (i.e. *basic*) level, and be established within the confines of a fiscal constitution promoting long-term fiscal sustainability (Berggren 2000). The low per capita rate and fiscally sustainable UBI are less likely to unduly discourage non-political mutual assistance throughout the communal order, thus minimising the potential for a return to a Samaritan's dilemma situation associated with public sector domination. To further enhance the appeal of such a reform of governmental welfare, the establishment of UBI should coincide with a "regulatory constitution," substantially reducing the economic burden of engaging with regulatory authorities (Rohac 2017).

It appears that much of the contemporary UBI literature presumes the continued presence of monocentric public governance within the mutual assistance space. This need not be the case. Mitchell (2013) recommends that lower-level political jurisdictions set up their own UBI models, providing for comparison and experimentation in presumably a system of welfare provision with polycentric tendencies. A particularly interesting proposal developed by Potts et al. (2018) goes even further, arguing for the use of the blockchain to establish a "decentralised universal income, built from smart personal equity contracts" (UBI-SPECs).

Under UBI-SPEC, participating individuals, irrespective of their location, can enter into a self-executing, blockchained smart contract committing all of them to "swap" fixed percentages of their incomes with each other. The financial resilience of UBI-SPEC will be influenced by the lack of correlation between income streams earned by counterparty contracted participants, but a significant appeal of this mechanism from a liberal perspective is surely that "[i]t is in effect a voluntarily entered but hard coded mutual financial constitution among a distributed community" (Potts et al. 2018). For those difficult cases whereby certain individuals cannot secure an income-swapping contractual arrangement on the blockchain, political enterprises could pose as default UBI providers presumably at much lesser cost than under the existing welfare state.

Finally, it is appropriate for us to contend that polycentricity is not incompatible with our insistence upon generality in fiscal and regulatory treatments. Conceiving federalism as a public governance system, which at least bears some similarities with the polycentric ideal, Buchanan and Congleton state: "[f]ederalism allows generality to be adhered to at the level of every governmental body responsible for making collective program decisions while it allows departures from uniformity in the federation as a whole" (Buchanan and Congleton [1998] 2003, p. 187). Surveying Buchanan's contribution to federalism theory, Lynch (2004) indicates that generality does not preclude differences in service provision across jurisdictions. Irrespective of the differences between jurisdictions, the fiscal constitution remains underpinned by observance of the non-discriminatory generality norm within a given political jurisdiction.

Towards a Regulatory Constitution

It would be unreasonable to consider the need for rules applicable to the fiscal domain without commensurate arrangements for regulatory activity. The discussion in Chap. 5 described how certain regulatory settings enacted by political agents had been complicit in the upward redistribution of income and wealth. Contrasting the pro-competitive sensibilities of the ordo-liberal school and other classical liberals, regulation has been cited as a major factor responsible "for slowing down the pace of transformation within the nexus of relationships, thereby conserving the wealth of otherwise threatened enterprises" (Wagner 2010, p. 121).

The enunciation of principles for a regulatory constitution—which respects, and conforms to, the fundamental constitutive principles of a liberal, market-based economic order—is not necessarily clear-cut in all circumstances. Regulation is a broad concept assuming a rather broad, and somewhat diffuse, meaning, and its application does vary by country and even within countries. Undeterred, we proceed to outline some generic principles for a regulatory constitution which suppresses the capacity of regulation, and the governance modes which support it, to worsen economic inequalities.

A number of classical liberals have given special attention to a rule indicating that governments should compensate individuals and businesses whose properties have been expropriated for public uses—for example, major infrastructure development—under compulsory acquisition schemes. This is known in the U.S. as "eminent domain," and, under the Fifth Amendment of the Constitution, governments are obliged to provide "just compensation" for those whose property has been taken. Similar constitutional or statutory provisions exist in Australia, Canada, Germany, New Zealand, and many other developed countries, even if the finer details of their applications vary by jurisdiction.

The merit of just compensation, according to one account, is that it "essentially introduces a price mechanism in a setting where the government has all the options, and in consequence acts as an effective constraint against excessive intervention" (Epstein 2000, p. 5). Fischel (2004) arrived at a similar judgement, to the effect that just compensation may serve to restrain over-regulation. With an affirming nod to ordo-liberal theory, Richard Wagner suggests that just compensation clauses principally reflect a political "interest in achieving conformability between the operating principles of private and public law, and with such conformability helping to keep the practice of political economy in line with liberal principles of governance" (Wagner 2017, p. 163).

An enunciation of the principle of just compensation for compulsorily acquired private property is one thing, while the propensity for political actors to faithfully adhere to such provisions is another. Writing in light of the American Supreme Court *Kelo v. City of New London* decision legally approving a politically sanctioned private property redevelopment in Connecticut, Somin (2015) illustrates how eminent domain provisions are manipulated by property developers and other interests to enrich themselves at the expense of those less well-off. Observing the baleful effects of eminent domain in condemning so-called blighted neighbourhoods, predominantly housing lower-income individuals and families,

Somin called for a prohibition on economic development takings. This example illustrates the risk that solemn inscriptions, advocating political self-control on pieces of parchment, are not self-enforcing when individuals, enterprises, interest groups, and political agents want to realise gains.

In theory, the principle of just compensation specifies that political agents should provide adequate, market-reflective compensation to people whose properties are being physically possessed for public purposes. This raises the question as to how individuals are to be compensated, if at all, in the event that regulation induces a change in property values (Fischel 2004). Consider that regulatory encroachments upon private property include (but are not limited to) the following cases:

> land use control and zoning regulations; building codes; occupancy restrictions and facilities requirements on property used for economic gain; restrictions on the donative ability of the possessor of property to bequeath or transfer possessions (through the testator) upon his demise; rent controls; acreage quotas for farmers; government trade controls or quotas on international exchanges; … "open housing" legislation that takes away from the seller the right to choose his own customers; government grants of exclusive access to certain markets; price supports; price ceilings; minimum wage laws; maximum profit laws; rate regulations; controls over utilities, travel, housing, communications, insurance, interest, banking, etc. (Younkins 2002, p. 60)

From a classical liberal perspective, the accumulation of such examples of governmental regulation, and more, unleashes socially tectonic episodes, deforms competitive economic conduct, and may entail pro-rich redistribution. Even so, the opacity of regulatory effects means that it is virtually impossible to provide compensation accounting for distributional effects in finely grained detail. Richard Epstein (1985) surmises, then, that perhaps the most appropriate remedy for inherently discriminatory regulation is constitutional invalidation. The elimination of regulations failing to conform to the constitutive principles of the economic order could suitably fall within the terms of Potts's (2010) "negative experiments" to downscale public sector activity more generally.

With respect to regulatory governance issues, a return to a past when legislators directly manipulated regulatory settings is best avoided. By the same token, the modern concern that discretionary power for regulators lacks political legitimacy is a reasonable one. Finding an appropriate avenue to reconcile these conflicting issues as posed by modern regulatory governance is difficult but, we suggest, not impossible.

Building on an intellectual tradition crafted by Michael Polanyi, Friedrich Hayek, and Elinor and Vincent Ostrom, modern classical liberals suggest a potential workaround is to acknowledge that objectives can be successfully met through effective modes of self-governance. In other words, interaction between heterogeneous agents provides ample opportunities to vet economic conduct and performance against the principles of property ("don't steal from others"), contract ("keep your promises to others"), and liability ("do not hurt others"), and to sanction those who violate these rules (Wagner 2016). Individuals immersed in market conduct can punish persistent rule-breakers by withholding engagement altogether, or to insist that business can still be conducted albeit with additional, and mutually agreed, commercial and other safeguards (Klein 1997).

Entanglement may be consistent with competition and the dissipation of inequality, or it could induce social tectonics and the "bad" inequalities derived from rent-seeking. An avoidance of monocentric styles of regulatory governance appears as a necessary condition to enable individuals and enterprises to generate effective and pro-competitive self-governance with respect to economic conduct. Systems of government regulation should not be organisationally concentrated in a meta-regulatory fashion and dominated by one intra-national jurisdiction, but polycentrically dispersed to keep tectonic clashes to a reasonable level and help facilitate policy learning about better practices.

Political agents within those jurisdictions wishing to act as "holdouts" against improving their regulatory policy standards will be unable to depredate the quality of the regulatory system as a whole. This is because polycentric regulatory governance is at least just as likely to encourage other jurisdictions to embrace more adaptive, flexible, regulatory arrangements, energising additional economic activity in the process. The capacity to compare the performance of "dynamist" versus "stasist" (Postrel 1998) regulatory regimes fosters learning for all participants beholden to regulatory structures. Over time, this should instigate rounds of policy entrepreneurialism which contestably modify government regulation, ensuring that meaningful economic and social improvements can be realised.

Regulatory governance reform in a polycentric direction should also help reduce the potential for regulation to be used as a redistributive tool. Mobility by regulated parties deleteriously affected by regulation, and "yardstick" interjurisdictional comparisons, is likely to maintain pressure upon policymakers to ensure that their regulations do not worsen inequality outcomes.

Alex Salter and Vlad Tarko ingeniously apply polycentricity and institutional robustness insights to the financial sector, which has been widely identified as a catalyst for economic inequality. Expressing antipathy towards monocentric modes of financial regulation, the authors submit that "[g]etting the 'rules of the game' right at the various levels of social interaction, rather than continuously tinkering at the edges of an existing regulatory apparatus, offers the best chance of securing a financial system that is robustly governed while still promoting sustainable growth via efficient capital allocation" (Salter and Tarko 2017, p. 6). An ecological tapestry of financial sector activity corresponding with "free banking" regimes will be more resilient to shocks. To this end, Salter and Tarko reaffirm Richard Wagner's (2012c) contention that entanglements consistent with a more willing embrace of liberal principles are likely to be less economically turbulent.

Political responses to emergent blockchain technology and its applications—most prominently "cryptocurrencies" such as Bitcoin, Ethereum, and Ripple—serve as another interesting case study into regulatory governance. The blockchain is a decentralised public ledger (i.e. data structured by rules) which is securely maintained on peer-to-peer computing networks around the globe. The kind of information that may be recorded on the blockchain is expansive—financial and economic transactions, personal identity records, contractual information, property ownership records, and so on.

Reducing the need for third-parties, such as large firms and governments, to record and store information, blockchains may be conceptualised in a number of ways, as shown by Davidson et al. (2018). The blockchain could be seen as an accompaniment to existing production processes, effectively a "general purpose technology" similar to rail and the Internet of the nineteenth and twentieth centuries, respectively. Another interpretation of blockchain is that it presents a means to reduce transactions costs via less costly verification of information potentially without the need for expensive intermediation. Finally, the blockchain may be perceived as a rival institutional technology altogether, or a new style of economic coordination supplanting the likes of already-established markets, clubs, firms, and states.

Given the critical importance of data and information for a functional economy, society, and polity, the third potential application of blockchain, being an institutional technology in its own right, is potentially the most profound. MacDonald (2015) and MacDonald et al. (2016) indicate that actors may use the blockchain as a means of "crypto-seceding" away from established organisations that insufficiently respect the need for privacy and security of information.

From an entangled political economy perspective, the practice of non-territorial crypto-secession would be reflected not only in a rearrangement of existing network connections, but by way of the introduction of entirely new elements (agents) altogether. It is possible to conceive of emergent "crypto-firms" creating new sources of economic value, "crypto-altruists" discovering new ways of generating mutual assistance, and other crypto-entities working to resolve collective action problems. It may be speculated that the animosity expressed towards blockchain applications by central bankers, financial regulators, and certain other participants within the political order is informed by an appreciation of the potential for crypto-secession to undermine inequality-inducing triadic exchange.

It is possible to conceive of a spectrum of regulatory engagement with blockchain, ranging from policy abstention ("pure crypto-friendliness") to outright policy suppression ("pure crypto-unfriendliness"). This spectrum generically corresponds with political receptions as to whether the blockchain fundamentally represents an "opportunity," or "threat," to existing modes of operation and interaction. Differential regulatory responses to blockchain, and resultant applications across jurisdictions, will help build a repository of learning with regard to the most effectual strategies to nurture the evolutionary growth and development of this technology.

The emergence of blockchain is relevant to Adam Thierer's call for a regulatory environment facilitating what is known as "permissionless innovation." The regulatory constitution should maintain the default position that new technologies, products, business models, management styles, and other facets of innovation should not be necessarily disallowed, curtailed, or pre-empted in any way. Specifically, "[u]nless a compelling case can be made that a new invention will bring serious harm to society, innovation should be allowed to continue unabated and problems, if they develop, can be addressed later" (Thierer 2016, p. 1).

A permissionless disposition lends itself to practical suggestions which are likely to reinforce the dynamic resilience of polycentrically ordered regulatory arrangements. These include the adoption of self-restraint and patience on the part of political enterprises specialising in regulation, relaxing antiquated rules upon incumbent meso-level economic and communal agents as new entrants challenge the *status quo*, and fostering "educate and empower" (instead of "legislate and regulate") responses to new challenges. In a similar vein, James Broughel recommends that regulators ought to "embrace a culture that respects new technologies. … Regulators should resist the demands of interest groups that are displaced by new technologies and should work to explain to the public the benefits of new technologies, even when those benefits also carry risks. Regulators who encourage safe experimentation with new technologies will promote growth more than those who act as gatekeepers to technological change" (Broughel 2017, p. 101).

The accumulation of regulatory artefacts has not only raised concerns about the growing burden of "red tape," however defined, but has focused initiatives upon improving regulatory quality. Many initiatives have been trialled or otherwise implemented amongst developed countries in this regard, sharing an aspiration to improve quality through better processes and structures of regulatory design and enforcement. These include regulatory cost-benefit analyses and impact statements, "sunset" and "grandfathering" clauses for legislation and regulatory provisions, regulatory review processes, establishing ministries and agencies responsible for deregulation or red tape reduction, and the list goes on. Ironically, these strategies have been implemented amidst the background of a policy environment in which political agents promulgate frequent regulatory adjustments. As such, these "quick-fix" measures do not appear situated within the same category of the more thoroughgoing attention to the underlying rules of regulation.

The "Special Case" of Competition Policy?

The ordo-liberal agenda, developed largely during the first half of the twentieth century, was centred upon the elucidation of rules which would maintain liberty as economically understood. As noted previously, the ordo-liberals outlined zero-order rules which aimed at constitutionalising competition as an ordering norm in economic affairs. Maintaining certain institutions consistent with the exercise of liberty provides an effective space in which agents rival each other to create novelties (embodied in goods and services, production methodologies, etc.) that spread useful economic knowledge.

The key is that the constitutive principles foster performance-based competition (*Leistungswettbewerb*) which would ultimately enhance the well-being of final consumers. This concept resembles Adam Smith's age-old observation that "consumption is the sole end of production." In opposition to this form of competitive conduct is *Behinderungswettbewerb*, a perverted sense of "competition" designed to impede and hinder a rival's capacity to perform—for instance, wherein market players lobby governments to enact policies impeding superior rivals from exercising their entrepreneurial flair (Vanberg 2001). The greater the prevalence of competition informed by the desire to instigate genuine performance improvements, the greater the capacity for economic action to undermine concentrated networks fomenting inequality.

As indicated in this book, ordo-liberal thought can be usefully reinterpreted through the lens of evolutionary market theory and, more broadly, entangled political economy. It is notable, however, that the original ordo-liberals, who lived through the "many monopolies" periods of Weimar and Nazism, were more sanguine about the ordering efficacy of competitive markets. The constitutive principles were even deemed insufficient to uphold *Leistungswettbewerb* and limit the concentration of private economic power. In response the ordo-liberals believed that governments had a duty, as informed by regulative principles, to prevent economic monopolisation with the aid of formal competition policy.

There was no uniform formula for an ordo-liberal competition policy. The key ordo-liberals, such as Walter Eucken, nevertheless considered that an independent regulatory authority was necessary to conserve the integrity of an economic order underpinned by competition. Using the market conformability criterion, the regulator would be charged with identifying "predatory pricing" and restraints on trade preventing the emergence of a diverse ecology of rivalrous economic enterprises. Measures would also be taken up to disband private cartels from the economy. It was appreciated by the ordo-liberals that some monopolies (e.g. enterprises providing network infrastructure services such as electricity, gas, and water) could not be readily dissipated. Leonhard Miksch (Gerber 1998; Goldschmidt and Berndt 2005) advocated pricing and investment regulations which would behove monopolies to act "as if" they acted in accordance with the perfect competition framework (or, as Eucken would say, "complete" competition accounting for the competitive state of both the producer and consumer sides of markets).

The economic environment motivating a call by the original ordo-liberals for prescriptive models of competition policy does not necessarily exist today. This is affirmed by the advent of falling trade barriers and reduced tax rates, encouraging the international mobility of capital, finance, and skilled labour. One could also assert that stringent competition policy, predicated on the desirability of first-order interventions "into the market," does not rest easily with the constitutive principles of ordo-liberalism. Indeed, generalised policy rules consistent with the constitutive principle of open markets are meant to ensure freedom of entry and exit by definition or, at least, ensure contestability threatening to undermine existing concentrated economic networks.

Additional questions may be asked about the applicability of competition policy in an evolutionary economy predominated by market processes. Scholars affiliated with the Austrian school of economics strongly criticise efforts to establish the competitive situation of an economy using a structure-conduct-performance paradigm (DiLorenzo 1988). This is not to claim, however, that monopoly is never problematic—only monopolies eliciting political support should be reformed. In this context, we also recall the evolutionary economics perspective of Dopfer and Potts (2008) suggesting that, so long as constitutive principles are respected, monopolies will tend to be frittered away by meso-level competition.

In truth, competition policy is not a panacea for concentrated positions giving rise to inequality within the networked structures of entangled political economy. Furthermore, ordo-liberal regulative principles are intended to integrate with constitutive principles via market-conformability criteria. If competition policy is to be in harmony with voluntaristic instances of economic entanglement, and not hamper the evolutionary potential of the economy, it must be *consistent* with other policy rules. Competition policy not consistent with zero-order constitutive principles should be ruled out as a legitimate regulatory stratagem.

The requirement that competition-friendly policies are to be appropriately nested within an economic constitution brings other policies into our field of consideration. Consider innovation policy, within which intellectual property is a key plank. The problems raised about intellectual property in Chap. 5 are hardly new; Walter Eucken himself harboured reservations about the anti-competitive effects of patent laws in Germany (Wörsdörfer 2012). In a posthumously issued tract, Eucken stated, "patent law has unexpectedly triggered powerful tendencies towards the formation of monopolies and concentration processes in industry" (Eucken [1952] 1982, p. 120). Eucken's dispositions were consistent with the fundamental ordo-liberal belief that the most important economic question is not what the government should do, but what rules and norms are most resonant with the ideal of preserving the liberal vision of a market-based economic order.

Conclusion

The German ordo-liberals, James Buchanan and public choice theorists, and the Austrians and evolutionary economists of today have demonstrated great intellectual novelty in specifying the institutional conditions conducive to entrepreneurial creativity and trade-tested betterment. A framework for inequality-dissipating competition by market participants was identified in the early stages of theoretical development as being a pivotal component to the overall success of a liberal economic order.

This chapter outlined a number of rules which should be observed if redressing income and wealth inequalities are of concern. The imposition of taxes whose structure embodies the generality principle of non-discrimination calls for the uniformity of tax treatment, deterring to some extent the incentive for the politically well-connected to effectively transfer their liabilities onto someone else. Uniformity in public services provision should apply to strictly pure public goods (or close approximation thereof), subjecting the provision of all other economic goods to competitive pressures in decentralised, polycentric settings comprising diverse economic, social, and political actors.

It is also suggested that regulation is a shared responsibility of the community, rather than for politicians and bureaucrats alone. All options for deregulation should be investigated to enable people to craft their own reputations for performance-oriented competition in the service of others. If regulation cannot be relaxed, then it is incumbent upon governments to justly compensate people and groups for the expropriations that regulatory policies generate. These recommendations are in stark contrast to the centripetal tendencies of regulatory policy in recent decades, whereby self-responsibility for regulating one's own behaviour and conduct has been replaced by monocentric and monopolised regulation in the hands of unaccountable mega-regulators.

We plainly concede that the interactions fostered in an entangled political economy are likely to depart, and greatly so, from the fiscal and regulatory rules proposed in this chapter. Recognition should also be given to concerns that individual policies intended to enshrine fiscal generality, and contain politically induced economic inequality, may themselves be susceptible to future rent-seeking contests to win discriminatory policy concessions (Boettke and Martin 2011). In the broader context, though, we concur with Mark Pennington's assessment to the effect that, "[a] 'pure' form of classical liberal order may well be unattainable, but the principles that inform the case for a movement 'towards the minimal state' may still prove more workable than any alternative" (Pennington 2011, p. 265).

We consider that there are significant upsides to reform realising an economic order grounded in *better* rules. Better rule structures would make for a more effectual fulfilment of liberty in our time, allowing us to achieve objectives in our own lights. A reform direction consistent with the constitutive principles of ordo-liberalism would be expected to drive the better outcomes most of us desire—including the reduction of inequalities of income and wealth driven by lobbying for particularised fiscal and regulatory favours.

Notes

1. Political actors in most developed countries have prepared a written constitution, usually in collaboration with political and legal peers, and with some degree of consultation with the general public. However, there are some countries (e.g. Israel, New Zealand, United Kingdom) that uphold constitutional principles without reference to a written constitution.
2. The division of powers between levels of government within a given country may be in the form of a confederation (with a weak central governmental authority deriving most or all of its powers from lower-level governments), federation (with powers shared between central and lower governments), or a unitary state (with strong central authority, and limited powers for lower governments as prescribed by the central government).
3. As had been mentioned in a previous chapter, public debt is not the subject of an extensive analysis for this book. It is noted, however, that the appropriate management of borrowings by political enterprises has long been of concern to classical liberal thinkers, and such matters are legitimately incorporated into an expansive conception of the fiscal constitution. Borrowing activities by political agents essentially generate intertemporal non-generality norms in fiscal politics, raising fundamental questions about the appropriateness of extending debt burdens onto future generations that lack current-day political access.

References

Bartholomew, James. 2004. *The Welfare State We're In*. London, UK: Politico's.

Beito, David T. 2000. *From Mutual Aid to the Welfare State: Fraternal Societies and Social Services, 1890–1967*. Chapel Hill, NC: University of North Carolina Press.

Berggren, Niclas. 2000. Implementing Generality While Reducing the Risk for Fiscal Explosion. *Constitutional Political Economy* 11 (4): 353–369.

Boettke, Peter J., and Adam Martin. 2011. Taking the "G" Out of BIG: A Comparative Political Economy Perspective on Basic Income. *Basic Income Studies* 6 (2): 1–18.

Broughel, James. 2017. *Regulation and Economic Growth: Applying Economic Theory to Public Policy*. Arlington, VA: Mercatus Center of George Mason University.

Buchanan, James M. 2008. Same Players, Different Game: How Better Rules Make Better Politics. *Constitutional Political Economy* 19 (3): 171–179.

Buchanan, James M., and Roger D. Congleton. (1998) 2003. *Politics by Principle, Not Interest: Toward Nondiscriminatory Democracy*. The Collected Works of James M. Buchanan, vol. 11. Indianapolis, IN: Liberty Fund.

Davidson, Sinclair, Primavera De Filippi, and Jason Potts. 2018. Blockchains and the Economic Institutions of Capitalism. *Journal of Institutional Economics*. Accessed January 30, 2018. https://doi.org/10.1017/S1744137417000200

DiLorenzo, Thomas J. 1988. Competition and Political Entrepreneurship: Austrian Insights into Public-Choice Theory. *Review of Austrian Economics* 2 (1): 59–71.

Dopfer, Kurt, and Jason Potts. 2008. *The General Theory of Economic Evolution*. London, UK: Routledge.

Epstein, Richard A. 1985. *Takings: Private Property and the Power of Eminent Domain*. Cambridge, MA: Harvard University Press.

———. 1995. *Simple Rules for a Complex World*. Cambridge, MA: Harvard University Press.

———. 2000. *Towards a Regulatory Constitution*. Wellington, New Zealand: New Zealand Business Roundtable.

Eucken, Walter. 1948a. On the Theory of the Centrally Administered Economy: An Analysis of the German Experiment. Part I, trans. T. W. Hutchinson. *Economica* 15 (58): 79–100.

———. 1948b. On the Theory of the Centrally Administered Economy: An Analysis of the German Experiment. Part II, trans. T. W. Hutchinson. *Economica* 15 (59): 173–193.

———. (1952) 1982. A Policy for Establishing a System of Free Enterprise. In *Standard Texts on the Social Market Economy: Two Centuries of Discussion*, ed. Wolfgang Stützel and Horst Friedrich Wünsche and trans. Derek Rutter, 115–131. Stuttgart, Germany: Gustav Fischer.

Fischel, William A. 2004. Takings and Public Choice: The Persuasion of Price. In *The Encyclopedia of Public Choice*, ed. Charles K. Rowley and Freidrich Schneider, vol. II, 549–553. Dordrecht, Netherlands: Kluwer.

Foldvary, Fred E., and Daniel B. Klein. 2003. *The Half-Life of Policy Rationales: How New Technology Affects Old Policy Issues*. New York, NY: NYU Press.
Geloso, Vincent, and Steven Horwitz. 2017. Inequality: First, Do No Harm. *The Independent Review* 22 (1): 121–134.
Gerber, David J. 1998. *Law and Competition in Twentieth Century Europe: Protecting Prometheus*. Oxford, UK: Oxford University Press.
Goldschmidt, Nils, and Arnold Berndt. 2005. Leonhard Miksch (1901–1950): A Forgotten Member of the Freiburg School. *The American Journal of Economics and Sociology* 64 (4): 973–998.
Green, David G., and Lawrence G. Cromwell. 1984. *Mutual Aid or Welfare State: Australia's Friendly Societies*. Sydney, Australia: George Allen & Unwin.
Hall, Robert E., and Alvin Rabushka. 2007. *The Flat Tax*. 2nd ed. Stanford, CA: Hoover Institution Press.
Hayek, Friedrich A. (1965) 1967. Kinds of Rationalism. In *Studies in Philosophy, Politics and Economics*, 82–95. London, UK: Routledge Kegan Paul.
Hebert, David, and Richard E. Wagner. 2013. Taxation as a Quasi-Market Process: Explanation, Exhortation, and the Choice of Analytical Windows. *Journal of Public Finance and Public Choice* 31 (1–3): 163–177.
Henderson, David R., Robert M. McNab, and Tamás Rózsás. 2005. The Hidden Inequality in Socialism. *The Independent Review* 9 (3): 389–412.
Hillman, Arye L. 2009. *Public Finance and Public Policy: Responsibilities and Limitations of Government*. New York, NY: Cambridge University Press.
Hume, David. (1741) 1985. *Essays, Moral, Political and Literary*. Indianapolis, IN: Liberty Fund.
Jakee, Keith, and Stephen Turner. 2002. The Welfare State as a Fiscal Commons: Problems of Incentives Versus Problems of Cognition. *Public Finance Review* 30 (6): 481–508.
Kasper, Wolfgang, and Manfred Streit. 1993. Lessons from the Freiburg School: The Institutional Foundations of Freedom and Prosperity. Centre for Independent Studies, *Occasional Paper No. 44*. St. Leonards, Australia: CIS.
Kasper, Wolfgang, Manfred E. Streit, and Peter J. Boettke. 2012. *Institutional Economics: Property, Competition, Policies*. 2nd ed. Cheltenham, UK: Edward Elgar.
Klein, Daniel B. 1997. *Reputation: Studies in the Voluntary Elicitation of Good Conduct*. Ann Arbor, MI: University of Michigan.
Kolev, Stefan. 2015. Ordoliberalism and the Austrian School. In *The Oxford Handbook of Austrian Economics*, ed. Peter J. Boettke and Christopher J. Coyne, 419–444. New York, NY: Oxford University Press.

Kuznicki, Jason. 2017. *Technology and the End of Authority: What is Government for?* London, UK: Palgrave Macmillan.

Lynch, G. Patrick. 2004. Protecting Individual Rights Through a Federal System: James Buchanan's View of Federalism. *Publius: The Journal of Federalism* 34 (4): 153–168.

MacDonald, Trent J. 2015. Theory of Non-Territorial Internal Exit, February 1. Accessed January 30, 2018. https://papers.ssrn.com/sol3/papers.cfm?abstract_id=2661226

MacDonald, Trent J., Darcy W.E. Allen, and Jason Potts. 2016. Blockchains and the Boundaries of Self-Organized Economies: Predictions for the Future of Banking. In *Banking Beyond Banks and Money: A Guide to Banking Services in the Twenty-First Century*, ed. Paolo Tasca, Tomaso Aste, Loriana Pelizzon, and Nicholas Perony, 279–296. Cham, Switzerland: Springer.

Madison, Gary Brent. 1997. *The Political Economy of Civil Society and Human Rights*. London, UK: Routledge.

McCloskey, Deirdre N. 2010. *BomEconomics Can't Explain the Modern World.* Chicago, IL: University of Chicago Press.

———. 2016. *Bourgeois Equality: How Ideas, Not Capital or Institutions, Enriched the World.* Chicago, IL: University of Chicago Press.

Mitchell, Dan. 2013. Decentralization and Federalism is the Libertarian Way to Determine Whether a Basic Income Is Practical or Desirable. Cato Institute, *libertarianism.org*, December 18. Accessed February 19, 2018. https://www.libertarianism.org/columns/decentralization-federalism-is-libertarian-way-determine-whether-basic-income-is-practical

Nell, Guinevere Liberty. 2017. *The Driving Force of the Collective: Post-Austrian Theory in Response to Israel Kirzner*. London, UK: Palgrave Macmillan.

Okun, Arthur M. 1975. *Equality and Efficiency: The Big Tradeoff.* Washington, DC: Brookings Institution.

Palagashvili, Liya, Ennio Piano, and David Skarbek. 2017. *The Decline and Rise of Institutions: A Modern Survey of the Austrian Contribution to the Economic Analysis of Institutions*. Cambridge Insights ed. New York, NY: Cambridge University Press.

Pennington, Mark. 2011. *Robust Political Economy: Classical Liberalism and the Future of Public Policy*. Cheltenham, UK: Edward Elgar.

Piketty, Thomas. 2014. *Capital in the Twenty-First Century: The Dynamics of Inequality, Wealth, and Growth*. Translated by Arthur Goldhammer. Cambridge, MA: The Belknap Press of Harvard University Press.

Postrel, Virginia. 1998. *The Future and Its Enemies: The Growing Conflict Over Creativity, Enterprise, and Progress*. New York, NY: Free Press.

Potts, Jason. 2010. Innovation by Elimination: A Proposal for Negative Policy Experiments in the Public Sector. *Innovation: Management, Policy & Practice* 12 (2): 238–248.

Potts, Jason, John Humphreys, and Joseph Clark. 2018. A Blockchain-Based Universal Basic Income, February 15. Accessed February 19, 2018. https://medium.com/@jason.potts/a-blockchain-based-universal-basic-income-2cb7911e2aab

Rajagopalan, Shruti, and Richard E. Wagner. 2013. Constitutional Craftsmanship and the Rule of Law. *Constitutional Political Economy* 24: 295–309.

Ratnapala, Suri. 2003. Securing Constitutional Government: The Perpetual Challenge. *The Independent Review* 8 (1): 5–26.

Raudla, Ringa. 2010. Governing Budgetary Commons: What Can We Learn from Elinor Ostrom? *European Journal of Law and Economics* 30 (3): 201–221.

Rohac, Dalibor. 2017. The Grand Bargain to Give the West Back Its Mojo. *The American Interest*, December 18. Accessed February 19, 2018. https://www.the-american-interest.com/2017/12/18/grand-bargain-give-west-back-mojo/

Röpke, Wilhelm. 1960. *A Humane Economy: The Social Framework of the Free Market*. Chicago, IL: Henry Regnery.

Salter, Alexander W., and Vlad Tarko. 2017. Governing the Financial System: A Theory of Financial Resilience. George Mason University Mercatus Center, *Working Paper*. Arlington, VA: Mercatus Center.

Salter, Alexander William, and Richard E. Wagner. 2017. Constitutional Catallaxy: Friends and Enemies in an Open-Ended Social Order. George Mason University, Department of Economics, *Working Paper No. 17-18*, May 9. Accessed September 15, 2017. https://papers.ssrn.com/sol3/papers.cfm?abstract_id=2965513

Siems, Mathias, and Gerhard Schnyder. 2014. Ordoliberal Lessons for Economic Stability: Different Kinds of Regulation, Not More Regulation. *Governance* 27 (3): 377–396.

Somin, Ilya. 2015. *The Grasping Hand: Kelo v. City of New London & the Limits of Eminent Domain*. Chicago, IL: University of Chicago Press.

Teles, Steven M. 2013. Kludgeocracy in America. *National Affairs* 17: 97–114.

Thierer, Adam. 2016. *Permissionless Innovation: The Continuing Case for Comprehensive Technological Freedom*. Revised and Expanded ed. Arlington, VA: Mercatus Center.

Vanberg, Viktor J. 2001. The Freiburg School of Law and Economics: Predecessor of Constitutional Economics. In *The Constitution of Markets: Essays in Political Economy*, ed. Viktor J. Vanberg, 37–51. London, UK: Routledge.

———. 2014. Ordnungspolitik, the Freiburg School and the Reason of Rules. *i-lex* 21: 205–220.

Wagner, Richard E. 1983. The Egalitarian Imperative. In *Against Equality: Readings on Economic and Social Policy*, ed. William Letwin. London, UK: Macmillan.

———. 1989. Fiscal Principle, Fiscal Politics, and Consumption Taxation. In *Heidelberg Congress on Taxing Consumption: Proceedings of the International Congress on Taxing Consumption, Held at Heidelberg, June 28–30, 1989*, ed. Manfred Rose, 247–263. Berlin, Germany: Springer-Verlag.

———. 1996. Economic Policy in a Liberal Democracy. *Locke Institute Shaftesbury Papers No. 8*. Cheltenham, UK: Edward Elgar.

———. 2007. *Fiscal Sociology and the Theory of Public Finance*. Cheltenham, UK: Edward Elgar.

———. 2010. *Mind, Society, and Human Action: Time and Knowledge in a Theory of Social Economy*. London, UK: Routledge.

———. 2012a. *Deficits, Debt, and Democracy: Wrestling with Tragedy on the Fiscal Commons*. Cheltenham, UK: Edward Elgar.

———. 2012b. Rationality, Political Economy, and Fiscal Responsibility: Wrestling with Tragedy on the Fiscal Commons. *Constitutional Political Economy* 23: 261–277.

———. 2012c. Viennese Kaleidics: Why It's Liberty More Than Policy That Calms Turbulence. *Review of Austrian Economics* 25 (4): 283–297.

———. 2016. *Politics as a Peculiar Business: Insights from a Theory of Entangled Political Economy*. Cheltenham, UK: Edward Elgar.

———. 2017. *James M. Buchanan and Liberal Political Economy: A Rational Reconstruction*. Lanham, MD: Lexington Books.

Watson, William. 2015. *The Inequality Trap: Fighting Capitalism Instead of Poverty*. Toronto, Canada: University of Toronto Press.

Wörsdörfer, Manuel. 2012. Walter Eucken on Patent Laws: Are Patents Just Nonsense on Stilts? *Economic Thought* 1 (2): 36–54.

Younkins, Edward W. 2002. *Capitalism and Commerce: Conceptual Foundations of Free Enterprise*. Lanham, MD: Lexington Books.

8

A Society of Dignified Equals and Inequality

Introduction

Entanglement is endemic to human affairs, and is the consequence of interactions between individuals and groups across the economic, communal, and political orders which can take on several degrees of complexity. The terms and conditions under which entanglements arise are numerous, but from a classical liberal perspective there is little doubt that certain kinds of knotted interpersonal relations are preferable to others. In the most general of terms, societal configurations which permit more members to engage with each other on a voluntary, non-coercive basis are preferred than others which constrict the scope of engagement.

The network structures of entangled political economy are not only a reflection of primarily economic matters such as relative resource endowments. The ways in which networks are formed and maintained also depend upon perceptions about the merit and worth of those agents proposing novelties into economic, social, and political affairs. However, as had been illustrated previously, if individual members of certain groups are deemed less entitled to basic human dignity and respect than others, then "option value" available to those deleteriously affected by groupish tendencies is greatly reduced.

M. Novak, *Inequality*, Palgrave Studies in Classical Liberalism,
https://doi.org/10.1007/978-3-319-89417-1_8

Out-group members are at risk of not having a seat at the negotiating table alongside in-group members. Group-based discrimination dividing the members of society into in- and out-group classifications could have a potentially telling, long-run effect upon economic inequality outcomes, representing a liberty-inconsistent source of inequality limiting the capacity of certain people to discover and implement their own modes of well-being and self-improvement (Geloso and Horwitz 2017). In the vernacular of Boettke and Candela (2017), the entrenchment of inequality on the basis of group status represents a violation of the liberally oriented "moral constitution."

The purpose of this chapter is to canvass issues concerning the intellectual position of social equality in the classical liberal tradition, and how this relates to entangled political economy. The next section outlines historical progress amongst developed countries to expand human liberties and rights. This is followed by a critical assessment of some recent suggestions to entrench hard-fought social gains, ranging from affirmative action and anti-discrimination legislation through to reparations. Acknowledging that the process of rights expansion has unfolded unevenly, we next consider the place of toleration as a pivotal rule-set in an entangled political economy context. This chapter concludes with some brief statements about how social relations grounded in greater toleration are likely to open up viable networking opportunities among disparate persons.

A Changing of the Rules: Emancipation Sequence and the Moderation of Group Biases

Identity represents an underrated, yet significant, influence upon the adaptive potential of entangled political economy. There are many identities that people assume, drawing upon cultural, social, and other forms of knowledge embraced by others. An individual may also bravely modify conventional understandings of identity by entrepreneurially fashioning themselves anew in comparison with peers and non-peers alike. Individuals can flexibly assume multiple identities which reflect their overlapping commitments in life, consistent with the thought of historian Otto von Gierke and sociologist Georg Simmel (Palmer 2008).

To summarise, an evolutionary perspective suggests that identity is fluid, contextual, and subjective (Berg et al. 2017; see also Davis 2003, 2011, and Hermann-Pillath 2013) and as such contributes to meso-level complexities.

The balance between continuity and change of individual and group identities is shaped by many forces. The alteration of a given person's sense of identity may be borne of feelings of dissatisfaction, or inadequacy, concerning certain forms of identity assigned to them at birth or during any other time prior to, or even during, adulthood. An individual may wish to change aspects of their identity with respect to occupation, religious affiliation, residential location, income level, gender identity, and so on. On the other hand, grounds for wanting to maintain a stable identity include the desire to be legible to others in order to earn recognition and esteem over time. Retention of identity is similarly informed by a propensity to form and maintain homophilous social networks.

Social distance plays its part in reinforcing identity. It is also observed that human beings have the tendency to show altruism and solidarity towards intimates, or people they least know well, but that those feelings dissipate when it comes to people identified as situated outside their favoured, in-group cliques. As stated by Barry Brownstein (2016) "[t]ribal identity fosters negative feelings, even hatred, toward those outside the tribe," starkly contrasting the "halo effect" of positive esteem that is dedicated to people regarded as belonging to the in-group.

As mentioned previously, one of the forces leaving a great impression upon identity, and the entrenchment of in- and out-group distinctions, has been governmental attempts to codify and cement identity for fiscal, regulatory, and other purposes. Whereas the ideal is that "[r]ights of ownership, contract, and tort that are not restricted by bloodlines, class, religion, or race are examples of a generality principle in law" (Buchanan and Congleton [1998] 2003, p. 87), the reality is that public sector actors have repeatedly failed to accede to such principles. Policy non-generality animated by group identity considerations has been reflected in racial identifiers in official census surveys (Thompson 2015), differential taxes imposed on the basis of race (Dowdy 2014), and public services subject to group-discriminatory provision (Halcoussis and Lowenberg 1998). These discriminatory practices were often accompanied by non-logical actions, such as the dissemination of political rhetoric, attempting to rationalise these manifestations of out-group animosity.

Discrimination and prejudice against members of out-groups may be evident throughout the annals of human history, and may still be evident in our age, yet it should not be submitted that group-based enmities are beyond rectification. If groupism is an unavoidable feature of our entangled lives, this would beg the following question: Why were government interventions deemed so pressing and necessary, in certain places and times, to entrench such norms? Our response is that mass subscription to in-group and out-group identity distinctions is not inevitable, or at least not fixed over time.

The famed "contact hypothesis" of Gordon Allport (1954) indicates that greater exposure to maligned out-group members would tend to calm discriminatory attitudes and allay stereotypical attitudes. In no small part, these effects result from the fact that those who engage across group divides are prone to discover that most individuals tend to share similar aspirations, hopes, and problems, and that each and all are roughly equipped with the same capacity for reflection and self-improvement. Stephanie Haefelle and Virgil Storr (2017) likewise contend that individuals quell their appetites for group-based discrimination by displaying acts of moderation, facilitating interpersonal engagement, sympathy, and, ultimately, peaceful coexistence.

Over the past few centuries, especially in developed countries since the British Industrial Revolution era, critical scrutiny of the efficacy and merits of group distinctions has proceeded apace. The interrogation of discrimination—as it has been manifested in policy terms, at the very least—has contributed to a succession of policy concessions breaking down group-based barriers to commingled economic, social, and political participation. The trends described here are loosely formalised in several terms in the political science and sociological literature, such as the "emancipation sequence" or the "rights revolution." The emancipation sequence has been otherwise referred to as the "Humanitarian Revolution" (Pinker 2011), the "Moral Arc" (Shermer 2015), or the "Expanding Moral Circle" (Singer 2011) in which members of previous out-groups become encompassed in the inner circle of in-groups. German political philosopher Christian Welzel explains the basis of the emancipation sequence as follows:

> Human empowerment is the emancipation of people from external domination. Emancipation requires equal freedoms, and such freedoms are granted through citizen rights. Ironically, as large as the theme of citizen rights loom in our time, it has literally been absent throughout most of history. But since the onset of preindustrial capitalism, starting with the abolition of slavery and feudal privileges, history takes a new turn: the granting of rights to common people, the steady differentiation of these rights, and their continuous extension to new groups and territories becoming a major trend of development—indeed a signature theme of modernity itself. (Welzel 2013, p. 278)

There are clearly numerous characterisations of the emancipation sequence. In common, these changes feature efforts to eliminate the range of what Jeremy Waldron (2017) calls "sortal status"—legal categorisation of people based on race, gender, and other group-identifiers—and those elements of "conditional status"—identity and status based on the conditions people find themselves in (e.g. financial solvency, marital status, occupation)—that attracted social disapproval and legal punishments.

Interpretations of the emancipation sequence will vary, but an attempt at a generic ordering of the sequence, roughly mapped to the chronology and contribution of key classical liberal figures in promulgating reforms, is described as follows:

- *Freedom of conscience*: Figures such as Desiderus Erasmus, Martin Luther, Jean Bodin, and Roger Williams argued that people should be free to exercise their own spiritual beliefs, without fear of persecution by the state or by adherents of other religious orders and belief systems.
- *Freedom of expression*: The English essayist John Milton and philosopher John Stuart Mill both argued for freedom of speech to facilitate the discovery of better ideas, and stressed the importance of preventing press censorship and other prohibitions against free expression.

- *Freedom to create economic value*: Adam Smith argued for the elimination of economic privileges advantaging certain producers, noting that empowering sellers and buyers to cooperate with each other fuels economic growth and improves material conditions for those less well-off.
- *Freedom from slavery*: Numerous thinkers of a classical liberal persuasion, including William Wilberforce, John Stuart Mill, William Lloyd Garrison, and Frederick Douglass, strenuously opposed servitude on racialist lines as a deprivation of fundamental individual liberties, including with respect to bodily integrity.
- *Freedom for women*: Beginning with the writings of Britain's Mary Wollstonecraft, classical liberal activists and scholars called for equality between women and men, including the abolition of discriminatory legal treatments and the subversion of cultural norms reinforcing a false stereotype of female inferiority.
- *Freedom to engage one's sexual preferences*: During the eighteenth century, English philosopher Jeremy Bentham and the Italian legal scholar Cesare Beccaria wrote against state punishments against gay men engaging in mutually consenting sexual conduct.

The observed wiping away of politically sponsored discrimination seems to have rested on little more than the ingenious discovery, articulate argumentation, and successful implementation of reform to weaken status differentials and to ensure that groups of people are regarded as more equal in their economic, political, and social capacities. A dissemination of socially reformist ideas often imaginatively tied arguments about freedom for all people with moral appeals to evoke support amongst in-group members and, ultimately, the political class itself (Powell 2013). Lockean notions of "natural rights" inherent in every human being were particularly influential. A contemporary interpretation of this vintage liberal proposition is that "we cannot fully respect people as morally equal, free, and autonomous human beings unless we respect them as right-holders" (Vossen 2013).

The concept of the rule of law, that all people be legally treated similarly and in generic, abstract terms (Hayek [1960] 2006), is also derived from philosophical considerations regarding the natural equality of each and all. These principles may be interpreted "negatively" in the sense that government should abstain from exacerbating groupish biases: "to respect others as free and equal moral persons is to refrain from claiming moral authority over them to demand that they do what they do not themselves have reason to endorse" (Gaus 2011, p. 19). It is from this vantage point that phenomena such as "[t]he institution of slavery—the subjugation of individuals by making them the property of others—represents the most profound nullification of equality under law" (Bolick 2008, p. 6).

In recent years, Sandra Peart and David Levy draw inspiration from classical economists such as Adam Smith and John Stuart Mill to expound a theory of "analytical egalitarianism." Peart and Levy state that, "analytical egalitarianism … presumes humans are the same in their capacity for language and trade; observed differences are then explained by incentives, luck, and history" (Peart and Levy 2005, p. 3). Countering the stereotypical portrayals of out-group members as somehow incapable of meaningful interaction, analytical egalitarians illustrate how the trying economic, social, and political positions faced by certain groups are traced to *illiberal government policies* preventing people from striking their own network connections.

The intellectual arguments for advancing liberty were accompanied by other, moralistic appeals which could be understood by in-group and out-group members alike. One method of non-logical persuasion was for members of out-groups, and their coalitional allies within in-groups, to analogise their disadvantaged situations with those of other groups in society. For example, the "first-wave" feminist movement of the eighteenth and nineteenth centuries compared the status of women with that of slaves, finding a shared cause of oppression: legal restrictions against the capacity of certain people to fully engage with others economically, socially, and politically (Novak 2016).

Individuals who were advantaged by discriminatory legal regimes were also challenged to contemplate putting themselves in the place of oppressed minorities. Expressed differently, in-group members were encouraged to use their imaginations to "enter" into another's situation and conceive how they would cope if they were to be discriminated against (Griswold 1999; Darwall 2004). Illuminating inconsistences by those favouring group-based discrimination also played its role in adjusting attitudes: "if we believe that men and women are equal, we cannot consistently maintain that sons should be favored over daughters. Discussions are one of the best ways to unearth such inconsistencies" (Bicchieri 2017, p. 157).

Any novel proposal to extend rights occasioned a degree of resistance from groups whose members enjoy privileges. Referring to groups as "castes," Ludwig von Mises notes that "[e]ach privileged caste aims at the attainment of new privileges and at the preservation of the old ones. Each underprivileged caste aims at the abolition of its disqualifications" (Mises [1945] 1978, p. 3). The potential insufficiency of arguments alone to counter group privileges points to the historically pivotal role of meso-level social movements—consisting of alliances and coalitions of like-minded individuals dedicated to eliminate government-entrenched discrimination—in pressing for greater social equality:

> Inspired by emancipative values, people take action on behalf of freedoms. This is evident in all kinds of social movement activity, the most vigorous of which voice emancipatory goals: people-power movements, equal opportunity movements, civil rights movements, women's rights movements, gay rights movements, children's rights movements, and so forth. (Welzel 2013, p. 396)

Activists engaged in a variety of additional strategies to promulgate their pro-equality causes. These included patient, "behind-the-scenes" engagement within policy and legislative networks, the promulgation of media campaigns (Bicchieri 2017), non-violent demonstrations, and acts of civil disobedience to attract public attention. As was famously demonstrated by Rosa Parks—who, upon refusing to obey race-demarcated seating arrangements on mass transit, was arrested and convicted in 1955 for violating U.S. Jim Crow segregation laws—activism grounded in non-violence can also be assumed by individuals.

While campaigning for emancipation is not cost-free, organising actions against governmental injustices need not be conducted at great cost. One relatively low-cost way in which social movements can influence the agenda is by engaging with members of the general public, changing their political attitudes concerning group biases. Charles

Johnson refers to, for example, the "women-led social movements to counter the effects of diffuse male violence outside, or beyond, the sphere of government and conventional political lobbying. C.R. groups, speakouts, culture-jamming, building grassroots networks of battered women's shelters, rape crisis centers, and other feminist spaces originally had little if any connection to hierarchical power-politics or the male-dominated state, and all could productively be understood as *voluntarily-coordinated*, *polycentric*, but *consciously organized* political resistance to a *polycentric*, *emergent*, *coercive* order of violent oppression" (Johnson 2013, p. 25).

For classical liberals, market effects also play a significant role in eliciting greater attention to the need to ameliorate discrimination. On some accounts, it is surmised there is a direction of causation running from economic prosperity to greater demands for emancipation and inclusiveness. As people are able to procure their own income, and accumulate their own wealth, their concerns transcend physiological considerations of survival for themselves, their kin, and other members of their immediate group, towards philosophical concerns regarding the attainment of individual liberties and rights. This process represents, in effect, an escalation up the scale of Abraham Maslow's (1943) famous "needs-hierarchy."

The development of markets *also* facilitates the breakdown of social distance between individual members of diverse groups. Arguably, the most famous statement in all of classical liberalism connecting market trades with social harmony and peace came in the form of Montesquieu's *doux-commerce* thesis, enunciated in his eighteenth-century tract *The Spirit of the Laws*. "Commerce cures destructive prejudices," stated Montesquieu, "and it is an almost general rule that everywhere there are gentle mores, there is commerce and that everywhere there is commerce, there are gentle mores" (Montesquieu [1748] 2008, p. 338).

To enhance opportunities for market-tested betterment, individual economic agents reach out to non-intimates possessing specialised (often tacit) knowledge about what, when, where, and how to produce. Reaching out successfully involves the need to understand and respect other agents, irrespective of those backgrounds and customs which have immaterial bearing upon a capacity to arrive at mutually beneficial exchange. To the extent that such dispositions are respected, the implication will be that, in effect, "movable effects, such as silver, notes, letters of exchanges, shares in companies, ships, and all commodities, belong to the whole world, which, in this regard comprises but a single state of which all societies are members" (Ibid., p. 352).

Some of the more interesting strands of research in contemporary classical liberalism question communitarian, and other market-antagonistic perspectives, contending that market activity corrodes human relationships grounded in altruism, care, and support for others. Virgil Storr (2008) illustrates that economic interactions facilitate interpersonal conversation and, through it, a better correspondence in intersubjective understandings. Building upon the work of Adam Smith and other early-stage classical liberals, Neera Badhwar states: "by breaking the shackles of inherited status, the market order made it possible for people to see themselves as equals and ends in themselves … In pre-commercial societies, friends and enemies were created by custom, station, and estate—and most strangers were potential enemies. The universalism of the new commercial society created a public space characterized by a hitherto unknown openness and friendliness" (Badhwar 2008, p. 319). These processes often turn initially commercial acquaintances into close friends over time.

All in all, the classical liberal position is that interaction by agents within the decentralised, market-based economic order is not only likely to dissipate income and wealth inequality. The *doux-commerce* thesis exemplifies the venerable liberal idea that market activities also promote social equality. It is in this spirit that Pérez-Diaz submits that, "[e]ngagement in markets should … be expected to bring home awareness of the fact that every individual is placed within an ever-expanding network of social relations" (Pérez-Diaz 2009, p. 61). Interaction in this context is, therefore, said to foster other-regarded attitudes towards others, including those people much unlike ourselves.

The realisation of a process dissipating in-group/out-group animosities is also reliant upon policy concessions to reduce discriminatory barriers against economic and social engagement. These concessions may come in the form of unilateral political decisions to unwind formal discrimination, or as responses to judicial decisions and other events, obliging government to cease its repression of minorities and other out-group members. As mentioned previously, economist Jayme Lemke expounded the intriguing hypothesis that the elimination of restrictions against married women owning their own property in the U.S. was influenced by competition between established American states and Western frontier jurisdictions for greater gender balance within their populations (Lemke 2012, 2016).

Figure 8.1 illustrates some of the properties underlying the propagation of a rule-set consistent with the emancipation sequence over time. There are numerous meso-level groups embedded within this entangled political economy—the non-political agents are represented by hexagon shapes and political agents by the triangles. The political system assumes a monocentric quality, given the presence of only one meso-set of political agents. To complicate this picture somewhat, suppose that all agents assume one of two generic identities—purple or green. It is clear that the agents assuming the purple identity represent a clear majority, although the inherent complexity of identity is underlined by the various shades of purple identities.

During time period *t* all members of society adhere to a discriminatory rule-structure (indicated by income-flow connections marked by thick

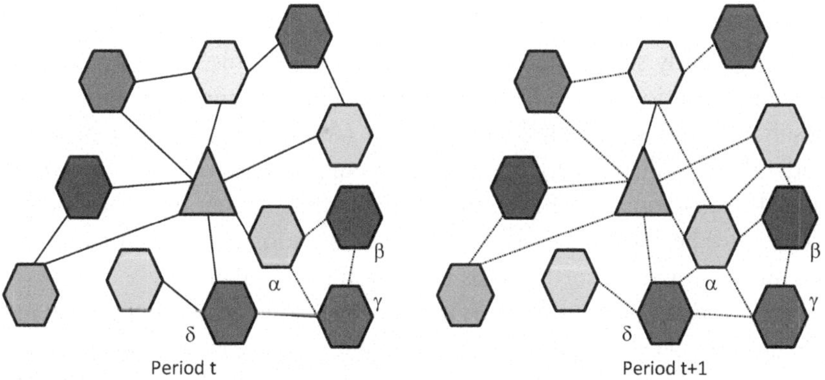

Fig. 8.1 Emancipation sequence effects. Source: Author's illustrations

black lines). This situation leaves members affiliated with the minority green identity (represented by α) in a position relatively isolated from the others. The α-agents have a direct, yet subordinated, relationship with the government (consisting of a meso sub-population of micro agents assuming a purple identity). The α-agents also have a small number of allies (β and γ) in a sub-network connected by a shared ethical and ideological adherence to non-discriminatory rules (expressed by connections marked by dashed black lines). Agent γ fortuitously has a connection with another set of purple meso agents (denoted by δ) who do not wish to deal directly with minority α but which, nevertheless, indirectly assist the reform-minded coalition to muster a sufficient level of action-resources campaigning for pro-egalitarian social change.

With a judicious admixture of convincing intellectual argument and moral rhetoric, combined with the use of novel campaigning techniques, the discriminatory rule against the α-agents is eventually displaced by a non-discriminatory rule allowing each meso-population sub-group to facilitate their own connections as they see fit. During period $t + 1$, agents α and former discriminators δ establish a direct connection, as have other agents within the entangled political economy. Similar changes to the network degree distribution suggest that ameliorating discrimination—in a way compatible with "a movement from Status to Contract," as famously stated by Sir Henry Maine—is likely to contribute towards a reduction in inequality.

Progress in easing discriminatory restraints against participation in economic, social, and political networks has been practically observed, more evidently so in some places than in others. This is simply because the emancipation sequence is not a deterministic trend. It is, rather, the result of meso-level utopia competition (Almudi et al. 2017) between individuals affiliated with alternating groups—generically, the in-group and the out-group. Utopia competition is in the end an intensely fought contest for hearts and minds over the basic question of social equality: the argument to reduce sortal status to a common humanity.

It is for these reasons that it is presumptuous to suggest that the emancipation sequence is complete. According to a recent account by philosopher Loren Lomasky and legal scholar Fernando Tesón, "[i]nnumerable practices—for example, slavery, enforced female subservience, persecution of homosexuals—were at one time taken for granted but now are clearly seen to be unjust. Moral myopia strikes in different ways in different environments and ages. To suppose that our current state of enlightenment has put all species of invidious discrimination behind us is an optimism called into question by that prior experience" (Lomasky and Tesón 2015, p. 92). Given that shifting legal rights result from emergent, participatory processes, it is, regrettably from a classical liberal perspective, not a foregone conclusion that discriminatory barriers will always recede.

Immigration appears to be a good case in point with respect to the intransigence of discrimination. Although some of the worst vestiges of race-based immigration policies have been abolished, many developed countries have introduced quotas capping the number of migrant entries, established elaborate visa authorisation processes, and have more stringently enforced passport restrictions for business and personal travel across national borders. Countries have also restricted the ability of migrants of various visa classes, especially those on short-term stays, to gain employment and access certain social services (e.g. education, housing). As Kunal Parker (2015) demonstrated in his historical account of U.S. immigration, more stringent regulations against migrants coincided with the emancipation sequence primarily benefitting groups of American citizens.

Loren Lomasky (2001) suggests that adherence to a principle of "softening borders" could play a pivotal role to ameliorate unwarranted discrimination between nationals and non-nationals. The "softening borders" phrase suggests that limitations on cross-border movement be eased, in effect so that inter-national borders more closely resemble the intra-national borders found in federal systems. According to some accounts, such an initiative risks a worsening of income inequality. In this case, an influx of lowly skilled migrants somehow depresses the wages of residents, especially those with lower skills, less education, and less work experience. Even if this prognosis is accepted in an uncritical fashion, the classical liberal approach would still endorse an extensive immigration flow, since any inequality attributable to immigration does not, *prima facie*, abridge liberty.

Alongside a reduction in the use of costly and violent border-security regimes by governments, less stringent immigration regulations could help undermine deeply entrenched economic and social networks as opportunities increase for more people to freely associate with each other (Lomasky and Tesón 2015; Tebble 2016). Both migrants and native-born citizens stand to benefit from the enhanced opportunities to interact with one another in closer proximity. The incomes received by migrants in wealthy developed countries are also likely to contribute to a reduction in global inequality, including if some of the proceeds are repatriated to friends and families in developing countries (Geloso and Horwitz 2017).

From Affirmative Action to Reparations: The Controversies Surrounding "Reverse Discrimination"

Over the past two centuries, there has been a clear trend amongst developed countries to ease legal constraints upon certain minorities, women, and other members of formally designated out-groups. The relaxation of discriminatory barriers has not only extended social equality. The reform process, all else being equal, is likely to have played some role in suppressing income and wealth inequalities. This effect results from more people being able to entrepreneurially contest incumbent patterns of production, distribution, and exchange promulgated by members affiliated with in-groups.

Noting the esteem for non-discrimination in majoritarian democracies, and wishing to signal their desire to rectify the deleterious legacies of previously government-supported group divisions, political actors in recent decades have gone further to invoke policies "designed to be the diametric opposite of the exclusionary ones. They would not only erase any law in the books that singled out an ethnic minority for unfavorable treatment, but would swing the opposite pole and mandate *anti*-exclusionary, *un*-eliminationist policies" (Pinker 2011, p. 389).

There are several forms in which "reverse discrimination" policies can take. The first we refer to are a somewhat related set of policies commonly referred to as "anti-discrimination." These are measures designed to eliminate discriminatory treatment of people based on background characteristics deemed irrelevant to economic and social considerations (e.g. race, ethnicity, gender, religious affiliation, and sexual orientation). Anti-discrimination policy generically covers interactions by people with regard to employment and workplace conduct, and accessing services provided by economic and political enterprises.

Legislative provisions proscribing discriminatory treatment against individuals on the basis of certain group characteristics appear to enjoy widespread support within developed countries. In practice, there seems little appetite for a return to the days in which formal segregation, employment discrimination, and group-differentiated service access were the norm. As is the case with legislation in many instances, anti-discrimination provisions in some way could be interpreted as an *ex-post* codification of the more inclusive community values which have built up as the emancipation sequence has unfolded over time.

As anti-discrimination legislation was crafted and implemented, several figures aligned with classical liberal or conservative intellectual traditions raised their concerns about the propriety of such actions. The critics suggested that statutes enshrining anti-discrimination may induce legal conflicts, as those refused employment or service could claim that such an event resulted from discrimination by the employer or provider, respectively. From a legal perspective, there are concerns that anti-discrimination provisions lead the burden of proof to effectively shift from the allegedly discriminated party to the alleged discriminator (Epstein 1992, 1995). The presence of anti-discrimination legislation could also create an arena for institutionalised conflicts between different groups in society, each striving to attain protection under relevant legislation. Similarly, it has been supposed that anti-discrimination legislation could threaten long-cherished liberal rights as freedom of association and speech, and the free exercise of religious beliefs (Bernstein 2003).

It must be said that such worries surrounding anti-discrimination legislation are not necessarily the final words on the matter. Other adherents of classical liberal philosophy argue that policies explicitly preventing the discrimination against certain groups need not rank highly in any listing of legislative reversal. During an online debate about the relationships between discrimination and liberty, David Bernstein (2010) suggested that Title II of the American *Civil Rights Act 1964*—which prohibited racial segregation in public accommodations—was justifiable as a pro-liberty counter to the punitive Jim Crow laws. There seems little doubt that the legitimacy of anti-discrimination legislation, and many other legislative edicts promulgated by government, will continue to be debated amongst liberal circles. The consistency of anti-discrimination statutes against tests that it be "simple, easy-to-understand … [and] … well supported by social norms and community understandings" (Kuznicki 2010) is likely to serve as one area of consideration among many in future debates.

Another policy development which has garnered some controversy is what is generically called "affirmative action." These kinds of policies can encompass anti-discrimination but invariably go further to ratify what might be perceived as "proactive" strategies to assist people identified as the subject of disadvantageous treatment in the past (e.g. indigenous peoples, persons with disabilities, women, people identifying as gay, lesbian, bisexual, transgender, or intersex). Some kinds of affirmative action may come in the form of unfunded regulatory mandates, in which political actors insist that economic enterprises provide favourable treatment to traditional out-group members in the provision of goods and services such as credit, education and healthcare, as well as advantageous contract provisions.

Other affirmative action policies encompass employment programmes such as numerical quotas to ensure adequate representation of certain groups within the workforce. Taking the case of policies aimed at promoting the economic status of women, several countries and regions (such as Belgium, Canada's Quebec, France, Iceland, and Norway) have adopted "gender quotas." These quota initiatives specify that a certain proportion of people hired within senior private or public sector employment positions must be women. In other countries, such as Australia, legislators occasionally threaten to impose formal quotas should major corporations not proactively take their own steps hiring more senior women.

The imposition of gender quotas has not gone unchallenged either, by certain classical liberals. In a statement reminiscent of Douglas Rae's (1981) distinction between individual- and bloc-regarding inequalities, Chandran Kukathas suggests:

> preferential policies to address inequalities of opportunity between groups may work to increase equalities between the general level of benefits enjoyed by particular groups as wholes, but at the expense of equality between individuals in society. Favoured individuals in poor groups may thus grow wealthy, making for wider differences not only between them and the poor of the richer groups, but also between them and the poor of their own, poor, group. (Kukathas 2003, p. 217)

Even figures sympathetic to affirmative action objectives, such as sociologist William Julius Wilson, have questioned the effectiveness of quotas (in this case, on a racial basis) in that such policies would benefit individuals already possessing extensive human capital, rather than those in genuinely disadvantaged circumstances (Wilson 1987).

The psychological literature has shown that affirmative action policies such as quotas not only do very little to improve the perceptions of others, particularly those harbouring misogynistic or biased views, towards women (Heilman et al. 1992). The policies may also adversely affect the perceptions of the women they intend to help. Some studies have shown that quotas could detrimentally affect beneficiary women's self-images, detrimentally affecting their work performance (Unzueta et al. 2010), whereas others suggest women who benefit under quota regimes in some circumstances may be ignored or sidelined in internal decision-making processes (Karpowitz and Mendelberg 2014).

There is also the concern that firms may overlook hiring some talented men in order to fulfil their gender quota obligations, which could somewhat compromise the ability of the economic enterprise to create additional value for their customers. Viewed from an entangled political economy perspective, the gender quota imposes triadic exchange effects, much like any other form of regulation—in this instance, legislators and bureaucrats set up a policy advantaging women as a group, whilst members of another group (i.e. men) must find alternative employment. It may also be speculated that a gender quota regime would be classified as non-market-conformable under criteria established by ordo-liberals for a functional economic order (Wagner 2016).

The seemingly widely held sentiment to eliminate employment discrimination is aptly encapsulated by the French phrase *la carrière ouverte aux talents* (translated into English, "careers open to talents"). It is insisted that people should have the same basic opportunity to improve their economic and social positions in accordance with their inherent capabilities and skills on merit, abstracting away from background characteristics and conditions irrelevant to performance. This laudable notion seems, if anything, to be undermined by quota policies which "run contrarily to most liberal democratic conceptualizations of equality and citizenship, which demand that the superficial phenological and morphological characteristics used to distinguish supposedly distinct … [groups] … matter not" (Thompson 2015, p. 115). In any event, by attempting to manipulate labour market outcomes, legislators and bureaucrats run, once again, the risk of entrenching group distinctions through the policy process.

Policymakers have also instigated a raft of measures, known as "pay equity" or "comparable worth." These policies are justified on the basis of rectifying the consequences of previously discriminatory policies, wherein women were paid less than men when performing comparable jobs. In the face of rising educational attainment by girls and young women, and increasing labour force participation rates, governments progressively relaxed gender-based discriminatory edicts by and large during the twentieth century. Going beyond this, however, developed countries also legislated pay equity regimes. The United States introduced an *Equal Pay Act* in 1963 applicable to both private and public sector employment, and Australia, New Zealand, and the United Kingdom introduced their own pay equity legislation or regulatory guidelines within roughly the following decade. Most other OECD-member countries have followed suit.

Defenders of these regulatory arrangements frequently invoke statistics showing, on average, women are still being paid less than men, suggesting that pay equity objectives are somehow not being met. Many classical liberals tend to concur with the findings of more sophisticated empirical analyses that—once occupational selection, different types of education and training, decisions to raise a family, and so on, are considered—much of the observed gender pay gap is accounted for by choice and effort. This discussion should not be taken to imply that nothing in the average women-men remuneration differential is attributable to persistent discriminatory tastes by employers. The key message is that the weight of evidence suggests such malign effects are relatively small in magnitude. It should not be presumed, in any event, that statistically averaged characteristics attributable to a group are replicated in every single individual identified with that group (Bowman 2017).

One should be mindful of Richard Epstein's point that "[t]he critical question about 'pay equity' is whether there is any precision in the term—something that decides that equity is going to be a collective determination or, alternatively, that equity is going to be determined by individual, subjective valuations as expressed in the marketplace" (Epstein 1995, p. 189). Genuine differences of perspective concerning the treatment of women and men in employment situations—reflected in, say, whether bloc-regarding inequalities revealed by average or median pay gaps are relevant to discussions about individual-regarding inequalities—are anecdotally observed to represent yet another source of tectonic clashing between regulators and the regulated.

Finally, we wish to consider reparations, a potential remedy that has largely remained within the confines of academic discussions but, nonetheless, has been recommended to redress past discrimination. Reparations could be very broadly defined to encompass the policy positions previously described in this section—that is, anti-discrimination and affirmative action is needed to make amends for past group-based discrimination. For our immediate purposes, however, we consider reparations as merely the provision of financial assistance to those harmed by the scourges of racism, sexism, xenophobia, or other vestiges of discrimination previously waged by political agents. In this context, reparations may come in the form of governmental transfer payments to historically victimised out-groups.

There are classical liberal (and libertarian) strains of thought providing support for a reparations regime to rectify previous injustices, which involve the taking of properties. John Locke once argued that "he who hath received any damage, has, besides the right of punishment common to him with other Men, a particular Right to seek *Reparation* from him that has done it" (Locke [1689] 1988, p. 273). The twentieth-century libertarian philosopher Robert Nozick outlined a theory of "justice as rectification," whereby those whose actions breach the principle of non-interference must compensate those whose rights have been violated (Nozick 1974). The Nozickian perspective, incidentally, dictates that distributions of income and wealth—of even a heavily skewed nature—are deemed just if they are the product of mutually agreeable transactions by economic agents, with no property confiscation or theft applicable.

Whilst reparations appear consistent with liberty principles under certain conditions, severe Hayekian knowledge problems would seem to make the achievement of well-targeted reparation schemes a very tall order. According to Tom Palmer, the case for reparations in response to historical slavery in the U.S., for instance, is a practically challenging task: "[t]here are no living persons who were either slaves or slave-holders. That fact does not dispense with claims for reparations; those who inherited less because the wealth of their ancestors was stolen could, after all, be compensated by those who inherited more because their ancestors stole. This argument, however, is difficult to maintain after the passage of so long a time. The populations are today so mixed and the strands so intertwined that we cannot determine the justice of inherited endowments" (Palmer 2009, pp. 318–319).

Given the proclivity of political agents to want "to specify the exact shape of things, to reify detailed categories" (Postrel 1998, p. 127), classical liberal reservations regarding the reintroduction of politically determined social group categories, through the prism of fiscal and regulatory policies, are not unwarranted. The virtue of the liberal support for an identity-blind legislative and policy agenda is precisely so that individuals, regardless of how they identify themselves and are identified by their compatriots, enjoy maximal scope for forging their own mutually agreeable connections with others. A politically "thin" conception of identity—in which each and all are respected and treated equally resulting from their shared humanity—avoids the worst effects of government-inspired discrimination.

Consistent with the extensive domain for freedom of action in a liberal society, it is true that willing individuals, agencies, and groups can establish their own affirmative action protocols on top of a political non-discrimination norm. An open, liberal society would be able to accommodate polycentrically centred experiments to appropriately acknowledge the harms caused by group-discriminatory government policies of times past (Bean 2016; Cohen 2016). A reparations scheme could even be subject to private and other non-political forms of financial support, through crowdsourcing or some other means, by a critical mass of individuals convinced of the need to promote justice.

As noted by Adam Tebble, "the stance of statutory silence endorsed by the epistemic liberal state means that individuals would be equally at liberty to impose discriminatory burdens upon one another, they would also be at liberty, either alone or in concert, to decide upon their own anti-discrimination and affirmative action strategies with respect to employment and education" (Tebble 2016, p. 223). Lest this position be misunderstood by all fair-minded, reasonable persons who rightly abhor discrimination, "[t]he repeal of most state-mandated affirmative action programmes … would not mean that the state endorses inequality of opportunity, or affirms the acceptability of discrimination *per se*, but rather that it upholds the idea that civil society is the proper locus for debate and decision-making about what responses to phenomena such as discrimination and lack of advantage are most appropriate, given the tacit understandings of and distancing between its members" (Ibid., p. 225).

Not by Formal Institutions Alone: Toleration as Binding Agent for Social Equality

Our intellectual journey towards an understanding of the basis of social equality in an entangled political economy frame brings us to a final set of considerations: the foundations and implications of toleration—arguably one of the most esteemed virtues in all of classical liberal philosophy.

There have been many attempts to arrive at a reasonably cogent definition of toleration, with recent contributions giving emphasis to three theoretical elements. First, there is a micro- or meso-level tolerating agent (α) and a tolerated agent (β). Second, there is an object of toleration ψ—generically, an attitude, attribute, belief, behaviour, characteristic, identity, or value—associated with β which arouses a sense of disapproval or negative sentiment on the part of α. Third, and finally, there is a deliberate decision made by α to not impose their will upon β in order to amend ψ in some way which would be more agreeable to α (Cohen 2014; Şahin 2010, 2015).

Classical liberalism emphasises the desirability of non-interference in the lives of others (agent β's), even if they undertake courses of action that we (in our capacity as agent α's) believe to be consequentially erroneous or morally wrong, though not socially harmful. Toleration appears closely aligned with liberal non-interference given that the person committing a given act (in our case, expressing the view or assuming the identity we find disagreeable) is, nevertheless, allowed to persist with that act. However, the following question does arise: How far should a tolerating person, or group of tolerating persons, abstain from interference?

Based on an appreciation that toleration need not connote indifference about what others do, and how others are to be, Karl Popper ([1945] 1995) presented what he labelled a "paradox of tolerance." This paradox asserts that extending a welcoming, all-encompassing hand of "unlimited" tolerance to each and all, especially to those who display intolerance, would undermine tolerance itself (for a response to Popper's paradox, and some modern interpretations of it, see Kuznicki 2017). There are a number of closely interrelated reasons why classical liberals, nonetheless, hold toleration as an ideal:

- *Autonomy*: a tolerant society respects the fundamental rights of the individual to partake in acts and indulge in beliefs (including in competition and collaboration with other people) adjudged to be most conducive for their self-development;
- *Competition*: a sense of toleration towards those wishing to challenge existing ideas and rules encourages Millian "experiments in living," which are themselves subject to competitive testing, economically, socially, and politically;
- *Diversity*: human environments characterised by a high degree of toleration create and encourage the development of new ideas and innovations (in all realms of human activity) without undue fear of nullification by the intolerant, unleashing greater diversity amongst meso-level populations;
- *Knowledge*: toleration enables heterogeneous individuals to act how they wish to act, and be who they want to become, and so produces and

disseminates a rich tapestry of knowledge and social learning throughout the economic, communal, and political orders concerning lifestyle, preference, and ethical rules;

- *Costs*: a lack of toleration necessitates imposing one's will unto other people, many of whom are unknown to us, and this would impose substantial enforcement and other costs to ensure common adherence with the allegedly "one, true way of life"; and
- *Détente*: we maintain a disposition of toleration—irrespective of irrelevant background traits of, and non-harmful kinds of conduct by, others—because intolerance risks retaliation from others with respect to the matters that we ourselves would seek toleration (Cohen 2014; Şahin 2015).

Toleration as a social norm and practice appears to be more prevalent in countries exhibiting a stronger commitment to liberal institutions which order activity in the economic and political realms. The economic order—whose activities are shaped by constitutive rules of property, contract, liability, and so on—is more effective in ensuring that market processes are ends-independent and non-discriminatory in character, both enabling and ennobling "everyone to contribute to the generation of new knowledge, be it as employees, employers or entrepreneurs" (Berggren and Elinder 2012, p. 290). It is conceived that markets can help foster tolerance in several crucial ways:

> People can internalize a positive outlook on others through transactions that demonstrate that those who are different can be trusted. … If people want to improve their lot, they realize that in a market economy this can come about through treating others on the basis of what they can contribute, not on the basis of characteristics such as race or sexual orientation. … The market process tends to transform society over time, from the small, closed group (that exerts pressure on people to conform to one way of life) to the great society, where people need not try to control and dislike those who deviate from majority practices and characteristics. (Berggren 2014, p. 56)

Contractual performance voluntarily rendered through markets is sharply contrasted with triadic exchanges grafted through political negotiation between legislators, bureaucrats, and typically highly organised interest groups. As described as Wagner, "[t]here is a fundamental clash between liberty, private property, spontaneous ordering, and a tolerance over outcomes on the one hand, and servility, relationships based on domination and subordination, collective property, and preferences over outcomes on the other" (Wagner 2002, p. 118). The rent-seeking, fomented by the dispensing of political favours, connotes interpersonal distinctions made on the basis of status, marking out winners and losers from the dispensing of privilege. The tendency to seek private gains through politics does, indeed, sit most awkwardly alongside voluntary exchanges which fructify the social value of tolerance.

A number of classical liberals contend it would be practically difficult for all (heterogeneous) individuals within society to reach binding agreement about distributive patterns and social justice arrangements (Kukathas 2003; Pennington 2011; Tebble 2016). This conferral does not entail a dispensing of political status, but necessitates an extensive realm of non-interference from legislative and bureaucratic actions. At the very least, "political forces must seek to encourage, or at least not actively retard, the process of micro units becoming generically different" (Dopfer and Potts 2008, p. 96). Therefore, it is desirable to preside over a minimal set of formal institutional rules conferring a high degree of dignity and respect to people interacting in the economic and communal orders.

The constitutive rules for a market-based economic order, mapped out by the German ordo-liberals, align reasonably neatly, with a range of long-standing ethical norms fostering mutually beneficial and cooperative relations between non-intimates. Within this, the ethical rules are fundamentally grounded in the values of toleration. In respect of private property, Leeson and Boettke (2006) submit that the maintenance of this regime encourages tolerance in two ways. First, "the private property system tells individuals that they are free to do what they want with their property and must refrain from interfering with others doing the same, even if they disagree with what others are doing" (Ibid., p. 204). Second, "in establishing maximal latitude to individuals to use their property as they see fit, liberalism limits the size and scope of the government to its role as protector of individuals' property rights" (Ibid.).

Based on theories developed by the likes of Elinor and Vincent Ostrom, classical liberals in recent years have made great strides elucidating the kinds of political institutions reconciling the imperatives of diversity (as a foundation for dynamism) and peace (as a foundation for cooperation). Polycentricity is increasingly viewed as a robust, "anti-fragile" framework to generate feedback, encourage social learning, and accommodate differences in ways of being, doing, and knowing. As noted by Boettke, "[a] humane liberalism, as well as a robust and resilient liberalism, may find its operationalizability in an institutional structure of overlapping competing jurisdictions, and in a public discourse that respects the limits of agreement on ultimate values, but insists on a general framework that exhibits neither discrimination nor dominion" (Boettke 2017).

The record of the emancipation sequence suggests that toleration also tends to flourish in those countries whereby commitments to eschew political influence over personal and social identities are most keenly applied. In an assessment of the effects of the emancipation sequence, Christian Welzel says, "[p]eople in knowledge societies experience weakening social control mechanisms, diminishing group norms, fading conformity pressures, and, more generally, individualization: a process that places behavioral control with people themselves" (Welzel 2013, p. 5).

Leeson and Boettke observed that some of the luminaries of classical liberalism played significant roles in propagating the merits of toleration. John Locke argued in favour of religious toleration, whereas Mill defended toleration of thought and speech. These figures bravely promulgated their landmark views during periods in which diverse perspectives were not necessarily welcomed by authority, or even by the majority of the general public. According to Leeson and Boettke, "[t]hese multiple conceptions of liberal tolerance are bound together by the overriding belief that (a) individuals have different, often conflicting values about how to live, and (b) individuals should be allowed to pursue their values to the greatest extent possible, free from encroachments by third parties, be they public or private" (Leeson and Boettke 2006, p. 203). In no uncertain terms, the liberal argument for toleration was instrumental in fostering the extensive economic, social, and political changes that we call the emancipation sequence.

The gradual disintegration of group-based discrimination ensures that less and less of the economic inequality observed is reflective of the morally disreputable, and socially corrupting, division of human beings into "boxed-in" identity categories bearing no connection to their aspirations, capabilities, and dreams. The trend improvement in social equality—represented by greater consistency of respect and treatment for individuals of all races, ethnicities, gender identities, nationalities, occupations, religions, and sexual orientations—is also of paramount importance, including to classical liberals, because of the way in which it has dramatically expanded the scope of economic, social, and political participation.

Conclusion

This chapter has advanced the claim that the treatment of certain groups of people under political authority, and by their peers, is linked with distributional economic outcomes. The human tendency to demarcate each other, and even ourselves, as a part of our either favourable in-groups or unfavourable out-groups has too frequently metastasised into political groupism and economic division. Group-oriented discrimination in politics carries significant risks for the simple system of natural, non-discriminatory liberty, simply because political actors can intertwine with rent-seeking non-political actors to reward insider cliques and punish designated outsiders.

The relationship between the social inequality of a common regard and inequalities of income and wealth may be considered as largely of an indirect nature. Nonetheless, the economic-social inequality nexus carries importance for the evolutionary resilience of orders comprising entangled political economy, not to mention the esteem for existing systems of private and public orderings in the estimation of the general public. In any event, there is something deeply disturbing within the core of the proposition that human beings are somehow not socially equal—if, for some reason, one believes that other people are their lesser, they are more likely to want to differentially regulate or tax them; in other words, treat others illiberally.

Seeking institutional arrangements rewarding domination nor subjection, classical liberalism applies the principles of legal neutrality to everybody in the same measure, without fear or favour. When equality refers to the consistent and widespread application of consensual dealings between individuals—without consideration to background attributes and beliefs which have no bearing on respecting other people's possessions, the keeping of promises, and compensating for wrongdoing—there exists no inconsistency between it and liberty, since both merely represent two sides of the same coin to be used to cash in an unfolding process of human betterment.

In an important statement of contemporary liberalism, Peter Boettke (2017) suggests that "[t]he liberal virtues of respect, honesty, openness, and toleration all entail a commitment to a way of relating to one another, not necessarily a commitment to agree with one another about sacred beliefs of lifestyle choices, or what commodities we desire, or what occupation we want to pursue." The appropriate legal representation of these principles was aptly described by John Tomasi as one which "neither impose[s] legal disabilities nor confer[s] advantages on the basis of ascriptive, status-based characteristics" (Tomasi 2012, p. 241).

The classical liberal of today is far from oblivious to challenges against the liberty-conforming emancipation sequence that has progressed, sometimes rather painstakingly so, over time. Recent political developments in the United States, Europe, and elsewhere have meant that racism, xenophobia, and anti-cosmopolitanism have returned to foment social discord and political turbulence. The unedifying political scenes before us sharply remind liberals that the phrase "eternal vigilance is the price of liberty" still holds true in the twenty-first century, inspiring them to reaffirm the age-old liberal traditions of social equality and toleration for our age.

References

Allport, Gordon W. 1954. *The Nature of Prejudice*. Cambridge, MA: Addison-Wesley.

Almudi, Isabel, Francisco Fatas-Villafranca, Luis R. Izquierdo, and Jason Potts. 2017. The Economics of Utopia: A Co-evolutionary Model of Ideas, Citizenship and Socio-Political Change. *Journal of Evolutionary Economics* 27 (4): 629–662.

Badhwar, Neera K. 2008. Friendship and Commercial Societies. *Politics, Philosophy & Economics* 7 (3): 301–326.

Bean, Jonathan. 2016. Say No to Reparations: Remembering Slavery, Forgetting the Classical-Liberal Values That Abolished It. Independent Institute, *The Beacon blog*, March 21. Accessed December 2, 2017. http://blog.independent.org/2016/03/21/say-no-to-reparations-remembering-slavery-forgetting-the-liberal-values-that-abolished-it/

Berg, Chris, Sinclair Davidson, and Jason Potts. 2017. The Institutional Economics of Identity. RMIT University, *Working Paper*, November 16. Accessed November 30, 2017. https://papers.ssrn.com/sol3/papers.cfm?abstract_id=3072823

Berggren, Niclas. 2014. The Soft Side of Economic Freedom. In *Annual Proceedings of the Wealth and Well-Being of Nations*, ed. Joshua C. Hall, vol. 6, 43–66. Beloit, WI: Beloit College Press.

Berggren, Niclas, and Mikael Elinder. 2012. Is Tolerance Good or Bad for Growth? *Public Choice* 150: 283–308.

Bernstein, David E. 2003. *You Can't Say That! The Growing Threat to Civil Liberties from Antidiscrimination Laws*. Washington, DC: Cato Institute.

———. 2010. Context Matters: A Better Libertarian Approach to Antidiscrimination Law. Cato Institute, *Cato Unbound blog*, June 16. Accessed December 2, 2017. https://www.cato-unbound.org/2010/06/16/david-e-bernstein/context-matters-better-libertarian-approach-antidiscrimination-law

Bicchieri, Cristina. 2017. *Norms in the Wild: How to Diagnose, Measure, and Change Social Norms*. New York, NY: Oxford University Press.

Boettke, Peter J. 2017. Cosmopolitanism is the Answer. *Foundation of Economic Education blog*, November 15. Accessed December 3, 2017. https://fee.org/articles/cosmopolitanism-is-the-answer/

Boettke, Peter J., and Rosolino A. Candela. 2017. The Liberty of Progress: Increasing Returns, Institutions, and Entrepreneurship. *Social Philosophy and Policy* 34 (2): 136–163.

Bolick, Clinton. 2008. Affirmative Action. In *The Encyclopedia of Libertarianism*, ed. Ronald Hamowy, 6–8. Thousand Oaks, CA: Sage Publications.

Bowman, Sam. 2017. Understanding Averages. *Medium blog*, August 8. Accessed December 2, 2017. https://medium.com/@s8mb/understanding-averages-253394f3512c

Brownstein, Barry. 2016. Is Tribalism the Worst Idea in History? *Foundation of Economic Education blog*, February 23. Accessed November 30, 2017. https://fee.org/articles/is-tribalism-the-worst-idea-in-history

Buchanan, James M., and Roger D. Congleton. (1998) 2003. *Politics by Principle, Not Interest: Toward Nondiscriminatory Democracy*. The Collected Works of James M. Buchanan, vol. 11. Indianapolis, IN: Liberty Fund.

Cohen, Andrew Jason. 2014. *Toleration*. Cambridge, UK: Polity Press.

Cohen, Andrew I. 2016. Americans Owe It to Themselves to Consider Reparations for Marginalized Minorities. Institute of Humane Studies, *Learn Liberty blog*, June 22. Accessed December 2, 2017. http://www.learnliberty.org/blog/americans-owe-it-to-themselves-to-consider-reparations-for-marginalized-minorities/

Darwall, Stephen. 2004. Equal Dignity in Adam Smith. *Adam Smith Review* 1: 129–134.

Davis, John B. 2003. *The Theory of the Individual in Economics: Identity and Value*. New York, NY: Routledge.

———. 2011. *Individuals and Identity in Economics*. New York, NY: Cambridge University Press.

Dopfer, Kurt, and Jason Potts. 2008. *The General Theory of Economic Evolution*. London, UK: Routledge.

Dowdy, Wayne. 2014. Poll Taxes. In *Race and Racism in the United States: An Encyclopedia of the American Mosaic*, ed. Charles A. Gallagher and Cameron D. Lippard, 955–956. Santa Barbara, CA: Greenwood.

Epstein, Richard A. 1992. *Forbidden Grounds: The Case Against Employment Discrimination Laws*. Cambridge, MA: Harvard University Press.

———. 1995. *Simple Rules for a Complex World*. Cambridge, MA: Harvard University Press.

Gaus, Gerald F. 2011. *The Order of Public Reason: A Theory of Freedom and Morality in a Diverse and Bounded World*. New York, NY: Cambridge University Press.

Geloso, Vincent, and Steven Horwitz. 2017. Inequality: First, Do No Harm. *The Independent Review* 22 (1): 121–134.

Griswold, Charles. 1999. *Adam Smith and the Virtues of Enlightenment*. Cambridge, UK: Cambridge University Press.

Haefelle, Stefanie, and Virgil Henry Storr. 2017. An Appeal to Moderation. *U.S. News & World Report*, August 7. Accessed November 30, 2017. https://www.usnews.com/opinion/economic-intelligence/articles/2017-08-07/adam-smith-on-why-moderate-politics-neednt-mean-compromising-beliefs

Halcoussis, Dennis, and Anton D. Lowenberg. 1998. Local Public Goods and Jim Crow. *Journal of Institutional and Theoretical Economics* 154 (4): 599–621.

Hayek, Friedrich A. (1960) 2006. *The Constitution of Liberty*. Routledge Classics ed. London, UK: Routledge.

Heilman, Madeline E., Caryn J. Block, and Jonathan A. Lucas. 1992. Presumed Incompetent? Stigmatization and Affirmative Action Effects. *Journal of Applied Psychology* 77 (4): 536–544.

Hermann-Pillath, Carsten. 2013. *Foundations of Economic Evolution: A Treatise on the Natural Philosophy of Economics*. Cheltenham, UK: Edward Elgar.

Johnson, Charles. 2013. Women and the Invisible Fist: How Violence Against Women Enforces the Unwritten Law of Patriarchy, May 3. Accessed December 1, 2017. http://charleswjohnson.name/essays/women-and-the-invisible-fist/women-and-the-invisible-fist-2013-0503-max.pdf

Karpowitz, Christopher F., and Tali Mendelberg. 2014. *The Silent Sex: Gender, Deliberation, and Institutions*. Princeton, NJ: Princeton University Press.

Kukathas, Chandran. 2003. *The Liberal Archipelago: A Theory of Diversity and Freedom*. Oxford, UK: Oxford University Press.

Kuznicki, Jason. 2010. Discrimination and the Growth of the Government. Cato Institute, *Cato Unbound blog*, June 25. Accessed December 2, 2017. https://www.cato-unbound.org/2010/06/25/jason-kuznicki/discrimination-growth-government

———. 2017. On the Paradox of Tolerance. Cato Institute, *libertarianism.org blog*, August 17. Accessed December 3, 2017. https://www.libertarianism.org/columns/paradox-tolerance

Leeson, Peter T., and Peter J. Boettke. 2006. Liberal Tolerance as Robust Political Economy. In *Tolerance in the Twenty-First Century: Prospects and Challenges*, ed. Gerson Moreno-Riaño, 201–212. Lanham, MD: Lexington Books.

Lemke, Jayme. 2012. Polycentrism, Self-Governance, and the Case of Married Women's Rights Reform. In *Annual Proceedings of the Wealth and Well-Being of Nations*, ed. Emily Chamlee-Wright, vol. 4, 69–88. Beloit, WI: Beloit College Press.

———. 2016. Interjurisdictional Competition and the Married Women's Property Acts. *Public Choice* 166 (3–4): 291–313.

Locke, John. (1689) 1988. *Two Treatises of Government*. Cambridge Texts in the History of Political Thought, ed. Peter Laslett. Cambridge, UK: Cambridge University Press.

Lomasky, Loren. 2001. Toward a Liberal Theory of National Boundaries. In *Boundaries and Justice: Diverse Ethical Perspectives*, ed. David Miller and Sohail H. Hashmi, 55–78. Princeton, NJ: Princeton University Press.

Lomasky, Loren E., and Fernando R. Tesón. 2015. *Justice at a Distance: Extending Freedom Globally*. New York, NY: Cambridge University Press.

Maslow, Abraham H. 1943. A Theory of Human Motivation. *Psychological Review* 50 (4): 370–396.

von Mises, Ludwig. (1945) 1978. *The Clash of Group Interests and Other Essays* New York, NY: Center for Libertarian Studies.

de Secondat Montesquieu, Charles. (1748) 2008. *The Spirit of the Laws*. Cambridge Texts in the History of Political Thought, ed. Anne M. Cohler, Basia C. Miller, and Harold S. Stone. Cambridge, UK: Cambridge University Press.

Novak, Mikayla. 2016. Feminism and Liberty's Emancipation Sequence. Cato Institute, *libertarianism.org*, January 15. Accessed November 12, 2017. https://www.libertarianism.org/columns/feminism-libertys-emancipation-sequence

Nozick, Robert. 1974. *Anarchy, State, and Utopia*. Oxford, UK: Blackwell Publishing.

Palmer, Tom G. 2008. Cosmopolitanism. In *The Encyclopedia of Libertarianism*, ed. Ronald Hamowy, 107–109. Thousand Oaks, CA: Sage Publications.

———. 2009. Madison and Multiculturalism: Group Representation, Group Rights, and Constitutionalism. In *Realizing Freedom: Libertarian Theory, History, and Practice*, ed. Tom G. Palmer, 299–347. Washington, DC: Cato Institute.

Parker, Kunal. 2015. *Making Foreigners: Immigration and Citizenship Law in America, 1600–2000*. New York, NY: Cambridge University Press.

Peart, Sandra J., and David M. Levy. 2005. *The "Vanity of the Philosopher": From Equality to Hierarchy in Postclassical Economics*. Ann Arbor, MI: University of Michigan Press.

Pennington, Mark. 2011. *Robust Political Economy: Classical Liberalism and the Future of Public Policy*. Cheltenham, UK: Edward Elgar.

Pérez-Diaz, Victor. 2009. Markets as Conversations: Markets' Contributions to Civility, the Public Sphere and Civil Society at Large. In *Markets and Civil Society: The European Experience in Comparative Perspective*, ed. Victoria Pérez-Diaz, 27–76. New York, NY: Berghahn Books.

Pinker, Steven. 2011. *The Better Angels of Our Nature: The Decline of Violence in History and Its Causes*. New York, NY: Allen Lane.

Popper, Karl. (1945) 1995. *The Open Society and Its Enemies, Volume 1: The Spell of Plato*. Routledge Classics ed. London, UK: Routledge.

Postrel, Virginia. 1998. *The Future and Its Enemies: The Growing Conflict over Creativity, Enterprise, and Progress*. New York, NY: Free Press.

Powell, Jim. 2013. To Defeat the Assault on Liberty, Our Appeals Must Be Moral. *Forbes Magazine*, February 13. Accessed December 1, 2017. https://www.forbes.com/sites/jimpowell/2013/02/13/to-defeat-the-assault-on-liberty-our-appeals-must be moral/#473d4dc21391

Rae, Douglas. 1981. *Equalities*. Cambridge, MA: Harvard University Press.

Şahin, Bican. 2010. *Toleration: The Liberal Virtue*. Lanham, MD: Lexington Books.

———. 2015. Toleration: The Liberal Path to Peace and Prosperity. *Atlas Network*, March 25. Accessed December 3, 2017. https://www.atlasnetwork.org/news/article/toleration-the-liberal-path-to-peace-and-prosperity

Shermer, Michael. 2015. *The Moral Arc: How Science and Reason Lead Humanity Toward Truth, Justice, and Freedom*. New York, NY: Henry Holt and Co.

Singer, Peter. 2011. *The Expanding Circle: Ethics, Evolution, and Moral Progress*. Princeton, NJ: Princeton University Press.

Storr, Virgil. 2008. The Market as a Social Space: On the Meaningful Extraeconomic Conversations That Can Occur in Markets. *Review of Austrian Economics* 21: 135–150.

Tebble, Adam James. 2016. *Epistemic Liberalism: A Defence*. London, UK: Routledge.

Thompson, Debra. 2015. What Lies Beneath: Equality and the Making of Racial Classifications. In *Equality and Public Policy*, ed. Mark LeBar, Antony Davies, and David Schmidtz, 114–136. New York, NY: Cambridge University Press.

Tomasi, John. 2012. *Free Market Fairness*. Princeton, NJ: Princeton University Press.

Unzueta, Miguel M., Angélica S. Gutiérrez, and Negin Ghavami. 2010. How Believing in Affirmative Action Quotas Affects White Women's Self-image. *Journal of Experimental Social Psychology* 46 (1): 120–126.

van der Vossen, Bas. 2013. More on Bleeding Hearts and Social Justice. *Bleeding Heart Libertarians blog*, May 31. Accessed December 1, 2017. http://bleedingheartlibertarians.com/2013/05/more-on-bleeding-heart-and-social-justice/

Wagner, Richard E. 2002. Complexity, Governance and Constitutional Craftsmanship. *The American Journal of Economics and Sociology* 61 (1): 105–122.

———. 2016. *Politics as a Peculiar Business: Insights from a Theory of Entangled Political Economy*. Cheltenham, UK: Edward Elgar.

Waldron, Jeremy. 2017. *One Another's Equals: The Basis of Human Equality*. Cambridge, MA: Belknap Press of Harvard University Press.

Welzel, Christian. 2013. *Freedom Rising: Human Empowerment and the Quest for Emancipation*. New York, NY: Cambridge University Press.

Wilson, William Julius. 1987. *The Truly Disadvantaged: The Inner City, the Underclass, and Public Policy*. Chicago, IL: University of Chicago Press.

9

Conclusion

It is an indisputable fact that economic inequality—the unequal distribution of income and wealth amongst the agents that comprise civil society—has emerged as one of the major cultural, economic, political, and social themes of modern times. The chief concern is that income and wealth disparities threaten significant and unwarranted harms not only to those unfortunate enough to have found themselves struggling with poverty. If left unaddressed, even wealthier individuals and families, who enjoy more fortunate circumstances, would not be left untouched by inequality.

The sense of apprehension about the nature and consequences of inequality has been reflected in the extensive research efforts by social scientists amongst an array of disciplines. This is aptly illustrated by the proliferation of academic papers, and even best-selling books, about what must be done to enshrine fairer shares of income and wealth. Strong advocacy by interest groups and vigorous demands by members of the general public, to ensure that governments suppress economic inequalities, have also resonated. Although it is anecdotally conceived that anti-inequality policy actions are mainly the preserve of progressive and social-democratic politicians, conservative governments across developed

M. Novak, *Inequality*, Palgrave Studies in Classical Liberalism,
https://doi.org/10.1007/978-3-319-89417-1_9

countries have also enacted fiscal and regulatory policy initiatives to ameliorate economic inequality.

Modern adherents of classical liberalism have engaged in the inequality debate in various ways. Numerous liberals question the view that income and wealth inequalities are problems necessitating policy rectification under all circumstances, raising doubts about the economic efficacy of redistributive efforts to ameliorate inequalities of income and wealth. The counteracting efforts by classical liberals have also challenged the methodological integrity and accuracy of empirical inequality studies. Although the liberal critiques in response to inequality analysis and policy have been important, the distinctive contribution of this book is to situate the classical liberal response to inequality within a holistic theoretical framework. Our support for the adoption of a theoretical framework borrows from philosopher Thomas Kuhn's insight that a framework helps illuminate what we see and even, to the extent that a given theory offers a clear study in contrast to others, that we cannot see (Kuhn [1962] 2012; Potts 2000).

Combining perspectives from complexity, evolutionary, and network theories to examine the substance of multifarious interactions by fallible-yet-capable individuals and their groups, we consider the work of Richard Wagner has succeeded in illuminating much of what appeared to be previously hidden before the advent of entangled political economy. Essentially, neoclassical economic policy is based on the unrealistic assumption of a disjunctive cohort of actors somehow charged with responsibilities to amend the aspirations and plans of everybody else, to the extent that those aspirations and plans are assessed as inefficient or unfair. The policymaker is akin to a player in the sport of curling, and the remainder of society is the object of a granite stone which will end up at an inappropriate place (that, we might say, is "inefficient") unless the curler takes up intervening action to move the stone elsewhere.

Taking its foundational insights from complexity and network theories, and evolutionary conceptions, entangled political economy enables us to see that politics as policy-injection into an inert society is implausible. For a start, "a market economy is simply the network of exchange relationships among people that arises when those relationships are governed by the principles of property, contract, and liability" (Wagner

1996, p. 8). To add to this, government "is a complex organization that is not subject to detailed central control, and rather represents to a large extent a network of exchange relationships within its constitutive rules" (Ibid., p. 42). Social organisations and institutions, such as families, neighbourhoods, charities, schools, hospitals, clubs, and civic associations, are also properly understood as the manifestations of decentred interactions among human beings (Horwitz 2015; Garnett et al. 2015).

Entangled political economy explains human phenomena as the result of interactions between, and among, economic, social, and political actors unfolding across time and space. Individuals attempt to achieve gains by exchanging with others in diverse institutional environments, oftentimes displaying entrepreneurial flair as they compete and collaborate to secure their objectives. The existence of complex and evolving multiplexes of institutional terrains, interests, and values not only enables mutual benefits to be secured but, along the way, may lead to socially tectonic clashes upsetting established patterns and preconceived notions.

In this book we push the boundaries of Wagner's entangled political economy by interpreting inequality using its key theoretical foundations. Essentially, economic inequality arises when non-uniform patterns of income and wealth connections form between various participants within society. Interaction between people within entangled political economy is also subject to change, and therefore inequality is not necessarily a fixed phenomenon. An exclusive reliance upon statistical artifices to represent inequality—such as the Gini coefficient or pay gaps between the genders or races—overlooks the complex, emergent properties of income and wealth connections between individuals and enterprises.

The structural relations emergent within entangled political economy come in many guises. Nonetheless, we can generically describe patterns of market interactions (e.g. selling and buying of goods and services) as being influenced by the principles of mutuality and exchange between people, whereas interactions within the political order (e.g. lobbying for, and negotiating, terms of fiscal and regulatory interventions) tend to be influenced by domination and compulsion.[1] We propose that broader inequality patterns are similarly affected by different underlying sources (Geloso and Horwitz 2017). Some forms of human congress generate income and wealth distributions but do not abridge harm-principle norms, because they fundamentally arise from voluntaristic action. These were defined throughout the book as "good," or socially harmless, inequalities. Other interactionist patterns, associated with coercive action, induce inequalities which do render harm, thus seen as "bad," circumscribing opportunities by certain individuals and groups for their own advancement.

The entangled political economy theorist appreciates that entanglement is an inescapable feature of living, with economic, communal, and political actors coming into contact with each other to some extent. In the interests of maintaining an open liberal society, lacking neo-feudalistic distinctions between rulers and subjects, non-discriminatory policy settings should be applied as broadly as practicable, and to each and all in the same measure. The critical ingredient for a "Great Enrichment" (McCloskey 2010), encompassing as many people as possible, is that economic action be undertaken in accordance with the "constitutive principles" of property, contract, liability, open markets, sound money, and consistent economic policy.

A dispensing of discriminatory fiscal and regulatory privileges through the state not only flouts the quintessentially liberal idea that all should be equals under the law. As this book has shown, policy-induced privilege can represent its own source of "bad" inequality which, at its worst, implicitly redistributes incomes from the poor to those on middle incomes, and from those on middle incomes to high incomes. It is at this point that the classical liberal calls for the minimisation of such ill-founded kinds of entanglement through less discriminatory policy forms, as well as the decentralised and polycentric flourishing of experiments in financing, service provision, and regulation (involving non-political and political players alike) to discover better methods of social cooperation.

Another contribution we make to the entangled political economy literature is to suggest that there are important relations between economic and social inequalities requiring due consideration. Specifically, an unequal distribution of income and wealth can perpetuate through deliberate acts of social exclusion of particular groups from opportunities to forge their own network connections with others.

Much of human history appears to have unfortunately been stained by the propagation of group-based animosities. These have been reflected through public policy in a variety of unedifying ways, enabling slavery to exist, denying women property and contracting rights, stifling free association, restricting cross-border movements, and so on. In developed countries, key restrictions differentially imposed on people, based on their identity, have been removed, representing an alteration of cultural, social, and political rules in the process. However, the removal of formal discrimination has not been uniformly implemented and nor is it complete.

An important, but underappreciated, dimension of the inequality debate is that reform allowing for a more open and competitive economic order would also reduce discriminatory pressures within society more generally. In other words, market operations assist in the reduction of "social distance" between strangers. Economic action filtered through markets can encourage diverse people to communicate, negotiate, and bargain over the terms of prospectively mutually beneficial exchanges, and to keep promises. These practices in turn would not only refine manners but can assist in bridging gaps in intersubjective understandings.

The *doux-commerce* thesis of classical liberalism is one manifestation of an entire range of pro-social behaviours which correlate with a shared sense of toleration. Although there are a range of activities and interactions that individuals may find unsavoury or displeasing, a tolerance ethic underlines a respect for others as social equals. As equals we recognise the possibility of mistakes by our peers but, by the same token, recognise that other people are capable of judgement and self-improvement. Abstaining from interference in the lives of others, certainly in situations whereby the activities are not causing harm, toleration facilitates a robustly dynamic entangled political economy welcoming "experiments of living" of an almost unimaginable scale and scope.

We have catalogued a number of scenarios in which inequalities of income and wealth are generated through catallactic political processes. This opens numerous prospects for liberal reforms aimed at eliminating abuses of political power, wherever they may be found. To the extent that reform, fundamentally attuned to the principle of freedom, and conditioned by the absence of domination and subjection, is implemented, we can say that "liberty-consistent" networks materialise throughout entangled political economy. What we cannot assuredly say is that liberty-consistent network structures will necessarily achieve outcome-*equality*: "[i]gnoring possible disincentive effects of complete equalization, perhaps the most damaging argument against perfect equality as an idea is that it is an ideal under which few people would want to live. With rare exception, people prefer to take a chance at earning an above-average income even though this implies they may end up with a below-average income" (Wagner 1974, pp. 16–17).

When studying complex network structures, the theorist—who, incidentally, is as much a societal participant as anybody else—cannot successfully pronounce finely grained and intricate predictions about the consequences of broad-scale change, such as the transition of political entanglements from discriminatory towards more non-discriminatory underpinnings. In such circumstances, one can, at best, elucidate "explanations of the principle" which refer to the principles regarding how or why a phenomenon presents itself, or, perhaps, "pattern predictions" concerning qualitative conditional predictions about the phenomenon (Hayek [1964] 1967; Caldwell 2004). Consistent with these Hayekian limitations, it is our contention that economic inequalities will certainly remain as an emergent by-product of human interaction under a scenario wherein the activities of political agents are constitutionalised to be limited in scale and non-discriminatory in scope.

The unleashing of economic openness within entangled political economy is also likely to lead to significant challenges against incumbent producers and providers by up-and-coming entrepreneurs. The up-and-comers will themselves be subjected to successive waves of entrepreneurship. Therefore, it is expected that any temporary monopoly position attained during the adoption phase of meso-level evolutionary trajectories will tend to be rapidly dissipated by new challengers.

Classical liberals such as Pennington (2011) and Tebble (2016) have analogised the concept of economic entrepreneurialism to questions of social and cultural change. As explained in the previous chapter, the dissipation of group-based discrimination formerly supported by legislative fiat is likely to reduce the implicit degree of "stickiness" typifying personal and group identities. Given that identity is a subjective and dynamic phenomenon, the easing of constraints which ossify identity should induce additional discoveries and learning between individuals, and groups of individuals, with regard to beings, doings, and knowings.

The freeing up of social and cultural experimentation is unlikely to eliminate tectonic clashes. However, even seemingly irreconcilable differences attributed to diversity can be accommodated. This was aptly explained by Chandran Kukathas's (2003) model of the "liberal archipelago" wherein people can enter into, and exit from, different groups against the background of toleration of difference. Under such arrangements there seems no urgent requirement for political action to enshrine "reverse discrimination" policies, and no pressing need for all-encompassing political recognition as proposed by the likes of Iris Marion Young (1990).

This book provides the first comprehensive sketch of principles comprehending inequality through the entangled political economy theoretical framework. It is not envisaged that this book serves as the "final word" about such matters, with ample scope for research to be prospectively embraced by scholars in an interdisciplinary frame. A potential avenue of investigation for researchers includes a deeper examination of inequality determinants and consequences using the analytical tools made available by entangled political economy theory. In addition, there is potential to develop additional case studies revealing policy to be the product of entanglement across orders of human action, and how those policies shape inequalities.

Speaking most broadly, proponents of classical liberalism should not decry the fact that economic inequality has emerged as a focal point for economic, social, and political discourse in the modern era. It is hoped that bringing to bear the principles of entangled political economy to the inequality discussion will enable classical liberals, and others, to engage in more meaningful discussions about the basis of inequality, the circumstances in which inequality is harmful (and not harmful), and the most appropriate institutional and policy reform measures to suppress inequality extremes (more often than not, the legacy of political action itself).

When all is said and done, classical liberals need not resile from engaging in inequality debates, now or whenever else they may be found. The pursuit of equality and the commensurate amelioration of inequality is, in the final analysis, a fundamentally liberal proposition.

Notes

1. Our present focus is upon drawing a distinction between the quality of economic and economic interactions; however, we note that exchange relationships within the communal order (consisting of families, friends, clubs, associations, etc.) are typically ordered by the principle of mutual assistance encompassing the likes of camaraderie, care, and emotional support.

References

Caldwell, Bruce. 2004. *Hayek's Challenge: Intellectual Biography of F. A. Hayek*. Chicago, IL: University of Chicago Press.

Garnett, Robert F., Jr., Paul Lewis, and Lenore T. Ealy. 2015. *Commerce and Community: Ecologies of Social Cooperation*. New York, NY: Routledge.

Geloso, Vincent, and Steven Horwitz. 2017. Inequality: First, Do No Harm. *The Independent Review* 22 (1): 121–134.

Hayek, Friedrich A. (1964) 1967. The Theory of Complex Phenomena. In *Studies in Philosophy, Politics and Economics*, 22–42. London, UK: Routledge Kegan Paul.

Horwitz, Steven. 2015. *Hayek's Modern Family: Classical Liberalism and the Evolution of Social Institutions*. New York, NY: Palgrave Macmillan.

Kuhn, Thomas S. (1962) 2012. *The Structure of Scientific Revolutions*. 4th ed. Chicago, IL: University of Chicago Press.

Kukathas, Chandran. 2003. *The Liberal Archipelago: A Theory of Diversity and Freedom*. Oxford, UK: Oxford University Press.

McCloskey, Deirdre N. 2010. *Bourgeois Dignity: Why Economics Can't Explain the Modern World*. Chicago, IL: University of Chicago Press.

Pennington, Mark. 2011. *Robust Political Economy: Classical Liberalism and the Future of Public Policy*. Cheltenham, UK: Edward Elgar.

Potts, Jason. 2000. *The New Evolutionary Microeconomics: Complexity, Competence and Adaptive Behaviour*. Cheltenham, UK: Edward Elgar.

Tebble, Adam James. 2016. *Epistemic Liberalism: A Defence*. London, UK: Routledge.

Wagner, Richard E. 1974. Death and Taxes: Some Perspectives on Inheritance, Inequality, and Progressive Taxation. In *Perspectives on Tax Reform: Death Taxes, Tax Loopholes, and the Value Added Tax*, ed. Richard E. Wagner, Roger

A. Freeman, Charles E. McLure Jr., Norman B. Ture, and Eric Schiff, 1–67. New York, NY: Praeger Publishers.

———. 1996. Economic Policy in a Liberal Democracy. *Locke Institute Shaftesbury Papers No. 8*. Cheltenham, UK: Edward Elgar.

Young, Iris Marion. 1990. *Justice and the Politics of Difference.* Princeton, NJ: Princeton University Press.

Index

M. Novak, *Inequality*, Palgrave Studies in Classical Liberalism,
https://doi.org/10.1007/978-3-319-89417-1

The manufacturer's authorised representative in the EU is Springer Nature Customer Service Centre GmbH, Europaplatz 3, 69115 Heidelberg, Germany. If you have any concerns regarding our products, please contact ProductSafety@springernature.com

Printed and bound by CPI Group (UK) Ltd, Croydon, CR0 4YY
05/10/2026
02228140-0006